GOD, SEXUALITY, AND THE SELF

God, Sexuality, and the Self is a new venture in systematic theology. Sarah Coakley invites the reader to reconceive the relation of sexual desire and the desire for God, and – through the lens of prayer practice – to chart the intrinsic connection of this relation to a theology of the Trinity. The goal is to integrate the demanding ascetical undertaking of prayer with the recovery of lost and neglected materials from the tradition, and thus to reanimate doctrinal reflection both imaginatively and spiritually. What emerges is a vision of human longing for the triune God which is both edgy and compelling: Coakley's *théologie totale* questions standard shibboleths on 'sexuality' and 'gender', and thereby suggests a way beyond current destructive impasses in the churches. The book is clearly and accessibly written, and will be of great interest to all scholars and students of theology.

SARAH COAKLEY is Norris–Hulse Professor of Divinity at the University of Cambridge. Her publications include *Religion and the Body* (Cambridge, 2000), *Powers and Submissions: Philosophy, Spirituality and Gender* (2002), *Pain and its Transformations* (2008), *The Spiritual Senses* (with Paul L. Gavrilyuk; Cambridge, 2011), and *Sacrifice Regained* (Cambridge, 2012). Coakley is also the editor of *Re-Thinking Gregory of Nyssa* (2003) and co-editor (with Charles M. Stang) of *Re-Thinking Dionysius the Areopagite* (2009).

GOD, SEXUALITY, AND THE SELF

An Essay 'On the Trinity'

SARAH COAKLEY

CAMBRIDGE
UNIVERSITY PRESS

CAMBRIDGE
UNIVERSITY PRESS

University Printing House, Cambridge CB2 8BS, United Kingdom

Published in the United States of America by Cambridge University Press, New York

Cambridge University Press is part of the University of Cambridge.

It furthers the University's mission by disseminating knowledge in the pursuit of education, learning, and research at the highest international levels of excellence.

www.cambridge.org
Information on this title: www.cambridge.org/9780521552288

© Cambridge University Press, 2013

First published 2013

Printed and bound in the United Kingdom by TJ International Ltd. Padstow Cornwall

A catalogue record for this publication is available from the British Library

Library of Congress Cataloguing in Publication data
Coakley, Sarah, 1951–
God, sexuality and the self : an essay 'on the Trinity' / Sarah Coakley.
pages cm
Includes index.
ISBN 978-0-521-55228-8
1. Trinity. 2. God (Christianity) 3. Spirituality. 4. Sex – Religious
aspects – Christianity. I. Title.
BT111.3.C63 2013
231′.044–dc23
2013005144

ISBN 978-0-521-55228-8 Hardback
ISBN 978-0-521-55826-6 Paperback

For J. F. C.

But we will have a way more liberal,
Than changing hearts, to join them, so we shall
Be one, and one another's all.

John Donne, 'Lovers' Infiniteness' (1633)

Contents

vii

Illustrations

Preface and acknowledgements

This book assumed its first, preliminary, shape a very long time ago, in the 1990s, when I was invited to give the Hulsean Lectures at Cambridge University. Soon afterwards, when I migrated to a new post at Harvard, I became rapidly – and vividly – aware of the barriers of cultural difference that made my undertaking, indeed my whole theological approach, bemusing to my new American interlocutors, and especially to those in the liberal religious tradition. The impenitent philosophical realism in this project, the absolute centrality granted to the practice of prayer, the talk of the entanglement of 'sexuality' and 'spirituality' (both terms laden with different cultural baggage in the two continents), the insistence that early Christian – and especially celibate, monastic – traditions could throw some crucial and positive light on celebrated current dilemmas about 'sex' and 'gender': these traits were seen as at best quaintly English or Anglican, and at worst manifestations of a feminist false consciousness. Thus, for a long time the project was shelved while I reflected with real seriousness on the force of such criticisms, adjusted to my new cultural milieu, and took stock of the concomitant resistance, in an era of postmodernity, to the very project of a Christian systematic theology.

At the same time, however, a set of ecclesiastical paroxysms was occurring: Christian churches worldwide, but especially Roman Catholics in Boston and Episcopalians and Anglicans in North America, England, and Africa, were thrown into new and profound crises by sexual scandals, divisive debates about homosexuality, and continuing disagreements about women, gender roles, and church leadership. In this context of simultaneous exposure and threatened schism, I became newly aware that the approach I had been essaying in my earlier lectures fitted neither the standard liberal nor conservative approaches to these debates; but it was not a compromise between them either. Rather, it cut across the disjunctive divides all too familiar from press coverage and mutual accusation, insisting instead that prayer and a renewed asceticism (not, note, repression) had to be at the heart of any attempt to solve the profound questions of desire with which the churches struggled; and – perhaps even more counterintuitively to many – it argued that only engagement with a God who has been ineluctably revealed and met as *triune* could hold the key to contemporary anxieties about sexuality, gender, and feminism. However, this was not the approach to the Trinity that had by this time become almost commonplace amongst 'social trinitarians', including some feminists, who looked to the persons of the Trinity as *imitable prototypes* for good political, ecclesial, and personal relations. On the contrary, I saw my approach as involving a much more profound, challenging, and disconcerting engagement with God in prayer and scriptural reflection to be easily subsumable into the existing range of political and ecclesial agendas. In short, it seemed I wanted to say something that was not otherwise being said, and which, in practice, proved difficult to be heard by the existing theological parties of dissent.

Yet thus it was that finally, after various other published prolegomena had been completed first, the last lap in the writing of this book was reached. I had written a book (*Powers and Submissions*) which had already focused centrally on the practice of contemplation; I had followed that with edited studies of Gregory of Nyssa and Dionysius the Areopagite. So now theological courage returned, and a reconceived version of my original text was forged into the first volume of a larger systematic project which, as it is planned, will eventually have several parts. As currently conceived, the second volume (*Knowing Darkly*) will adumbrate my theological anthropology of the 'spiritual senses', and at the same time turn to the vexed modern category of 'race'. The third volume (*Punish and Heal*) will address the public realm of the polis with its secular institutions of prison and hospital, and so re-examine the doctrines of sin and atonement. Christology (*Flesh and Blood*) will advisedly be left till last, not as demotion but as climax: the mystery of the incarnation will be approached via a theology of the eucharist.

The rationale for my newly conceived understanding of the task of systematic theology, and for its intrinsic connection to these pressing contemporary questions about sex, sexuality, and gender (terms to be carefully defined), is provided in the opening sections of this book. This volume on the Trinity, however, is just the initial segment in the larger systematic project, to be entitled overall, *On Desiring God*. Thus to reconceive questions of sexuality and gender in relation to the trinitarian God is but the first, albeit adventurous, step in a new theological landscape.

This book is also an experiment in a form of writing that academic theology unfortunately increasingly eschews. It aims to be comprehensible to the general educated reader as well as to the professional theologian, but without – I trust – any loss of scholarly acumen. It is written, certainly, for colleagues and students; but no less too for those in the churches – and those who hover agonizingly at the edges of institutional religion – who occasionally wonder how Christianity remains intellectually defensible as a worldview at all, and how it may go forward in the face of the exposure of its massive historic collusion in gender blindness and abuse of power, its tragic (and continuing) mismanagement of the economy of desire. In short, it is written for all those who continue to seek a vision of God for today, one attractive enough to magnetize their deepest human longings so as to *order* their desires in relation to God.

To set oneself this task of communication to a wider theological readership is not easy, and involves a certain risk for the established academic, especially one who is now subject to regular government 'assessments'. The author in the academy habitually writes with one eye on the reviewer, friend or foe; and the tendency to heap up extraneous references, to engage in self-aggrandizing polemics, or to employ impressive, if inflated, jargon is at times almost irresistible. Here, however, I have consciously attempted to deflect such traits; and I have enlisted the help of several long-suffering students, friends, and parishioners to call me to account on this score. If the academic reader seeks further references, or indications of my own engagement in current scholarly debates, I here refer also to my other writings; and I provide in the bibliographic notes at the end of each chapter the detailed links to the material that has informed my argument. In this way I have kept the number of footnotes to a minimum. I have also supplied a glossary of technical terms at the end of the volume. I take this calculated risk – of relatively simple and direct communication – for a reason. For even as systematic theology today undergoes a remarkable revival, it is in grave danger of rendering itself socially insignificant by sheer obscurity of expression.

Yet my alternative form of writing is in no way a resort to a popular mode, let alone to anti-intellectualism. Indeed, I strongly resist certain false and stereotypical disjunctions: between belief and practice, thought and affect, or, for that matter, academic and accessible writing. As the argument of the book unfurls, it will become evident why the theological method employed here is appropriately conjoined with a direct style of writing. For the book is written for all those who struggle at the intersection of the theological, the political, the spiritual, and the sexual, as well as for those whose particular theological vocation it is to interpret this nexus. The method I here call *théologie totale* involves a complex range of interdisciplinary skills; and to link the theoretical to the pastoral in this way is a task of some considerable spiritual and intellectual delicacy, just as to write so as to be 'understanded of the people' makes its own ascetical demands on the author.

So much by way of brief introduction to this book's undertaking. The rest of this preface must now be devoted to the giving of thanks.

Despite the long delay in production, I remain much indebted, first, to the Hulsean electors at Cambridge for the honour of my original election; and I am especially grateful to those who gave me hospitality and friendly criticism during my weekly visits to Cambridge from Oriel College, Oxford, where I was then teaching. Nicholas Lash, David Ford, John Milbank, Tim Jenkins, Brian Hebblethwaite, and Janet Martin Soskice must be singled out for my special thanks, and their influence may be detected at points in what I have written. But I am no less grateful to the other senior members at Cambridge who attended the lectures, and to the gratifyingly large audiences of students, who also offered their comments.

At Harvard I was fortunate to enjoy the criticism (sometimes deservedly severe) of graduate students in several seminars and classes devoted to the subject of the Trinity. Their influence is particularly evident in Chapters 1 and 2 of this book. I thank them all, and trust that what I have learned from them, and also from my Harvard feminist colleagues, as I gradually became attuned to the American theological milieu, will be manifest in what I have written. Others outside Harvard did me the honour of engaging meticulously – whether approvingly or critically – with the substantial argument about patristic trinitarianism, and its systematic import, that lies at the heart of this book: Lewis Ayres, Brian Daley, SJ, Kevin Hector, Andrew Louth, Kilian McDonnell, OSB, Robert Murray, SJ, the late Lloyd Paterson, Columba Stewart, OSB, Kallistos Ware, Robert Wilken, and the late Maurice Wiles.

Various Harvard research assistants – Philip McCosker, Robert St Hilaire, Philip Francis – were a considerable help to me in gathering bibliographical materials and nobly lugging them to my door. The two Philips, especially, ensured in their distinctive ways that this book got finished, Philip McCosker invaluably assisting me again in Cambridge with the bibliographic notes in the final push, as did Mark McInroy and David Grumett as research associates there earlier. Michon Matthiesen (then a doctoral student at Boston College) was a constant source of encouragement at a time when I was despairing of completion. I must also mention the continuing luxury of a 'priest's hole' in which to hide, pray, and write, which was for a while vouchsafed to me by the rector of the local Jesuit community in Cambridge, Massachusetts, John Privett, SJ, who claimed he was paying me back for some hiding done by Jesuits in English houses 'in more turbulent times'. My parishioners in Boston, Deborah and Joseph Dyer, also gave me such sanctuary. For me, the solitude they provided was an invaluable aid to reflection.

Despite the cultural shifts I underwent during my sojourn in North America, this book remains – I am assured by my critics – a discernibly Anglican product. Be that as it may, I am glad to record my indebtedness to the Church of England Doctrine Commission (on which I served for ten years long ago, from 1982 to 1992) for the stimulus it provided to my thinking at that time; and more especially to Bishop Alec Graham (sometime chair of the commission), and to Church House Publications, for allowing me to reuse the material on charismatic spirituality that I originally wrote for one of the Doctrine Commission reports (*We Believe in the Holy Spirit*, London, Church House Publications, 1991, ch. 2). As will be clear from that material (now reworked as Chapter 4 of this book), I owe a great deal to the people in both of the charismatic groups in Lancashire whose membership I investigated. They welcomed me into their worship, and in their interviews with me generously gave me their time, their trust, and the depth of their spiritual insights. As I hope Chapter 4 will show, there is much buried theological treasure in the parochial life of contemporary churches and groups. The late Mary Douglas was a constant source of inspiration and encouragement as I sought to bring social science and theological methods creatively together in this regard.

Without two periods of sabbatical leave from Harvard, the first generously funded by the Henry Luce III Fellowship programme, the second by the Lilly Foundation, this book – and the other related projects, mentioned above – could never have been completed. The first period of leave also allowed me to spend some time in Princeton gathering materials for the iconographical chapter of this volume at the Index of Christian Art; the staff there were particularly gracious and helpful. On the practical publishing side, Alex Wright at the Cambridge University Press, and then his successors Ruth Parr and Kevin Taylor, encouraged and assisted me all along the way. When I asked for yet more time to redevelop this text as the first volume of a proposed systematic theology, Kevin Taylor remained unflappably supportive. And Kate Brett, Laura Morris, and Anna Lowe *firmly* helped to bring the project to completion.

Finally, as any honest author knows, and especially any feminist scholar, books are not written (let alone finished) without certain costs and compensatory adjustments to the lives of others in the family. Our daughters Edith and Agnes have over the years developed a good line in lampooning technical trinitarian jargon, and will doubtless be glad to see this particular project complete; while I have struggled with the Trinity they have grown into womanhood. My beloved husband Chip can alone count the cost to domestic comfort, or to the speed of his own research, and he must be mightily tired of hearing about the 'progress' of this book. He thought it would never be done. My thanks to him may be inadequate, but to him I dedicate this first volume of systematics in its final form.

Trinity Sunday, 2012

Abbreviations

The following acronyms are to be found within the bibliographical notes and footnotes:

ACW   Ancient Christian Writers
CCSL   Corpus Christianorum Series Latina
CSCO   Corpus Scriptorum Christianorum Orientalium
CSEL   Corpus Scriptorum Ecclesiasticorum Latinorum
CSS   Cistercian Studies Series
CWS   Classics of Western Spirituality
FC   Fathers of the Church
GNO   Gregorii Nysseni Opera
LCL   Loeb Classical Library
PPS   Popular Patristics Series
PTS   Patristische Texte und Studien
SC   Sources Chrétiennes
ST   *Summa Theologiae*
TCL   Translations of Christian Literature

Prelude: the arguments of this book

Institutional Christianity is in crisis about 'sexuality'. Its detractors in the supposedly secularized and liberal climes of Northern Europe, who nonetheless yearn for what they call a satisfying 'spirituality', see this crisis as a sign of its failure to engage the contemporary world. Its conservative defenders, to be found mainly in religiously observant parts of North America and throughout the southern hemisphere, take it as an indication of cultural decadence and a deficiency in scriptural obedience. Probably both sides are right, but perhaps neither, exactly; this book notably does not aim to solve the problems in the terms currently under discussion. Instead, it aims to go deeper: to come at the issue that is now called sexuality through a different route – that of the divine itself.

For this is a book about God, and more specifically about the Christian God. It is written for those who puzzle about how one might set about coming into relation with such a God in the first place; and who wonder how – without sacrificing either intellectual integrity or critical acumen – one might discover this baffling, alluring, and sometimes painful encounter to require thematizing in trinitarian terms: 'Father', 'Son', and 'Holy Spirit'. Further (and this may seem odd to the contemporary reader), this book is written in the fundamental conviction that no cogent answer to the contemporary Christian question of the trinitarian God can be given without charting the necessary and *intrinsic* entanglement of human sexuality and spirituality in such a quest: the questions of right contemplation of God, right speech about God, and right ordering of desire all hang together. They emerge in primary interaction with Scripture, become intensified and contested in early Christian tradition, and are purified in the crucible of prayer. Thus the problem of the Trinity cannot be solved without addressing the very questions that seem least to do with it, questions which press on the contemporary Christian churches with such devastating and often destructive force: questions of sexual justice, questions of the meaning and stability of gender roles, questions of the final theological significance of sexual desire.

It is the purpose of this introductory prelude to explain in advance how the various lines of argument in this book fit together. An overview will supply a perspective on the whole.

DESIRE, PRAYER, AND THE TRINITY IN THE 'FATHERS'

A perception of the significance of the right ordering of desire was not, of course, alien to some of the greatest early Christian thinkers of the late antique era; and a central part of my task in this book will be to explore how, for them, the perception of 'perfect relation in God' (the Trinity) was fundamentally attuned, and correlated, to their concomitant views about men and women, gender roles, and the nature of 'erotic' desire. Not that we can oblige any contemporary reader to accept their positions without critique (they are in any case various); but rather I shall aim, first, to lay bare the subtle – and forgotten – ways in which these elements in their thought connect, such that they may now illumine contemporary theological choices. At the same time it will become clear that the way they speak of desire has a different valence from today's post-Freudian context, and one as yet not cognizant of modern evocations of 'sexuality'.

This difference is itself revealing, as I shall show. Some of the most significant figures in the historical development of the doctrine of the Trinity (Origen, Gregory of Nyssa, Augustine, especially) feature large in this volume because of the fascinatingly *different* ways in which they relate their perceptions of intense desire for God, their often problematic feelings about sexual desire at the human level, and their newly creative understandings of God as Trinity.

Yet the modern textbook account of the development of the doctrine of the Trinity has largely obscured these crucial points of connection, often by concentrating more on philosophical issues of coherence than on the fathers' biblical exegesis or ascetical exercise. It is not customary, therefore, to study the fourth-century Gregory of Nyssa's (fascinating) views about virginity and marriage while *simultaneously* exploring his contribution to the development of technical trinitarian terms; it is not usual, either, to reflect on Augustine's understanding of sexual relations while studying his magisterial theological reflections on trinitarian analogies. But this omission is odd, not least because these two authors – prime progenitors of different, but mammothly influential, trinitarian visions of the Godhead – *themselves* saw these points of connection and discoursed upon them explicitly (see Chapter 6). And they did so under the impress both of scriptural injunction and of ascetic dictate, not merely by taking thought philosophically. Both of them, too, had extremely sophisticated ways of insisting how God cannot be compared or likened to anything creaturely (how a relationship with God is necessarily *unlike* any other), as well as a keen sense of how one's particular vision of God nonetheless also informs the whole realm of the personal and the political. Once one grasps these nexuses of association which they offer, one is also able to see – intriguingly –

that their two trinitarian traditions are not as disjunctive as they have long been presented; and here I contribute to a growing body of scholarship that seeks to reconsider the supposed gulf between early 'Eastern' and 'Western' views of the Trinity.

In addition to misrepresenting (or flattening) the trinitarian developments of the fourth and fifth centuries, the standard modern textbook narrative has more fundamentally and fatally obscured, as is argued in some detail in the earlier part of this book (Chapter 3), much of the richness of the earlier, *emergent* stage of trinitarian thought forms in the first three centuries of the Christian era. The picture here is more complicated than is the case with the Cappadocian fathers and Augustine; because it must be admitted that polemical patristic authors of huge significance (the great fourth-century defender of the council of Nicaea, Athanasius, par excellence) have themselves been strongly implicated in purveying the conciliar-based narrative I now seek to query or complexify. That is, it is not just the story of councils and creeds and dominant ecclesial and political personalities to which one should attend in an account of developing trinitarianism; and nor should the only principle of selectivity be a focus on an approximation to a presumed later 'orthodoxy' (in the sense of assent to creedal propositions). By repressing or marginalizing much of the early history of the doctrine of the *Spirit* (messy and erratic as it may seem), accounts of early trinitarianism that give sole attention to the status of the 'Son' vis-à-vis the 'Father' up to the mid fourth century, miss much of the drama: *at one and the same time* the crucial prayer-based logic of emergent trinitarianism is missed, and the related, and complicated entanglements with questions of human gender, power, and desire mutely disregarded.

So at the heart of this book is a proposed rereading of the formative, patristic sources for the origins of the doctrine of the

Trinity (Chapters 3 and 6). This task in itself already involves – in addition to the primary scriptural and doctrinal exegesis – the application of some contemporary scholarly methods (sociology of religion, cultural theory, gender analysis, for instance) not generally brought, even now, to the textbook account of the 'history of dogma'. But this – it should be stressed immediately – is not a *reductive* reading. It does not presume, that is, that the history of doctrinal development can be explained away in terms of something else: bids for power, for instance, or sociological forces, or manifestations of repressed sexuality, or devious attempts to occlude the voices of the oppressed. Some of these factors were indeed undeniably in play, to one extent or another, in this narrative history, and will be duly acknowledged; but they cannot exhaust the account of what was taking place theologically and *spiritually*.

My own reading of this early patristic period, then, neither reduces the history of the development of trinitarian doctrine to non-theological forces, nor assumes that the achievement of classical orthodoxy is the arrival at some stable place of spiritual safety. 'Orthodoxy' as mere propositional assent needs to be carefully distinguished from 'orthodoxy' as a demanding, and ongoing, spiritual *project*, in which the language of the creeds is personally and progressively assimilated. Nor, on the other hand, does my approach see the very emergence of Nicene orthodoxy as a kind of patriarchal plot – or a suppression of a more subtle, if élite, engagement with 'gnostic' wisdom. Rather, my proposal is both more modest and more complex. It is to set the story of the development of the orthodox doctrine of the Trinity within a constellation of considerations – spiritual, ascetical, sexual, social – which the dominant modern textbook tradition has tended either to ignore, or to sideline, in favour of its more purely cerebral account of the intellectual issues, along with the imperial political backdrop. But it is just as much to query, and correct, some of the more simplistic and reductive *reactions* to that textbook tradition, as well.

So my approach involves the highlighting of certain neglected patristic texts, and the collocation of texts not usually brought together, in order to expose a narrative of an explicitly prayer-based access to the workings of the divine. This form of access, I argue, not only begged trinitarian shape from its inception, but *simultaneously* raised insistent questions about the relation of sexual desire and desire for God. My thesis is that this nexus of association (between trinitarian thought, prayer of a deep sort, and questions of 'erotic' meaning), caused sufficient political difficulty to press the prayer-based approach to the Trinity to the edges of the more public, conciliar discussion of the doctrine, even in the patristic period itself, and further marginalized it as far as modern histories of dogma were concerned.

But by the end of the book it will be argued that the critical retrieval of this spiritual nexus today has great potential theological importance. It provides the resources for the presentation of a contemporary trinitarian *ontology of desire* – a vision of God's trinitarian nature as both the source and goal of human desires, as God intends them. It indicates how God the 'Father', in and through the Spirit, both stirs up, and progressively chastens and purges, the frailer and often misdirected desires of humans, and so forges them, by stages of sometimes painful growth, into the likeness of his Son. Here ethics and metaphysics may be found to converge; here divine desire can be seen as the ultimate progenitor of human desire, and the very means of its transformation. Moreover, this ascetic approach brings its own distinctive solution, finally, to the ongoing feminist problem of divine naming: the right language for God is not something to be 'fixed' at the outset by mere political fiat, but is part and parcel of the programme of the ascetic transformation of desire (Chapter 7).[1]

THE MEANING OF 'DESIRE'

Before I go any further in this account I must say something important about the very category of 'desire' in this book, and its relation to words more commonly utilized in contemporary debates about religion and sexual ethics: 'sex', 'sexuality', 'gender', and 'orientation'. When people talk about 'sex' and 'sexuality' today, they often presume that the first and obvious point of reference is sexual intercourse or other genital acts. (This is especially true in North America, I have found, where the word 'sexuality' has more of these overtones of actual physical enactment than in Britain.) The presumption, then, is that *physiological* desires and urges are basic and fundamental in the sexual realm; and to this is often added a second presumption: that unsatisfied (physical) sexual desire is a necessarily harmful and 'unnatural' state. From such a perspective, priestly or monastic celibacy is indeed monstrous – a veritable charade, necessarily masking subterfuge and illicit sexual activity. A popularized form of Freudianism is often invoked in support of this latter view about the 'impossibility' of celibacy. But this is odd; because Freud himself – who changed his mind more than once about these matters in the course of his career – never taught that social harm comes from what he called 'sublimation'. On the

---

[1] For this reason I must beg feminist readers not to prejudge my reasons for continuing to use the language of 'Father' in the trinitarian context. In my view, neither the straightforward obliteration of 'Father' language, nor the 'feminization' of the Spirit (or indeed of the Son), constitute in themselves satisfactory strategies in the face of the profound feminist critique of classical Christian thought forms and patterns of behaviour. These problems can only be met satisfactorily by an *ascetic* response which attacks idolatry at its root. These conclusions are finally drawn in Chapter 7 below.

contrary, he argued that sublimation is entirely necessary for civilization to endure. Chaos would ensue otherwise.

Freud's own views about desire ('Eros', in his later work) became, in the course of his life, more attuned to the Platonic view of desire that he had earlier eschewed. However, he never himself subscribed to the view, expressed classically in Plato's dialogue the *Symposium*, that 'erotic' desire has a propulsion to the eternal form of 'beauty', and that one must therefore spend one's life in an attempt to climb back up the ladder of (progressively purified) desire to that divine realm where the full 'revelation' of beauty may occur.[2] Freud, in rejecting the God of classical Jewish and Christian monotheism, of course rejected also the possibility of such a *divine* meaning in 'Eros'. But early Christianity, in contrast – at least those strands of it heavily influenced by forms of Platonism – was enormously drawn to the *Symposium*'s vision of 'desire'; and from the second and third century onwards it began to discourse on this matter intensively. Although it could find little or nothing in Jesus's teaching about *erōs* as such, it did not read his views on love (*agapē*) as in any way disjunctive from the Platonic tradition of *erōs*. And what it did inherit from Jewish scripture, and then from the earliest rabbinic exegesis of scripture, was a fascination with the symbol of sexual union as a 'type' – indeed, in the *Song of Songs* the highest type – of God's relation to Israel or Church.

The entanglement of this Platonic tradition of 'desire' with the emergence of ascetic forms of Christian life enjoining celibacy on its members, however, has made it a strand of thinking that is particularly problematic, not only for contemporary 'sub-Freudianism' (as I may perhaps dub the 'sexual teaching' of the secular newspapers and glossy magazines), but more especially for contemporary feminism. If

[2] *Symposium*, 210 A–212 C.

'desire' is *really* about desire for God, and involves some sort of 'purification' of physical expressions of sexual love, how can Plato's programme not involve a kicking away, at some point in the ascent, of the ladder that connects the divine to everything classically associated with the 'woman': materiality, physical desire, marriage, childbirth? Is not this tradition of ascetic Platonist Christianity arguably the one most *inimical* to feminist concerns? And is it not equally – if not more – problematic for the contentious contemporary issue of homoeroticism, which the Platonic text both assumes, and then rises 'above'?

It is nonetheless the central project of this systematic theology as a whole to give new coinage to this tradition of Christian Platonism, but to re-evaluate it and re-express it in ways that meet and answer some of the most difficult challenges that contemporary culture presents to the churches. Not the least of these challenges is the demonstration of the way in which the wisdom of this tradition is as applicable to those who are sexually active as to those who are not – whether 'heterosexual' or 'homosexual'. There is no denying, then, that such a re-expression of this tradition is required, even as it raises its own implicit critique of a contemporary erotic malaise. My primary patristic interlocutors in this volume, as I have already intimated, are Origen, Gregory of Nyssa, and Augustine; to them is added (later, in Chapter 7) some borrowings from the distinctive metaphysical framework of the early sixth-century Christian Platonist, Dionysius the Areopagite.[3] But for the purposes of this

---

[3] It should be added that each volume of this systematic theology concentrates on a different period of the classical Christian tradition. As volume II of this systematics will reveal, it is finally the view of desire proposed by the sixteenth-century Carmelites (Teresa of Ávila and John of the Cross) which most significantly informs the systematics as a whole; but since their own thought was profoundly informed by the patristic heritage that is under scrutiny in this book, the effect of looking at the *epistemic* significance of their thinking in volume II will build cumulatively on what is discussed here.

contemporary systematic project, I have to make these authors speak afresh; and the undergirding ideas are these.

First, Freud must be – as it were – turned on his head. It is not that physical 'sex' is basic and 'God' ephemeral; rather, it is God who is basic, and 'desire' the precious clue that ever tugs at the heart, reminding the human soul – however dimly – of its created source. Hence, in a sense that will be parsed more precisely as this book unfolds, *desire is more fundamental than 'sex'*. It is more fundamental, ultimately, because desire is an ontological category belonging primarily to God, and only secondarily to humans as a token of their createdness 'in the image'. But in God, 'desire' of course signifies no *lack* – as it manifestly does in humans. Rather, it connotes that plenitude of longing love that God has for God's own creation and for its full and ecstatic participation in the divine, trinitarian, life.

It follows that, if desire is divinely and ontologically basic, not only is human 'sex' to be cast as created in its light, but 'gender' – which nowadays tends to connote the way embodied relations are carved up and culturally adjudicated – is most certainly also to be set in right subjection to that desire. In short, the immense cultural anxiety that, in a secular society, is now accorded to 'sex' and 'gender' (and to their contested relations) can here be negotiated in a different, theological light. Not that 'sex' and 'gender' do not *matter*; on the contrary, the profound difference that incarnation makes to Christian Platonism will prove that they do indeed so 'matter', and deeply so. But it is not in the way that contemporary secular gender theory would (almost obsessively) have it. Such an obsession, I dare to suggest, resides in the lack of *God* as a final point of reference. As for 'orientation', too (another modern verbal invention): what orientation could be more important than the orientation to *God*, to divine desire? That is why this particular book will not divert to a detailed discussion of the so-called 'problem' of 'homosexuality'. For it is concerned with a deeper, and more primary, question: that of putting desire for God above all other desires, and with judging human desires only in that light. Ascetic transformation, ascetic fidelity: these are the goals which so fatally escape the notice of a culture bent either on pleasure or on moral condemnation. And to escape between the horns of that false dilemma is necessarily a spiritual and bodily task, involving great patience and commitment. From 'sexuality' and the 'self' to participation in the trinitarian God: this way lies a long haul of erotic purgation, but its goal is one of infinite delight.

How, then, am I to pass, in this book, from the patristic story of desire and its trinitiarian modulations to the contemporary realm of spiritual struggle and transformation? In fact I go via a rather unexpected route.

THE TRINITY IN SOCIAL CONTEXT: GOD IN THE FIELD

For my reassimilation of the patristic story of the development of trinitarian doctrine does not occur in this book without a critical testing of its contemporary veracity 'in the field'. As a systematic theologian, one cannot stop merely at the point of retelling a historical narrative: from there one looks to reapply the lessons to current social and ecclesiastical concerns. As discussion of the patristic analysis has suggested, the prayer-based approach to the Trinity is no mere individualist affair; it involves no naïve philosophical presumption that one can read doctrine straight out of 'subjective experience', nor does it isolate the individual knowing subject from her social context. Just as it did in the era of earliest Christianity, it again comes into being today – and calls forth rebuke or riposte – in *specific* intellectual, political, social, and ecclesiastical circumstances, which demand theological discernment and assessment. It is for this reason that this book forays into a seemingly unlikely realm for the investigation of trinitarian dogma: the fieldwork analysis of two contemporary Christian groups themselves deeply invested in the life of prayer (Chapter 4).

Just as the chapters on patristic trinitarianism probe neglected dimensions of the patristic story, pose previously sidelined questions about the 'erotic' nature of prayer in the Spirit, and bring together texts that are usually disjoined, so here – in the current context of postmodern spiritual renewal – I attempt another reconfiguration of trinitarian thinking. Instead of assuming that popular religious movements cannot yield high theological reflection, I analyze the specific conditions (social, ecclesiastical, political, personal) in which the pressure towards explicitly *trinitarian* thinking about God may become manifest – not as a merely obedient accession to imposed orthodoxy, but as an urgent spiritual necessity sweated out of the exigencies of prayer.

The significance here of highlighting the *social* matrix of such thought is not something, I argue, that can be left to the supposedly reductive analysis of the sociologist of religion (see Chapter 2). On the contrary, an awareness of the specific conditions in which such a pressure towards trinitarianism is located provides me with another crucial piece in the jigsaw of my avowed theological method. If, as I argue, revived trinitarianism of a vibrant sort – earthed in particular bodily practices of devotion, and tested in the crucible of chastened desire – tends to have its locus in *particular* social, ecclesiastical, and political conditions, then the sensitive theologian should become fully attuned to such connections. The social sciences, for these purposes, may become handmaids of theological awareness, not tools of theological reduction (as is often presumed). With the aid of the insights they afford, I come at the end of this fieldwork excursus to the somewhat startling conclusion that true trinitarian orthodoxy (in which the divine persons are perceived as radically and substantially one, while also distinct in relation to one another) flourishes more naturally at the *boundaries* of 'established' forms of Christianity than under its protective guardianship. For the political or ecclesiastical taming of the Spirit always comes with cost; and the dead hand of ecclesiastical authoritarianism is therefore no guarantor of orthodoxy in its qualitative sense (Chapters 3, 4). Indeed, as tragic contemporary events have shown, ersatz 'orthodoxy' can simultaneously become the silent protector of an abusive sexuality.

THE SPIRIT IN THE TRINITY: DESIRE CHASTENED AND PURIFIED

It is worth noting, at this particular point in my sketch of the book's fundamental logic, that the investigation of the workings of the Spirit in past text and contemporary context already reveals a double and paradoxical pressure about the workings of desire. For it seems that to step intentionally into the realm of divine, trinitarian desire, and to seek some form of participation in it through a profound engagement with the Spirit, is both to risk having one's human desires *intensified* in some qualitatively distinct manner, and also to confront a searching and necessary *purgation* of those same human desires in order to be brought into conformity with the divine will.

For, on the one hand, there is the neglected patristic evidence, already alluded to, that deep prayer in the Spirit (such as Paul describes in Romans 8. 27: 'with sighs too deep for words') may be understood as intrinsically 'erotic' in a primal sense. It veritably magnetizes the soul towards God, yet often with the simultaneous danger of a confusion of this attraction to divine love with human sexual loves that, in a fallen world, may well tend to sin or disorder. Here the Spirit is that which propels the one who prays towards union with the divine, but whose tug is felt *analogously* also in every erotic propulsion towards union, even at the human level. This is a nexus of association about which the patristic authors I discuss (especially Origen, in the third century) show great moral concern, and not without reason (see again, Chapter 3); for so much hangs here on how this analogy between human and divine loves is to be rightly discerned and understood, given the extraordinary capacity for human self-deception in the arena of the erotic. Yet on the other hand, and no less significantly, there is the evidence of the contemporary fieldwork (Chapter 4) that the Spirit may just as much be encountered as that which *checks* human desires, and stops their triumphalism; the apparent failure of prayer 'in the Spirit' for a desired human outcome may prove to be the pressure towards a truer and deeper perception of the unity of Spirit, Father, and (cruciform) Son.

To put this last point in more densely doctrinal terms: when one thinks rightly of God as Trinity, the Spirit cannot bypass the person of the Son, or evade thereby his divine engagement in Gethsemane and Golgotha; for that is a fundamental implication of the principle of the unity of Father, Son, and Spirit (expressed creedally in the phrase 'of one substance'). Whatever is true divinely, ontologically, of the Son, is true also of Father and Spirit – otherwise the persons are divided. The principle that the trinitarian persons are 'indivisible *ad extra*' (cannot be separated in their operations) is here given pointed application. One might say then, of human engagement with God at its most profound, that the Spirit progressively 'breaks' sinful desires, *in and through* the passion of Christ. And hence, at the pastoral, practical level, what I shall call the Spirit's 'protoerotic' pressure, felt initially as a propulsion towards divine union, must inexorably bring also – as the Spirit of the *Son* – the chastening of the human lust to possess, abuse, and control. This breaking, stopping, and chastening is a necessary prelude to the participatory transformation of all human, and often misdirected, longings – so that they may become one with God's.

So it seems possible to glimpse, even in apparently tangential fieldwork endeavours such as those charted later in this book, that the Spirit's activity in the world, because always in concert with the other two persons, has the capacity both to draw humans together in union and also subtly to interpose *between* them, acting as the guardian of human integrity. Or to put it in the language of Pauline theology, it is the same Spirit that inflames the heart with love (Romans 5. 5), and also imparts the (much neglected) 'gift' of 'self-control' (Galatians 5. 23).[4] Here lies the crucial difference between authentic, Spirit-endowed union (with Christ and each other), and *abuse*, in which sin and blindness pervert the workings of desire from their Godward direction.

Indeed, it is a chastening thought that clergy sexual abuse may, oftentimes, arise from this demonic perversion of a profound truth: that sexual desire finds it final meaning *only* in (the trinitarian) God.

THEOLOGY IN VIA: AN ASCETIC RECOMMENDATION FOR LIFE

I have now charted the ways in which a new type of case for the doctrine of the Trinity might proceed from the consideration of neglected patristic texts (especially the fathers' exegesis of certain

---

[4] Note that 'self-control' (*egkrateia*) in Paul does not mean 'repression' in the terms of modern Freudian psychology; this spiritual 'gift' belongs with 'love, joy, peace, patience, kindness, generosity, faithfulness, [and] gentleness' (Gal. 5. 22–3).

rich strands of biblical witness on prayer 'in the Spirit'), and from a central theological focus on that activity of prayer – whether past or present – as a matrix for trinitarian reflection. But once it is granted that a particular set of bodily and spiritual practices (both individual and liturgical) are the *precondition* for trinitarian thinking of a deep sort, one is already admitting that the task of theology – on this view – cannot simply be 'conformed to the world' and its current philosophical or cultural presumptions without a remaining excess of meaning, and an implicit critique of that 'world'. Simply put, and conversely: if one is resolutely *not* engaged in the practices of prayer, contemplation, and worship, then there are certain sorts of philosophical insight that are unlikely, if not impossible, to become available to one. So it now becomes clear why theology, thus understood, must be a form of intellectual investigation in which a *secular*, universalist rationality may find itself significantly challenged – whether criticized, expanded, transformed, or even at points rejected. In other words, an Enlightenment-style appeal to a shared universal 'reason' can no longer provide an uncontentious basis for the adjudication of competing theological claims.

But to take such an 'anti-foundationalist' view (one that, in varying forms, has almost become a new orthodoxy in theological circles in the era of postmodernity) is not without its own intellectual dangers. And here I wish to distinguish my position rather carefully from various contemporary alternatives with which it might well be confused. The problems with a *generically* anti-secular – and even anti-philosophical – position in theology are manifold. Such a posture can give the impression (real or imagined) of a rigid sort of Christian sectarianism which withdraws from the duties of public democratic discussion, and may even consider itself removed from the dictates of universal 'human rights' language. It can seem to indulge in rhetorical polemics against 'the world'

without giving any clear indication of its own rational accountability. It can thus play into the hands, conversely, of those secular
detractors from Christian commitment who argue that theology is
not even appropriate to the life of politics or the university – that is,
to reasoned public discussion in any rigorous sense.

So to give up now on the possibility of continuing rational debate
between denominations and religions, and especially across the
secular–religious divide, is in my view a fatal move for contemporary theology, particularly in the light of the newly charged significance of religion in world politics. (Ironically, the loss of the
possibility of a brokered *religious* rationality may be more fatal for
democracy and world peace than its maintenance and protection:
religious belief, religious *hope*, may ultimately be crucially important for such a discussion, rather than an impediment to it.)
Similarly, to decry the significance for Christian theology of clear
and well-ordered thinking, or of the responsible and critical use of
texts, historical evidences and philosophical arguments in theological work, is no less lethal. For all these undertakings remain both
apologetic and scholarly duties, however probingly certain secular
methodological presumptions met in the course of these tasks must
be assessed and challenged.

Further, as I shall argue later in Chapter 2, an entirely hostile
attitude to Enlightenment traditions of moral philosophy is a similarly
grave strategic mistake for contemporary theology, and especially for
those concerned with political justice for women and socially
oppressed people: an ardent 'trumping' of the Enlightenment tradition can lead all too easily to a strange amnesia about precisely those
people whom the Enlightenment originally set out to benefit. It
follows that the theological method proposed here fully endorses
the significance of ongoing *interaction* with modern and postmodern
secular philosophy – as a vital apologetic exercise, as a challenge to

the internal analytic clarification of the Christian faith, and as a commitment to pragmatic, justice-seeking ends. One does not need, as a Christian, to be either seduced by, or wholly averse to, contemporary secular philosophy in order to continue to engage with it, both critically and creatively: one might say that a *contrapuntal* relationship is what is required, but with Christian thought and practice, not secular philosophy, providing the *cantus firmus.*[5] Outright rejection of secular philosophy is as dangerous an alternative as outright submission: there has to be a 'more excellent way' than the two false alternatives (fideism versus secularism) that currently feature large in the theological culture wars. Ironically, Barth's dogmatics and ordinary language ('analytic') philosophy – perhaps the most important developments in the twentieth century for theology and philosophy, respectively – have together combined in a pincer movement to help entrench this false disjunction. Yet it is such an alternative third way, which precisely eludes this false choice, that I shall seek to exemplify in this volume and its successors.

What, then, is distinctive about the idea of theology that this book proposes? The central theme (and this is vital to the understanding of systematic theology to be unfurled in the next two chapters) is that the task of theology is always, if implicitly, a *recommendation for life.* The vision it sets before one invites ongoing – and sometimes disorienting – response and change, both personal and political, in relation to God. One may rightly call theology from this perspective an ascetical exercise – one that demands bodily practice and transformation, both individual and social. And to admit this is also to acknowledge that the task of theology is always in motion (*in via*), always undoing and redoing itself, not only in response to shifting current events, but

---

[5] And even this *cantus firmus* is of course not a merely human product (not a human 'foundation'), but a line sung precisely in response to God's prior tuning.

because of the deepening of vision that may – and should – emerge from such ascetical demand and execution. Such deepening of vision will eventually also involve at some point a profound sense of the mind's *darkening*, and of a disconcerting reorientation of the senses – these being inescapable fallouts from the commitment to prayer that sustains such a view of the theological enterprise.[6] The willingness to endure a form of naked dispossession before God; the willingness to surrender control (not to any human power, but solely to God's power); the willingness to accept the arid vacancy of a simple waiting on God in prayer; the willingness at the same time to accept disconcerting bombardments from the realm of the 'unconscious': all these are the ascetical tests of contemplation without which no epistemic or spiritual deepening can start to occur. What distinguishes this position, then, from an array of other 'post-foundationalist' options that currently present themselves in theology, is the commitment to the discipline of *particular* graced bodily practices which, over the long haul, afford certain distinctive ways of knowing.

Once this transformational feature of theology is granted (and it is worth pointing out once more that it is a peculiarly modern aberration to refuse it), then it is not only the false quest for pre-Christian secular-philosophical foundations for theology that falls away. At the same time, the project of being *in via* is seen as purposive: as a 'journey into God' rather than as a floundering on perilous, non-foundational quicksands. What shifts, on this view of theology, is not merely the range of vision afforded over time by the interplay of theological investigation and ascetical practice, but the

---

[6] I give a full (and wholly practical) account of what is meant by the practice of 'contemplation', as a simple form of dark, naked waiting before God, in my *Powers and Submissions: Philosophy, Spirituality and Gender* (Oxford: Blackwell, 2002), ch. 2. Since so much hangs on the appeal to contemplation in this book, it is vital that the reader understand what is at stake in this practice, and how different it is from any sort of exercise in narcissistic self-cultivation.

very capacity to see. What is being progressively purged, in this undertaking, is the fallen and flawed capacity for idolatry, the tragic misdirecting of desire. One is learning, over a lifetime – and not without painful difficulty – to think, act, desire, and *see* aright. But such seeing has a peculiar property, as must now be considered.

THEOLOGY AND SEEING GOD: IDOLATRY
AND THE IMAGINATION

Let me return once more to my account of the ordering of the individual chapters of this book. I have been arguing here, albeit briefly, that theology involves not merely the *metaphysical* task of adumbrating a vision of God, the world, and humanity, but simultaneously the *epistemological* task of cleansing, reordering, and redirecting the apparatuses of one's own thinking, desiring, and seeing. And that is why this first volume of systematics, on the Trinity, cannot bypass another neglected, but vital, arena for theological reflection on God as Trinity, that of the history of Christian iconography (Chapter 5). What may appear to influence one only from the subliminal realm of fantasy or the imagination is a vivid source of theological power – both for good and ill – and thus must receive its due attention and analysis. I shall say more later of my conception of the theological project as fundamentally purgative of idolatry, of the vital difference of such a project from straightforward iconoclasm, and of the strange power of the imagination both in the maintenance of such idolatry and in its transformation. The impetus simply to smash and bury an idolatrous image must face the charge that such violence may leave the broken shards curiously and remainingly powerful; a subtler approach, more cognizant of the psychology of the imagination – and its capacity for plasticity and transformation – is demanded.

It may by now be clear why an ascetic perception of theology leads inexorably into an examination of what it could mean in theology to seek the divine 'face' – to explore with intensity the fundamental religious desire to 'see God' (Exodus 24. 10–11; Psalm 27. 8; Matthew 5. 8), yet constantly to have that desire chastened and corrected (Exodus 20. 4–5; John 1. 18). This tension runs right through the Bible, and cannot therefore be said to be unproblematically 'solved' through the incarnation, despite the central Christian claim that Jesus uniquely manifests the invisible God (see John 12. 45; 2 Corinthians 4. 4–6; Colossians 1. 15). Yet if all the faculties and senses (intellect, feeling, will, imagination, aesthetic sensibility) are to be drawn into the realm of the systematic endeavour, then the enormous power of the visual and the imaginative – perhaps never so powerfully felt than in the age of advertising, television, and the internet – cannot be bypassed or gainsaid. The evidence of the history of the iconography of the Trinity here is, for a contemporary theology sensitive to issues of power and gender, as revealing an alternative account of the doctrine's development as is the turn to the prayer-based logic of the early patristic story. Here (Chapter 5) much is revealed about the difference between official, creedal accounts of trinitarian orthodoxy and the rather different messages – often explicitly coded in political or gendered guise – that have been purveyed in the visual representation of 'perfect relations in God' (the Trinity). All is not what it seems; the Trinity has to be reflected upon not merely as a pure item of dogmatic orthodoxy, but via its more elusive associations at the level of cultural production. Once again, the iconographical material presses one towards an ascetic test: the chastening of fallen desire, the darkening of previous certainties, and the reimagination of God's trinitarian relation to the created order. The double pressure of the Spirit is once more felt – building up and breaking down. For if the artistic evidence often reveals embarrassingly heterodox ways of painting the Trinity anthropomorphically, it also throws a stark light on the religious impoverishment in overzealous attempts to portray visual orthodoxy with exactitude. As I shall show, some strange three-nosed and three-headed monsters have been created in the attempt to paint 'three persons in one substance' *literally*. When one compares these freaks with more subtle visual symbolizations of the Trinity, one becomes newly aware of the delicate art of theological representation, whether verbal or visual – the significance of what cannot be stated or painted, as well as what can. In other words, art too, and in its own distinctive way, can be 'apophatic' (it can say by unsaying). It can gesture beyond words while also 'giving rise to thought' – sometimes fresh and disturbing thought.

BEYOND REPRESSION AND LIBERTINISM: THE SPIRIT IN THE TRINITY

And this brings me to the final strand in this first volume of systematics, 'On the Trinity'. In my last chapter (Chapter 7), having shifted the kaleidoscope on the history of the doctrine of the Trinity in this variety of new ways (from text to spiritual practice to field-work to art, exposing new vulnerabilities and new richnesses), I end with a proposal that draws together the lessons learnt about the ascetical demands of such a theological method and its significance for current speech, imagination, and reflection on God. I come back to the pressing contemporary concerns about sexuality and gender with which I started, and ask afresh how a specifically trinitarian understanding of the divine might radically challenge and transform the way in which a secular culture approaches these concerns.

The understanding of the Trinity that has emerged from the cumulative impact of the patristic, sociological, and iconographic investigations is now explicitly aligned with a theology of *divine desire*, one in which a particular form of human participation (not, note, direct human imitation) is deemed possible, but only in virtue of what one might call a posture of contemplative 'effacement'. To accept and even court such effacement, to seek to enter into such divine participation, is not only to embrace change – morally, intellectually, and spiritually – but to learn, diffidently at first, how to speak a new language. For to speak properly of God as Trinity (indeed to speak properly of God at all) involves a necessary form of noetic slippage – an acknowledgement of profound intellectual vertigo. The turn towards divine desire is itself transformative, not only of particular human desires (as outlined earlier in spiritual and ethical terms), but also of the very capacity to think, feel, and imagine. What is here playfully called the 'apophatic turn' is not limited merely to *linguistic* negations (although, to be sure, there has to be a constant and disciplined self-reminder that what one says of things in the created realm can never be said in the same way of God). Rather, what is blanked out in the regular, patient attempt to attend to God in prayer is *any* sense of human grasp; and what comes to replace such an ambition, over time, is the elusive, but nonetheless ineluctable, sense of *being grasped*, of the Spirit's simultaneous erasure of human idolatry and subtle reconstitution of human selfhood in God. Darkness as the condition of revelatory presence is, it emerges, importantly different from darkness as mere absence or 'deferral'.

In sum: by the end of this first volume of Christian systematics, an account has been given of what it might be to enter, willingly and consciously, into the life of divine desire; of how what occurs in this ascetic process might need to be described, albeit haltingly, in trinitarian terms; of how costly and transformative this might prove, both epistemically and ethically; and of how subtle, and how necessary, to escape thereby beyond the false modern disjunction of sexual libertinism and sexual repression. It has been seen, through a variety of lenses and perspectives, that the Spirit is the vibrant point of contact and entry into the flow of this divine desire, the irreplaceable mode of invitation for the cracking open of the crooked human heart. The Spirit is the constant overflow of the life of God into creation: alluring, delighting, inflaming, in its propulsion of divine desire. But the Spirit is no less also a means of distinguishing hiatus: both within God, and in God's relations to creation. It is what makes God irreducibly *three*, simultaneously distinguishing and binding Father and Son, and so refusing also – by analogous outreach – the mutual narcissism of even the most delighted of human lovers. It would be misleading, therefore, to call the Spirit an 'excess', as has become fashionable of late; for its love presses not only outwards to include others, but also inwards (and protectively) to sustain the difference between the persons, thus preserving a perfect and harmonious balance between union and distinction.

From this perspective I am forced, finally, to think afresh about some of the theological shibboleths that have divided the Christian tradition 'trinitarianly' – East and West, ancient and modern: what this view means, for instance, for the vexed and technical issues of trinitarian 'relations', 'persons', and 'processions', and for the doctrinal contention that ostensibly caused Eastern and Western Christendom to split (the so-called *filioque* dispute).[7] My solutions to these conundrums will turn out to be surprisingly irenic ecumenically, despite the apparent disturbance to traditional formulae effected by this new emphasis on the Spirit, and on the intrinsic

---

[7] *Filioque* means 'and from the Son' (in the creedal phrase 'And I believe in the Holy Spirit . . . who proceeds from the Father [and the Son]'). It was inserted into the Nicene Creed by the West without the agreement of an ecumenical council.

connection of trinitarian reflection to questions of human desire and gender.

Finally, one charge that might be levelled against the theological approach outlined here should perhaps be faced and deflected immediately, at the close of this Prelude. That is, is the appeal to the life of contemplation, or deep prayer in the Spirit, necessarily tainted with subjectivism? Is it just another form of wish-fulfilment or projection, spun out of a misguided inner need for comfort or certainty? My answer to that charge would be a firm no; and at least three reasons will emerge, in this book and its successors, for countering that charge. The first is that, as already intimated, this approach does not involve a philosophically naïve appeal to 'subjective experience', as if that were somehow separable from the exercise of biblical exegesis, patient examination of tradition, reasoned theological exposition, and testing by the criterion of 'spiritual fruits'.[8] Rather, the practice of prayer provides the context in which silence in the Spirit *expands* the potential to respond to the realm of the Word, and reason too is stretched and changed beyond its normal, secular reach. This can be strangely far from 'comforting' as a new undertaking – indeed deeply anxiety-making in its initial impact. It cannot therefore be claimed to be an exercise in mere wish-fulfilment: its spiritual impact far exceeds what it finds to be confirming of original expectation.

Second, as will be spelled out in more detail in due course in this systematics,[9] this venture leads to a vision of theology in which the hard philosophical task of justification of truth claims is nonetheless actively embraced rather than avoided – albeit in a way that takes

---

[8] Indeed, as this book – and this systematic project as a whole – unfolds, it will become apparent how the (seemingly) private or individual act of contemplation is in fact the most intensely corporate Christian activity of all, and thus too, the lifeblood of liturgical life.

[9] In volume II.

on the complication of states in which the mind is first darkened in order to relate to God more intimately and accurately. Third, as we have already seen in this Prelude, the theological approach that is proposed in this undertaking examines a much *wider* range of evidences than is normally employed in contemporary theology; and one might therefore claim that this contributes to an expanded objectivity of standpoint, rather than an intensified subjectivity.

CONCLUSION

It has been the task of this Prelude, now completed, to give a succinct forecast and overview of the interweaving themes that are to come, and of how the cumulative theses of this book hang together. I started with the contemporary obsessions of an over-'sexualized' culture, and came to the trinitarian God – not an obvious journey, but one that may perhaps be sufficiently intriguing to sustain further interest. I shall end with a vision of selfhood reconstituted participatorily in the triune God, in such a way that misdirected desire (sin and blindness) is radically purged and chastened. Desire, on this view, is the constellating category of selfhood, the ineradicable root of the human longing for God. To uncover this root, and give it *theological* valence, is to be forced to an equally radical rethinking of contemporary presumptions about sexuality, gender, and selfhood.

This book represents, it must already be clear, an approach to theology that invites the reader – however hesitantly and uncertainly – to step inside this realm of contemplation of the divine, and to 'taste and see' what insights fall out from such a perspective. As will emerge, each chapter of this book, each insight, is an essay in its own right; and without too much loss of coherence, the different chapters in this volume may be read first as distinct units. This method of gathering such discrete pieces into a theological basket has its own appropriateness to the type of systematic theology that is to be propounded in this work and its planned successors: some would say it is the only form of theology that can appropriately be undertaken in a postmodern age. So to the task of explaining further what exactly this theological method is – why I propose to call it *théologie totale*, how it relates no less to the discomforting authority of Scripture as to the disconcerting blanking of the mind in contemplation of which I have just spoken, and why it cannot be undertaken at all without close attention to prayer and to the workings of desire – I now turn.[10]

* * *

BIBLIOGRAPHIC NOTE

The following works may usefully be consulted for further background to the arguments developed in the Prelude above. I have divided the bibliography into paragraphs under key themes, and will continue to follow this format in the bibliographic notes throughout the book.

DEVELOPMENTS AND TRENDS IN TRINITARIAN THEOLOGY
IN THE TWENTIETH CENTURY

The latter part of the twentieth century saw a remarkable revival of trinitarian thought, and this forms the wider backdrop of my project. Both Karl Barth (see his *Church Dogmatics* (Edinburgh: T&T Clark, 1956–75), esp. vols. I/I, II/I, and IV/I) and Karl Rahner (*The Trinity* (London: Burns & Oates, 1970)) presented fresh approaches to the Trinity founded in the concept of

---

[10] Readers who are not trained in theology or philosophy may like to skip the next two chapters and come back to them later, after savouring the arguments of content about the patristic tradition, contemporary 'lived religion', and artistic representations of the Trinity. Discussions about theological method are, alas, necessarily more abstract than discussions about theological content. Nevertheless, I try even here to keep arcane or jargonistic language to a minimum.

revelation, and Eastern Orthodox theologians simultaneously revived trinitarian thought in their own tradition, in conscious and polemical differentiation from 'Western' models: see especially Vladimir Lossky, *The Mystical Theology of the Eastern Church* (Cambridge: James Clarke, 1957), and John Zizioulas, *Being as Communion: Studies in Personhood and the Church* (London: DLT, 1985). What followed, ironically, was a wave of Western imitations of such 'Eastern' models, often by appeal to a reading of the Greek fathers as 'social trinitarians' (see Colin Gunton, *The Promise of Trinitarian Theology* (2nd edn; Edinburgh: T&T Clark, 1997); Catherine Mowry LaCugna, *God for Us: The Trinity and Christian Life* (San Francisco: Harper, 1991); and, rather differently, Jürgen Moltmann, *The Trinity and the Kingdom: The Doctrine of God* (London: SCM Press, 1981), and Miroslav Volf, *After Our Likeness: The Church in the Image of the Trinity* (Grand Rapids, MI: Eerdmans, 1998)). Feminist theology, when interested in maintaining trinitarianism (e.g., Elizabeth A. Johnson, *She Who Is: The Mystery of God in Feminist Theological Discourse* (New York: Crossroad, 1992)) has tended to be strongly attracted to this 'social' approach, finding in the trinitarian God an imitable prototype for egalitarian human relations. More recently, however, there has been a significant reaction to the 'East–West' disjunction theory, as well as to the idea that a 'social Trinity' can form a straightforward model for human emulation (see especially Lewis Ayres, *Nicaea and its Legacy: An Approach to Fourth-Century Trinitarian Theology* (Oxford University Press, 2004), and the essays in Sarah Coakley, ed., *The God of Nicaea: Disputed Questions in Patristic Trinitarianism* in *Harvard Theological Review* 100/2 (2007)). For a survey of these developments, see my introduction to that journal issue (125–38).

Yves Congar's *I Believe in the Holy Spirit* (3 vols.; London, Chapman, 1983) has proved in retrospect to be a prescient account of how ecumenical advance might be aided by a stronger emphasis on the doctrine of the Spirit and a resistance to overplayed 'East–West' disjunctions: his work has also inspired aspects of Chapters 6 and 7, below.

'ORTHODOXY', 'HERESY', AND CRITICAL FEMINIST READINGS OF EARLY CHRISTIAN TRADITION

In this book I am picking my way, methodologically, between a set of scholarly contentions about 'orthodoxy' and 'heresy' which have been notable in scholarship dating from after World War II. Walter Bauer's generative study, *Orthodoxy and Heresy in Earliest Christianity* (orig. 1934; Philadelphia: Fortress Press, 1971), argued that the terms *orthodoxy* and *heresy* should not be straighforwardly identified with the views espoused by the 'majority' and 'minority' in early Christianity: the map of early Christian commitments was from the start more localized, contentious, and complex than that would suggest, and it was a 'myth' that 'orthodoxy' had come *first*. Although Bauer's work has been variously assessed (see, e.g., Thomas Robinson, *The Bauer Thesis Examined: The Geography of Heresy in the Early Christian Church* (Lewiston, NY: Edwin Mellen, 1988)), its effects were to render any story of a smooth unfolding of Christian truth problematic. In the wake of Bauer, one creative development was a feminist rediscovery of 'heretical' gnostic texts (see, e.g., Elaine Pagels, *The Gnostic Gospels* (New York: Random House, 1982), and Karen King, *What is Gnosticism?* (Cambridge, MA: Harvard University Press, 2003)), and with it the demonstration that emergent Christian 'orthodoxy' had sidelined women's interests and leadership. Operating in a parallel paradigm inspired by Michel Foucault's conception of power, Alain le Boulluec, *La Notion d'hérésie dans la littérature grecque*, IIe–IIIe *siècles* (2 vols.; Paris: Études Augustiniennes, 1985) has effected a further shift, moving the discussion beyond Bauer's matrix and representing 'orthodoxy' and 'heresy' as necessarily intertwined from the beginning.

One of the unfortunate effects of these otherwise exciting scholarly developments has been to range *theological* approaches (often associated with old-style dogmatics or 'patristics') over against *social science* analyses of power or gender. I resist this disjunction, supporting neither an intrinsic suspicion of the category of 'orthodoxy' (as can be seen in, e.g., Elizabeth Schüssler Fiorenza, *Jesus: Miriam's Child, Sophia's Prophet. Critical Issues in Feminist Christology* (New York: Continuum, 1994), or in Virginia Burrus, *'Begotten, Not Made': Conceiving Manhood in Late Antiquity* (Stanford University Press, 2000)), nor a straightforward valorization of traditions previously dubbed 'heretical' (as in the works of Pagels and King, already mentioned). Thus, while my own approach is distinctively theological, and more interested in prayer and *spiritual* power than is le Boulluec, I write against the background of his shift and its effect on the current scholarly consensus. Yet I also take very seriously the entanglement of such spiritual forms of power with questions of (gendered) ecclesiastical authority, without reducing the former to the latter. Everything depends on careful contextual analysis.

THE PLATONIC HERITAGE IN CHRISTIANITY AND THE
NATURE OF 'DESIRE'

The classic modern study of the role of *erōs* in patristic thought, and its purported *contrast* with *agapē*, is Anders Nygren's *Agape and Eros* (London: SPCK, 1953). In Nygren's work a sharp dichotomy is presented in which selfless Christian *agapē* draws one upwards, and selfish Greek *erōs* downwards. This present book does not accept such a dichotomy, and explores the productive intertwining of *erōs* with *agapē* from the time of the early marriage of Christianity and Platonic philosophy. A critical response to Nygren was already mounted by Martin D'Arcy, SJ, in his *The Mind and the Heart of Love* (London: Faber, 1954); and one can find a more recent, historically nuanced, rejection of Nygren's dichotomy in Catherine Osborne's *Eros Unveiled: Plato and the God of Love* (Oxford: Clarendon Press, 1994). Discussion of love in late antiquity and later is of course further complicated by the modern analyses of Sigmund Freud (for whom love has its origins in libidinal instincts formed in childhood: see especially his *Three Essays on the Theory of Sexuality* (London: Imago, 1949)), and Michel Foucault (for whom love is a negotiation of power and sexual desire: see his *The History of Sexuality* (3 vols.; New York: Pantheon, 1978–86)). The brilliant work of Peter Brown (*The Body and Society: Men, Women, and Sexual Renunciation in Early Christianity* (London: Faber & Faber, 1988)) and his pupils is often strongly inflected by influence from the Freudian school; whereas – in contrast – this volume seeks to probe back behind these modern presumptions about 'sexuality' to re-explore distinctive early Christian views of asceticism and desire. My essay, 'Pleasure Principles: Towards a Contemporary Theology of Desire', *Harvard Divinity Bulletin* (2005), 20–33 (also in Sarah Coakley, *The New Asceticism: Sexuality, Gender and the Quest for God* (London: Bloomsbury, 2013)), provides a charter account of this project, as well as analyzing the developments in Freud's own thought on sexual desire and his relation to the Platonic heritage.

HOMOSEXUALITY AND THE CHURCH OF ENGLAND

Analyses of homosexuality in the Church of England (and beyond) range from the theological and scholarly – for example Charles Hefling, ed., *Ourselves, Our Souls and Bodies* (Boston, MA: Cowley Publishing, 1996);

Eugene Rogers, *Sexuality and the Christian Body: Their Way into the Triune God* (Oxford: Blackwell, 1999); Eugene Rogers, ed., *Theology and Sexuality: Classic and Contemporary Readings* (Oxford: Blackwell, 2002) – through to more journalistic offerings linked to much publicised ecclesial ructions: for example, Stephen Bates, *A Church at War: Anglicans and Homosexuality* (London: I. B. Tauris, 2004), and William L. Sachs, *Homosexuality and the Crisis in Anglicanism* (Cambridge University Press, 2009). Although the present book only intersects with these Anglican crises implicitly, I provide a view beyond the usual conservative–liberal divide in 'Beyond Libertarianism and Repression: The Quest for an Anglican Theological Ascetics', in Terry Brown, ed., *Other Voices, Other Worlds* (London: DLT, 2006), 331–8.

THEOLOGY, POSTMODERNITY, AND PHILOSOPHICAL NON-FOUNDATIONALISM

In this volume, 'postmodernity' is taken to mean the (purported) end of a shared 'grand narrative' between differing cultural and philosophical contexts (see Jean-François Lyotard, *The Postmodern Condition: A Report on Knowledge* (Manchester University Press, 1984)), a matter which is closely related to the rejection of philosophical 'foundationalism'. Non-foundationalism denies the possibility of identifying universal epistemological criteria that could then form the basis ('foundation') for all other claims to truth. As such, it signals a massive assault on the 'Enlightenment project', which was designed precisely to pin down such criteria by reference to the basic capacities of the knowing subject. Postmodern theology has to a remarkable degree embraced this non-foundationalist fashion with enthusiasm, finding in it an opportunity to undermine a complacent secular universalism. But the religious ploys utilized thereby have been enormously varied: they range, for example, from Alasdair MacIntyre's (more appropriately labelled 'late-modern') adjudication between competing historical paradigms of rationality (*Whose Justice? Which Rationality?* (University of Notre Dame Press, 1988)), through Stanley Hauerwas's distinctive marriage of Barthian and Thomist thought (*The State of the University: Academic Knowledges and the Knowledge of God* (Oxford: Blackwell, 2007)), John Milbank's exposé of secular modernity and re-espousal of Augustinian Thomism (*Theology and Social Theory: Beyond Secular Reason*

(2nd edn; Oxford: Blackwell, 2006)), and analytic philosophy of religion's 'Reformed epistemology' (Nicholas Wolterstorff, *Reason within the Bounds of Religion* (Grand Rapids, MI: Eerdman, 1999), Alvin Plantinga, *Warranted Christian Belief* (Oxford University Press, 2000)), to – very differently – the various theological followers of Derrida's literary project of 'deconstruction' (see *Of Grammatology* (Baltimore: Johns Hopkins University Press, 1998)). David Tracy, commenting on these various trends, describes systematic theology as now irretrievably 'fragmentary' in the conditions of postmodernity ('Fragments: The Spiritual Situation of our Times', in John D. Caputo and Michael J. Scanlon, eds., *God, the Gift and Postmodernism* (Bloomington: Indiana University Press, 1999), 170–81).

As I shall discuss further in Chapter 2 below, this notable recent theological enthusiasm for non-foundationalism comes with dangers and costs which need to be faced. Amongst other things, it leaves generic ethical appeals to 'human rights' in a state of aporia, and discussion between theology and science problematically divided into apparently incommensurable *magisteria*. For further comment on these dangers, see my Cambridge inaugural lecture, *Sacrifice Regained: Reconsidering the Rationality of Christian Belief* (Cambridge University Press, 2012).

CHAPTER 1

Recasting 'systematic theology': gender, desire, and *théologie totale*

In the Prelude I sketched out the way that the various pieces of the argument that will follow in this book cohere. The metaphor was chosen advisedly: these pieces are not to be seen as merely broken shards, but as *tesserae* to be variously reconstellated in a kaleidoscope, or – by the end of this project – as eucharistic fragments to be gathered into a shared basket. I have attempted, in other words, to give just a brief glimpse of the multifaceted vision that informs this treatise 'On the Trinity'. I have also hinted at the sort of reconception of the task of theology that is involved here: this will be a theology *in via*, as I called it, founded not in secular rationality but in spiritual practices of attention that mysteriously challenge and *expand* the range of rationality, and simultaneously darken and break one's hold on previous certainties. Before I turn back to the world of early Christianity and to the origins of trinitarianism, I need to explain in more detail what such an ascetic, contemplative, proposal for theology actually entails.

Yet an 'excursus on method' is definitely something to be avoided: such a ponderous undertaking has been memorably derided as mere 'throat-clearing'.[1] Thus in this chapter and the

---

[1] See Jeffrey Stout, *Ethics after Babel: The Languages of Morals and their Discontents* (Boston, MA: Beacon, 1988), 163.

next I shall not so much be clearing my throat as redirecting the mind. Without this theological redirection, the pieces on the Trinity that follow might seem strangely disconnected; without this initial analysis of my intent, a range of misleading, but currently standard, theological disjunctions might still be exercising the reader, with negative imaginative and spiritual consequences.

So in Chapter 1, first, I shall set out to explain further why systematic theology (to be defined) must go on, even in a post-modern age; and also why it cannot credibly go on without urgent attention to matters of desire ('sex', 'sexuality', and 'gender', in secular parlance). The combination of these particular two sides to my argument is admittedly unusual. It is customary, that is, for postmodern gender theorists and feminists (insofar as they have dealings with matters of religion at all) to be extremely sceptical about the project of systematic theology, for reasons I shall discuss. It is perhaps even more common (conversely) for systematic theologians to be dismissive, even derogatory, about theologians interested in feminism or gender. It is rare indeed – although not completely unknown – for systematic theologians of any stature to take the category of gender as even a significant locus for discussion; and when they do, they tend to import a gender theory from the secular realm without a sufficiently critical *theological* assessment of it. I shall be concerned to show why this false disjunction between systematic theology and gender studies needs not so much to be overcome, but rather to be approached from a different, and mind-changing, direc-tion. A robustly theological, indeed precisely *trinitarian*, perspective on gender is required, and not one that merely smuggles secular gender presumptions into the divine realm at the outset. It is the very threeness of God, I shall argue, transformatively met in the Spirit, which gives the key to a view of gender that is appropriately founded in bodily practices of prayer. In this way, more of my proposed method of *théologie totale*[2] will thereby be disclosed: I shall show more closely how the activity of contemplation relates to the systematic task, and what changes it makes to it. I shall chart, too, how the ascetic undertaking, most paradoxically, makes the issue of desire the more acute, and gender rendered labile to it from the perspective of a theology *in via*. In short, I shall aim to bind questions of theological method, contemplative practice, and desire into a new tether. For they do belong together; and one can see all the more pressingly that they do once one grasps the implications for them of a specifically trinitarian understanding of God.

In Chapter 2 I shall then be able to turn back to the social and political questions with which an earlier generation of feminisms and concomitant feminist theologies was concerned. Much of the feminist theology from this earlier period now looks dated or methodologically flawed; but the social and political issues it attempted to solve have by no means gone away. In fact, if anything, they have intensified. Yet more recent gender study, especially that of postmodern philosophical allegiance, has tended in contrast to eschew the 'liberal' agenda of universal rights for women. It has thereby attracted the opprobrium of feminist political scientists still committed to such a global perspective. Here I shall extend my argument (already sketched in the Prelude), that secular, modernist philosophy, political thought, and sociology, along with the liberal feminist thinking that has classically been their partner, must at least remain as what I have called 'contrapuntal' voices in the contemporary theological task. The denigration of such thought is a theological and ethical mistake of grave consequence; yet the

---

[2] My use of this term (already fleetingly introduced in the Prelude) is based, although only loosely, on an analogy to the French Annales School's *l'histoire totale*, and on its goal of uncovering every level of an historical culture. As will shortly be explained, the evocations of *totale* are decidedly *not* 'totalizing' in the political sense.

critique, extension, and transformation of it is no less a matter of spiritual and theological urgency. Once again we shall discover that an apparently unconnected but distinctly *theological* matter – the issue of iconoclasm and the contemplative remaking of the imagination – is key to a right understanding of how such political and social thinking should proceed. Matters which appeared to have little to do with each other – liberal or socialist feminism and the problem of idolatry – come, in the perspective of a contemplative theology *in via*, into vital relation.

This methodological pincer movement in Chapters 1 and 2 will complete my purpose of disclosing the chief characteristics of a *théologie totale*. By the end of this discussion we shall have before us, and I shall have explained with some care, a new vision of systematic theology. Such a vision is not, I shall again insist, a compromise between long-standing ideological disjunctions in the practice of theology, but represents a subtle shifting of the terms of the discussion. The game can be replayed, and creatively so.

But first one has to understand what systematic theology has meant in the past, what it could mean now, and why it has come under such particular fire in this contemporary, postmodern era.

WHAT IS SYSTEMATIC THEOLOGY?

'Systematic theology' is itself a modern category, but one that has a certain family resemblance relation – albeit loose – to other, historic, ways of attempting to present a complete, and inviting, vision of Christian doctrine in its various parts. A brief mention of a variety of such attempts in the tradition – which have proved themselves by their sheer creative staying power – will help me present an argument both for systematic theology's indispensability, and also for its malleability.

The great Alexandrian theologian Origen, for instance, wrote in the third century a text he entitled *De principiis* (*On first principles*), and which has often been read in the modern period as his attempt to do 'systematic theology'. But it would be a grave mistake, as well as an anachronistic one, to see his undertaking in that one text as summing up everything he had to say about central Christian doctrines, let alone – as has also been charged – as a mere capitulation to Platonic philosophy. Origen's exegetical writings, and his treatises on particular subjects (such as *On prayer*, to be reflected upon in Chapter 3), fill out the picture of his doctrinal vision in infinitely richer ways, which complement and expand on the central 'principles' of Christian philosophical theology enunciated in the *De principiis*. So Origen is indeed, in a sense, one of the first systematic theologians in Christian tradition; but one needs to look at a wide variety of his different sorts of writing to divine his full vision. This is already a telling lesson, because it indicates that systematic theology cannot necessarily be undertaken simply in one genre of writing; and hence the false disjunction of the *De principiis* from different sorts of texts like the *De oratione* is a mistake of some gravity.

Much later, in the eighth-century East in a context of increasing Islamic ascendancy, John Damascene's *De fide orthodoxa* (*On the orthodox faith*) was another quite different, and much more succinct and focused, attempt to be systematic, reflecting the *cumulative* sense of doctrinal tradition in Greek Christian thought at the time. John of Damascus wrote to codify and clarify what was by then normatively orthodox in the East, and had been painstakingly learnt and refined through many centuries of theological and conciliar dispute in the post-Constantinian era. The representation and analysis of historic orthodoxy, then, can be another way of being systematic; but it is only one form, and a relatively restricted one, amongst many possible variations.

The later Western medieval tradition of commenting on
'Sentences', a different and strongly philosophical genre epitomized
in the work of Peter Lombard and his commentators, has been said, in
some contrast to John Damascene's work, to be inherently without
totalizing intent, a necessarily 'fragmentary' undertaking (albeit one
undertaken with a strong impetus to convict and persuade). One
could, nonetheless, count it as another type of intellectual endeavour
bent on unfolding a systematic account of Christian truth, but one
focused on punctiliar and particular challenges and questions about
the faith. In contrast, Thomas Aquinas's great *Summa Theologiae*
(along with his earlier apologetic *Summa contra Gentiles*), represents
one of the most breathtaking attempts in Christian tradition to
provide a *complete* inventory of Christian doctrine, ethics, and sacramental practice, and their relation to contemporary philosophical and
interreligious discussion. Here a full vision of Christian truth is
unfolded with due attention to Bible and tradition, yet sustained by
extraordinary argumentative power and continuous consideration of
alternative approaches (as is appropriate to a *Summa* founded in the
practice of philosophical 'disputation').

The early modern genre of 'Dogmatics' was, one might say, the
Protestant answer to the Catholic magisterial account of authoritative doctrine, and in part also a belated mimicry and riposte to
classic Catholic scholasticism. Here the so-called *loci* (standard
points of doctrinal discussion, roughly based on the main items in
the historic creeds)[3] received a distinctively Protestant form. It was

---

[3] The list of such *loci* has not remained static or unchanged in Christian 'systematic'
tradition, but characteristically contains at least the following: God/Trinity;
Christology (doctrine of Christ, divine and human); pneumatology (doctrine of the
Spirit); anthropology (doctrine of the human person); sin and atonement; sacraments;
ecclesiology (doctrine of the church); eschatology (doctrine of the end times). These are
often supplemented by other items for discussion, such as: creation and providence; love
and other divine attributes (or 'names'); epistemological and ethical topics; prayer;
Christianity's relation to Judaism, Islam and to non-'Abrahamic' religious traditions.

one that was more scholastically formalized than that originally envisaged by the sixteenth-century lawyer and exegete John Calvin, who might be said to have founded Protestant systematic theology in Reformed mode. He had laid out his own programmatic theological vision for Geneva in his so-called *Institutes*, a doctrinal discussion in four parts which he consciously moulded on Paul's *Epistle to the Romans* and the Reformed practice of scriptural commentary.

Much later, Friedrich Schleiermacher, reacting in the early nineteenth century to what he perceived as the dead hand of established Protestant scholasticism in this Calvinist mode, freed his own revisionary account of Christian doctrine into a descriptive account of 'the current religious consciousness', and renamed it *Glaubenslehre* ('teaching on the faith'). This was a ploy that allowed him the opportunity to reorder the loci in a strikingly creative way, starting with an analysis of human dependence on God, and only then unfolding a new distribution of the older doctrinal themes. Famously, or notoriously, he put human religious 'feeling' at the heart of his systematic undertaking.

Reacting fiercely to Schleiermacher's liberal Calvinism (but at the same time covertly assuming many of its inherent features), Karl Barth in the twentieth century championed an equally innovative form of exposition which he first playfully titled 'irregular dogmatics', and later 'Church Dogmatics'. His approach, refounded in the primary authority of the biblical Word, allowed him also a signal freedom to unfold his own creative thought – even as it changed and developed – across a lifetime of prophetic political resistance and increasing (albeit somewhat covert) engagement with post-Enlightenment philosophy. It established him as the premier Continental theologian of his era. His work, with its resounding '*Nein!*' uttered against secular power politics and against any attempts to moor theology in an analysis of the human, is probably still the dominating influence in new, contemporary attempts at systematic theology. Not the least of its attractions is its *apparent* rejection of philosophical apologetics, at a time when post-Kantian secular philosophy had appeared to place a roadblock across all attempts at speculative metaphysics.[4]

Fascinating respondents to Barth, however, even as he unfurled his vision, were the Roman Catholic systematic theologians Karl Rahner and Hans Urs von Balthasar, both of whom chose rather different forms of writing and starting point, even as they acknowledged their indebtedness to Barth: Rahner the essayist, who nonetheless eventually undertook a one-volume synthesis of his vision, starting from the anguished existential questionings of secularized 'man'; and von Balthasar, the lover of 'form', who – by reversing the order of Kant's three philosophical *Critiques* – chose to revision the core of Christian theology first through an *aesthetic* evaluation.

SYSTEMATIC THEOLOGY FOR TODAY

Even to rehearse this selective (and admittedly Western-oriented) account of some famous systematic endeavours in the Christian tradition, is to demonstrate that attempts at a complete vision of Christian doctrine have taken many forms – appropriate to the philosophical, cultural, and political ethos of their times, or sometimes in conscious reaction to the same. It has been as effectively advanced in very short documents, on occasion, as in magisterial compendia of volumes at other times. One cannot therefore speak of

---

[4] Barth thus might be seen as the reverse side of Kant – through an appeal to biblical authority which reaches into the realm of what Kant called the *noumenal*, if only by theological fiat.

systematic theology as a fixed or unchanging entity in Christian tradition. Even its starting points, criteria of theological truth, and fundamental philosophical presuppositions have been constantly open to renegotiation and debate, perhaps especially at the richest periods of its advance. Today, despite – and perhaps partly because of – the manifold objections to its very continuance in postmodern critique, systematic theology is in a remarkable state of regeneration. In some cases it takes the form of a careful, newly formulated Protestant scholasticism, albeit one heavily under the shadow of Barth; in other cases (and here one must locate the current endeavour) it is undertaken with a felt freedom to *recast* the central categories of thought at its disposal and to sit light to the burden of the traditional *loci*, even as the classic appeals to Bible, tradition, and reason are re-embraced and recast. If necessary, that is, one must start from a new perspective if this is the best way to recapture the contemporary imagination for Christ, or to reinvite reflection on the perennial mysteries of the gospel. Such is the inspiration of the notion of systematics that informs this work. Systematics, in other words, does not convey the hubristic idea of a totalizing discourse that excludes debate, opposition, or riposte; but on the other hand, it does not falter at the necessary challenge of presenting the gospel afresh in all its ramifications – systematically unfolding the connections of the parts of the vision that is set before us.

In short, it is an *integrated* presentation of Christian truth, however perceived, that 'system' connotes here: *wherever one chooses to start has implications for the whole, and the parts must fit together.* However briefly, or lengthily, it is explicated (and sometimes, as we have seen, the shorter versions have been at least as elegant, effective, and enduring as the longer ones), 'systematic theology' must attempt to provide a coherent, and alluring, vision of the Christian faith.

WHY IS SYSTEMATIC THEOLOGY DISTRUSTED?

But why, then, is systematic theology deemed contentious in our own postmodern age, even as it – paradoxically – enjoys such a notable period of revival? Why is 'order' so often perceived as a front for abuse, and 'system' as an assumed repression?

Three, often interlocked, contemporary forms of resistance to systematic theology can readily be identified, and cumulatively they might seem to be powerful. To examine them, however, is to enter the complex intellectual worlds of postmodern philosophy, political theory, and psycholinguistics: jargon and arcane theory abound, but I shall try to give a succinct, but fair, account of the issues. After I have done so, I shall return to the issue of desire which animates this whole volume, and show how these problems importantly connect to it.

The first resistance to systematic theology resides in the philosophical critique of so-called 'onto-theology': it claims that systematic theology falsely, and idolatrously, turns God into an object of human knowledge. The second resistance arises from the moral or political critique of so-called 'hegemony': it sees systematic theology (amongst other discourses that provide any purportedly complete vision of an intellectual landscape), as inappropriately totalizing, and thereby necessarily suppressive of the voices and perspectives of marginalized people. The third resistance is a feminist critique, arising from a particular brand of French, post-Freudian psychoanalytic thought. It accuses systematic thinking (of any sort) of being 'phallocentric', that is, ordered according to the 'symbolic',[5] 'male' mode of thinking which seeks to clarify, control, and master. It is thereby repressive of creative materials

---

[5] Meaning, in Jacques Lacan's use of this term, something like 'clear', 'analytical', 'demonstrable'.

culturally associated with 'femininity' and the female body, which are characteristically pushed into the unconscious.

I shall need to look briefly at each of these stringent criticisms in turn, but with a particular eye to assessing how they might be answered with the aid of the insights of a contemplative *théologie totale*. For the very act of contemplation – repeated, lived, embodied, suffered – is an act that, by grace, and over time, inculcates mental patterns of 'un-mastery',[6] welcomes the dark realm of the unconscious, opens up a radical attention to the 'other', and instigates an acute awareness of the messy entanglement of sexual desires and desire for God. The vertiginous free-fall of contemplation, then, is not only the means by which a disciplined form of unknowing makes way for a new and deeper knowledge-beyond-knowledge; it is also – as I have already argued – the necessary accompanying practice of a theology committed to ascetic transformation. When one looks at the three resistances to systematic theology I have just outlined, one can already note how revealingly themes of knowledge, power, and gender are entangled and woven into these three objections. One begins to glimpse why it is that issues of sexuality, desire, and gender cannot by mere fiat, or simple denial, be dissociated from the claim to be able to continue the task of systematic theology. But from what has already been argued in the introductory Prelude, and now here, it may perhaps also be guessed that these three objections to systematic theology may be fully answerable, once the properly contemplative matrix of theology is acknowledged. Nonetheless, what there is to learn from these

---

[6] I coin this term deliberately, to distinguish it from Milbank's and others' '*non*-mastery' (see John Milbank, *Theology and Social Theory: Beyond Secular Reason* (Oxford: Blackwell, 1990; 2nd edn 2006), 6). The desire *not* to 'master' cannot be summoned by mere good intention or fiat. It is a matter, I submit, of waiting on divine aid and transformation, a transcendent undoing of manipulative human control or aggression.

critiques is still highly significant and instructive. One cannot simply look away.

ANSWERING THE CHARGES AGAINST SYSTEMATIC
THEOLOGY: A RESPONSE FROM THE PERSPECTIVE
OF THÉOLOGIE TOTALE

That systematic theology should be perceived as necessarily engaged in a false reification of God, first, is the accusation made when systematics is seen as a form of 'onto-theology'. But what exactly does this accusation mean? The charge goes back to the claim that Greek philosophical metaphysics was already engaged in a hubristic and inappropriate attempt to explain the divine, the ultimate Cause, and so to extend metaphysics beyond its proper reach; and, further, that classical and scholastic Christian theology, in its dependence on Greek metaphysics, unthinkingly extended such a trait into its projects of philosophical and systematic theology. Even Thomas Aquinas has been (falsely) accused of such an 'onto-theological' error.

But the mistake in the charge itself is that it has failed to understand the proper place of the apophatic dimensions of classic Christian thought (as already briefly discussed in the Prelude). Once there is a full and ready acknowledgement that to make claims about *God* involves a fundamental submission to mystery and unknowing, a form of unknowing more fundamental even than the positive accession of contentful revelation, the 'onto-theological' charge loses its edge. Indeed, one might say it becomes a mere shadow-boxing. For 'God', by definition, cannot be an extra item in the universe (a very big one) to be known, and so controlled, by human intellect, will, or imagination. God is, rather, that without which there would be nothing at all; God is the source and

sustainer of all being, and, as such, the dizzying mystery encountered in the act of contemplation as precisely the 'blanking' of the
human ambition to knowledge, control, and mastery. To know God
is unlike any other knowledge; indeed, it is more truly to *be* known,
and so transformed.

So, if the 'onto-theological' charge misses its mark, is its accusation simply 'much ado about nothing'? Not exactly; for its concerns
rightly chide those forms of theology which show an inadequate
awareness of the *sui generis* nature of the divine, and of the ever-
present dangers of idolatry. In short, systematic theology without
appropriately apophatic sensibilities is still potentially subject to its
criticism. The question then presses: what constitutes such an
'appropriately apophatic sensibility'? Can this be gained simply by
taking thought (or, rather, by taking thought and then negating it)?
Or is it that this first accusation against systematic theology has
rightly isolated a deeper problem than that of mere intellectual or
semantic hygiene – that is, the modern problem of the dissociation
of theology from *practices* of un-mastery?

It is here that one of the key dimensions of my proposed
theological method becomes crucial. As I have already argued,
systematic theology without contemplative and ascetic practice
comes with the danger of rending itself void; for theology in its
proper sense is always implicitly *in via* as practitional. It comes, that
is, with the urge, the fundamental desire, to seek God's 'face' and
yet to have that seeking constantly checked, corrected, and purged.
The mere intellectual acknowledgement of human finitude is not
enough (and in any case is all too easily forgotten); the false
humility of a theological 'liberalism' which remakes God as it
wishes under the guise of a Kantian nescience is equally unsatis-
factory; it is the actual *practice* of contemplation that is the condition
of a new 'knowing in unknowing'. It must involve the stuff of

learned bodily enactment, sweated out painfully over months and years, in duress, in discomfort, in bewilderment, as well as in joy and dawning recognition. Apophatic theology, in its proper sense, then, can never be mere verbal play, deferral of meaning, or the simple addition of negatives to positive ('cataphatic') claims. Nor, on the other hand, can it be satisfied with the dogmatic 'liberal' denial that God in Godself can be known *at all*: it is not 'mysterious' in *this* sense. For contemplation is the unique, and wholly *sui generis*, task of seeking to know, and speak of God, unknowingly; as Christian contemplation, it is also the necessarily bodily practice of dispossession, humility, and effacement which, in the Spirit, causes us to learn incarnationally, and only so, the royal way of the Son to the Father.

The first, 'onto-theological', objection to systematics therefore does still have continuing point, even as one answers it. It serves as a reminder that the problem of idolatry is an enduring one, and that it can never be dealt with by mere mental fiat or a false sense of intellectual control. It draws attention, too, to the fact that not all theology adequately reflects on its apophatic duties: insofar as it fails in them, it is indeed implicated in 'onto-theological' temptation. Finally, it hints therefore also at the need to make important distinctions between different levels, or types, of approach to doc-trinal truth (a point which will become clearer once I have examined all three of the contemporary criticisms of systematic theology). That is, there are different ways in which doctrines can be purveyed, whether by symbolic power, indirect allusion, or analytic clarity; but even when these are judiously combined, there can be no intrinsic guarantee of an effective apophatic reminder in any attempt to speak truly of God – unless such reminders are *practised*. One of the rightful requirements of systematic theology, then, is for it to indicate what sorts of different 'forms' of expression it is using, and for what purpose, and how such forms relate to intentional practices of un-mastery. Only thus can one consciously guard against the 'onto-theological' danger.

The second charge against systematic theology is less to do with technical issues of speech about God, and more about falsely generalizing strategies of power. The social theorists who have decried 'hegemony' are rightly calling attention to ways in which powerful discourses, especially ones that aspire to a total picture, can occlude or marginalize the voices of those who are already oppressed, or are being pushed into a state of subjection. 'System' here tends to connote 'systemic' oppression, deep-seated political violence, or abuse; 'hegemonic' discourses – consciously or unconsciously – seek to justify such oppression. Does systematic theology do this too?

The short answer, again, is that it certainly can do, and most manifestly has done in many contexts in Christian tradition. Liberation theology, in all its guises, witnesses to the felt perception that classic, official church theology (systematic or otherwise) has often failed in any sustained theological response to problems of social and political oppression. And that 'gender', 'race', and 'class', amongst other categories related to such oppression, are still matters not generally discussed in systematic theology, is a telling comment on the state of the undertaking. So long as such topics are excluded a priori from systematic theology's *loci* for discussion, or pushed aside as irrelevant to theological truth, the charge that they are being occluded from theological sight will continue to have a point.

But the method of *théologie totale* is again of crucial significance here, and this is for at least two reasons. First, the ascetic practices of contemplation are themselves indispensable means of a *true* attentiveness to the despised or marginalized 'other'. It is easy, from a privileged position, to be morally righteous about justice for the oppressed, while actually drowning out their voices with the din of one's own high-sounding plans for reform. Likewise, there is much talk of the problem of attending to the otherness of the 'other' in contemporary post-Kantian ethics and post-colonial theory; but there is very little about the intentional and embodied practices that might enable such attention. And this is particularly ironic, given the claims of (largely secular) post-colonial theorists to speak for deeply religious populations. The moral and epistemic stripping that is endemic to the act of contemplation is a vital key here: its practised self-emptying inculcates an attentiveness that is beyond merely good political intentions. Its practice is more discomforting, more destabilizing to settled presumptions, than a simple intentional *design* on empathy.

Secondly, the method of *théologie totale* (as has been seen, and will be explored further in the next chapter) is not only founded in ascetic practices of attention, but also rooted in an exploration of the many mediums and levels at which theological truth may be engaged. It is in this sense that it deserves the appellation *totale*: not as a totalizing assault on worldly power, but as an attempt to do justice to every level, and type, of religious apprehension and its appropriate mode of expression. Thus it is devoted precisely to the excavation and evaluation of what has previously been neglected: to theological fieldwork in a variety of illuminating social and political contexts (not merely those of privilege, in fact especially not); to religious cultural productions of the arts and the imagination; to neglected or sidelined texts in the tradition; and to examination of the differences made to theology by such factors as gender, class, or race. In short, *théologie totale* makes the bold claim that the more systematic one's intentions, the more necessary the exploration of such dark and neglected corners; and that, precisely as a theology *in via*, *théologie totale* continually risks destabilization and redirection. In an important sense, then, this form of systematic theology must always also remain, in principle, *unsystematic* – if by that one means open to the possibility of risk and challenge. This playful oxymoron ('unsystematic systematics') applies just to the extent that the undertaking renders itself persistently vulnerable to interruptions from the unexpected – through its radical practices of attention to the Spirit.

And that point forms a natural transition to the third, and last, charge made against systematic thinking: that it is intrinsically 'phallocentric' (that is, that it operates intellectually in a mode symbolically linked to the male body); and that it is inherently repressive of 'feminine' imagination, creativity, or of the destabilization of ordered thinking that may arise from the unconscious. This objection will make little sense unless one is familiar with the thought forms and presumptions of French post-Freudian psychoanalytic theory; and thus one's immediate response to this last critique must be that it precisely *begs the question* of one's assumed theory of gender (an issue I am about to tackle at greater length in the last part of this chapter). However, there is something irreducibly important at stake in this charge: it concerns the embodied nature of all theological thinking.

For this last critique starts from the assumption that there is a distinctively 'feminine' mode of reflection (termed the 'semiotic' in Lacanian terminology), which is linked to the female body and female sexuality, and incapable of capture – without destructive 'phallocentric' distortion – in *clearly enunciated* forms. To attempt systematics in such forms would thus be an intrinsic offence to 'feminine' sensibility, and would crush the creative destabilizations that are unique to the realm of the semiotic. This particular understanding of the gender divide, we should note, can come in more or less hardened forms of dogmatism. The more subtle exponents of this school of thought by no means intend an essentialist view of gender (which would link female bodies inexorably and normatively to certain kinds of creative, but non-analytic, thought). Instead, they wish to draw attention to the undeniable cultural dominance of 'male' thinking, and its repressive and distorting effects on both women and men: if the so-called 'feminine imaginary' is accorded no worth, they argue, then psychic life remains distorted and stultifying for all.

The main problem with this line of thought is that it risks reinstituting the problem it seeks to resolve. If the gender division is so strongly bound to genital shape and symbolism, and so disjunctively construed, then a pessimistic ideology tends to dominate: the so-called 'feminine imaginary' can never, it is averred, be brought into effective play in the realm of existing systematic discussion. Instead it has to found its own, distinct, form of discourse. It is as if such pessimism, and such dogmatized gender dualism, reconsigns the 'feminine' to an eternal marginalization, ironically recreating the conditions of powerlessness from which it arose. Semiotic explosions may become the only means of redress: at best, they are the deliciously subversive ripostes of the marginalized ('noises off', as it were), but never harbingers of actual psychic or social change. Systematic theology, on this view, remains an irredeemably 'male' undertaking.

But it is to address such a false disjunction as this that the contemplative method of *théologie totale* is, once again, attuned. As the last part of this chapter will now seek to display, it is possible to acknowledge the full *theological* significance of bodily and gendered difference (in a sense to be discussed), but to avoid the stuckness of a theory in which the so-called semiotic realm fails in any substantial or transformative impact on the systematic. For the contemplative method of *théologie totale* of course already welcomes what is here called the semiotic at more than one level: it welcomes it in the very act of contemplation, in which practices of unknowing precisely court the realm of the unconscious; and it welcomes it in the arts, as a way into those levels of doctrinal truth, via the imagination and aesthetic artifacts, that more drily intellectual theology often misses. What this third critique of systematics has so rightly seen, then – that gender and bodily difference cannot be irrelevant to systematics – is capable of a different response than the dismissive one that it itself envisages.

THE TANGLED ROOT OF DESIRE

I have now surveyed the three major contemporary objections to systematic theology, fully acknowledging their force. But I have also suggested that a contemplative approach to systematics, by virtue of its very practices of un-mastery, is one capable of address-ing the deeper issues raised. Indeed, if I am right, it can change the terms of the debate in such a way that seemingly irresolvable dilemmas in secular approaches to these problems may be fruitfully addressed.

For the three objections to the task of systematic theology turn out to have a shared, or at least tangled, root. Each presumes that the systematician idolatrously *desires* mastery: a complete under-standing of God, a regnant position in society, or a domination of the gendered 'other'; and each presumes that the same systematician will thereby abuse his knowledge, his power, or his 'male' mode of thinking, for purposes of intellectual, social, or sexual dominance. The deeper issues, then, involve the insidious entanglement of knowledge, power, and gender. But their shared root, let me now suggest, is the yet deeper problem of *desire*. It is the idolatrous desire to know all that fuels 'onto-theology'; it is the imperious desire to dominate that inspires 'hegemony'; it is the 'phallocentric' desire to conquer that represses the 'feminine'. To speak theologically: *unredeemed* desire is at the root of each of these challenges to the systematic task. It is to this deeper problem that I must now attend.

I said at the beginning of this chapter that systematic theology cannot credibly go on without urgent attention to matters of desire, sex, sexuality, and gender. I am now in a better position to say why this might be so, and how these particular issues might themselves be ordered and rooted – in the category of desire itself. On the one hand, the contemplative task, which rightly sustains systematics, is itself a progressive modulator and refiner of human desire: in its naked longing for God, it lays out all its other desires – conscious and unconscious – and places them, over time, into the crucible of divine desire. (Sexual desire, from this contemplative perspective, is thus drawn into an inexorable tether with all other desires, judged by its approximation, or lack thereof, to the purity of divine charity.) On the other hand, the tumultuous obsessions of a secularized and sex-saturated culture, and the current political intensities of debates over gender, make it imperative for the systematician to give *theological* thematization to these divisive and contested topics. In the Prelude I already suggested that desire, when understood as rooted in the divine, could thus be seen as more basic a category than physical 'sex'. I now want to extend that analysis to the issue of gender, and to hypothesize that *desire is also more fundamental than gender*; and that the key to the secular riddle of gender can lie only in its connection to the doctrine of a trinitarian God.

WHY DOES GENDER MATTER?

But what *is* gender, in any case, and why does it matter? To contemporary secular theorists of gender, first, it matters intensely, since for them it is the powerful symbolic means by which culture slices humanity normatively into *two* (and only two), and thereby imposes, by continually repeated rituals of reinforcement (both conscious and unconscious), an oppressive and restricted form of life on those who do not fit the binary alternatives. Gender is – on this view – implicitly linked to oppression. Only 'performative' acts of public dissent from the so-called 'gender binary' may hope to shift its cultural hold – by a form of acted-out resistance.

To biblical fundamentalists and conservatives, by contrast, and especially to the anti-gay lobby, gender 'matters' no less intensely: not only is modern 'heterosexuality' read as normatively prescribed by the Bible, but a particular, subordinationist, understanding of the relation of female to male is seen to follow as well.

There is another possible theological approach to gender, however, which by no means decries biblical authority, indeed still takes it as primary; but it sets the exegesis of complex scriptural texts in full relation to tradition, philosophical analysis, and ascetic practice. Here gender 'matters' primarily because it is about *differentiated, embodied relationship* – first and foremost to God, but also to others; and its meaning is therefore fundamentally given in relation to the human's role as made in the 'image of God' (Genesis 1. 26–7). Gender 'matters' to systematic theology, too then, insofar as it is a crucial dimension of its *theological* analysis of the human: to fail to chart the differences and performances of gender would be to ignore one of the most profound aspects of human experience, whether felt as joy or as curse. Where this approach differs from secular gender theory, let me now suggest, is in three crucial areas, which transform its capacity to deal with seemingly insoluble dilemmas for the secular realm of discussion.

Whereas secular gender theory argues, and agonizes, about how it can shift and transform cultural presumptions about gender that are often unconsciously and unthinkingly replicated, a contemplative theology *in via* has at its disposal, first, theological concepts of creation, fall, and redemption which place the performances of gender in a spectrum of existential possibilities *between* despair and hope. What one might call the fallen, 'worldly' view of gender relations is open to the future, and to change; it is set in an unfolding, diachronic narrative both of individual spiritual maturation and of societal transformation.

Secondly, and correlatively, a theological view of gender thereby also has an eschatological hope, one that it sees not as pious fiction or wish-fulfilment, but as firmly grounded in the events of Christ's incarnation and resurrection. Gender, in the sense just given, is ineradicable (I am always, even after death – assuming I believe in that possibility – a particular sort of 'differentiated, relational being'); but gender is not unchangeable: it too is *in via*. What is fallen can be redeemed and sanctified – indeed rendered sacramental by participation in Christ. In this sense, gender may be seen not merely as a locus of oppression, but just as much as the potential vehicle of embodied salvation.

Third, then, and most fundamentally, gender is understood differently for a contemplative asceticism precisely because it claims through its practices of devotion to encounter and embrace a holy *reality*, a reality revealed as three (yet thereby transformative of any two).[7] What contemporary gender theory jargonistically calls 'performativity' and 'ritualization' – whether as reiteration of a repressive gender regime, or as a 'destabilization' of it – finds its *theological* counterpart in the *sui generis* 'performances' of contemplation. These performances, however, are not primarily intended as acts of resistance to worldly oppression (although they will give courage for such!); and nor are they therefore merely human strategies of resistance. Rather, they are acts of 'submission' to a unique power beyond human power – and, as

---

[7] I shall explain the relation of 'three' and 'two' in the next section. The metaphysical realism in my approach is important: it is not *we* who fix this problem of fallen gender, as I understand it, but God.

such, are of course already 'gendered', in a particular and unique sense denoting relationship to God. What makes *this* gendering 'different' from worldly gender, then, is its being rendered labile to the logic and flow of trinitarian, divine desire, its welcoming of the primary interruption of the Spirit, and its submission to contemplative unknowing so that the certainties of this world (including the supposed certainties of fallen views of gender) can be remade in the incarnate likeness of Christ. Gender (embodied difference) is here not to be eradicated, note, but to be transformed; it still 'matters', but only because God desires it to matter and can remake it in the image of his Son.

GENDER, THE TRINITY, AND INCARNATION

Threeness and twoness. Let me reflect a little more at the close of this chapter on the symbolic significance of these numbers for Christian doctrine, but also for gender. I can only spell out baldly here a thesis that may seem unfamiliar and strange, but which will gather impetus theologically throughout the coming chapters.

I have already intimated in the Prelude how this book is going to approach the early doctrine of God as Trinity in a distinctive way. The claim will be made in greater detail and substance later, especially in Chapter 3, that prayer (and especially prayer of a non-discursive sort, whether contemplative or charismatic) is the chief context in which the *irreducible* threeness of God becomes humanly apparent to the Christian. It does so because – as one ceases to set the agenda and allows room for God to be God – the sense of the *human* impossibility of prayer becomes the more intense (see Romans 8. 26), and drives one to comprehend the necessity of God's own prior activity in it. Strictly speaking, it is not I who autonomously prays, but God (the Holy Spirit) who prays in me, and so answers the eternal call of the 'Father', drawing me by various painful degrees into the newly expanded life of

'Sonship'. There is, then, an inherent reflexivity in the divine, a ceaseless outgoing and return of the desiring God; and insofar as I welcome and receive this reflexivity, I find that it is the Holy Spirit who 'interrupts' my human monologue to a (supposedly) monadic God;[8] it is the Holy Spirit who finally thereby causes me to see God no longer as patriarchal threat but as infinite tenderness; but it is also the Holy Spirit who first painfully darkens my prior certainties, enflames and checks my own desires, and so invites me ever more deeply into the life of redemption in Christ. In short, it is this 'reflexivity in God', this Holy Spirit, that makes incarnate life *possible*.

So when, from this perspective in prayer, I count three in God, the Holy Spirit cannot be a *mere* 'third'. The Spirit cannot be an add-on, an 'excess', or a 'go-between' to what is already established as a somehow more privileged dyad (the 'Father' and 'Son'). Instead, the Holy Spirit is intrinsic to the very make-up of the Father–Son relationship from all eternity; the Spirit, moreover, is that without which there would be no *incarnated* Son at all, and – by extension – no life of Sonship into which we, too, might enter by participation. The Spirit, then, is what interrupts the fallen worldly order and infuses it with the divine question, the divine lure, the divine life.

So this irreducible threeness in God cannot be insignificant for the matter of gendered twoness, since the human is precisely made 'in God's (trinitarian) image', and destined to be restored to that image. It must be, then, that in this fallen world, one lives, in some sense, *between* twoness and its transfiguring interruption; so one is not, as in secular gender theory, endlessly and ever subject to the debilitating falseness of fallen gender, fallen twoness. In fact, in Christ, I meet the human One who, precisely in the Spirit, has

---

[8] It is important to underscore that *this* 'interruption' does not bludgeon or suppress the human, but 'comes to our aid' as the Holy Spirit.

effected that interruptive transfiguration of twoness. He has done so by crossing the boundary between another 'twoness' more fundamental even than the twoness of gender: the ontological twoness of the transcendent God and the created world. In crossing that boundary in the incarnation, Christ does not re-establish the boundary as before, but nor – significantly – does he destroy it; rather, we might say that he 'transgresses' it in the Spirit, infusing the created world anew with divinity. And just as, in the Spirit, he crosses that ontological twoness transformatively, but without obliteration of otherness, so – I now suggest, and analogously – the interruptive work of the trinitarian God does not obliterate the twoness of gender, either, but precisely renders it subject to the labile transformations of divine desire. Whatever this redeemed twoness is (and there are remaining mysterious dimensions to this question), it cannot be the stuck, fixed, repressive twoness of the *fallen* 'gender binary'.

So one might say that there are two different sorts of 'difference' that the fundamental doctrines of Christianity (Trinity and Incarnation) hold before one, as symbolically and theologically relevant for the 'differences' of gender. One is the 'difference' of the three in God – different but *equal*, a difference only of relation and not of distinct activities or powers. The other is the quite different 'difference' between God and the world, a fundamental line of ontological difference that has been crossed and overcome in the Incarnation, yet also not obliterated. The Christian tradition has, of course, been constantly tempted to figure the difference of gender straightforwardly on the latter difference: to align 'masculinity' with God and 'femininity' with the world (and so to subordinate women to men, while tacitly undermining their status as fully redeemed). More recently, some feminist theology has attempted – in reaction – to model gender on the former difference –

straightforwardly to *emulate* a trinitarian 'equality in difference'. The position proposed here is that neither of these more familiar alternatives is possible, nor even obviously mandated by the complex authorities of Scripture and tradition. Rather, in the case of human gender there is a subtle transformation of both models caused by their intersection: the 'fixed' fallen differences of worldly gender are transfigured precisely by the interruptive activity of the Holy Spirit, drawing gender into trinitarian purgation and transformation. *Twoness, one might say, is divinely ambushed by threeness.*

This is *not*, I must strongly underscore in closing, a theory of a 'third gender', or a theory either of the insignificance, or obliteration, of gender. On the contrary, it is a theory about gender's mysterious and plastic openness to divine transfiguration.[9]

CONCLUSIONS

I wrote earlier, in the Prelude, that 'desire is the constellating category of selfhood, the ineradicable root of one's longing for God'. By the end of this complex chapter, I am now in a better position to see why I wish to say that this is so. Power, sex, and gender currently garner much attention in secular political, philosophical, and psychoanalytic discourses; and in this chapter I have acknowledged how revealing are the criticisms of systematic theology that emerge from those discourses. But a *theological* analysis such as I propose puts desire at the root – both anthropologically in the human, and theologically in the divine. Desire, I now suggest again – even fallen desire – is the precious

---

[9] Ascetic materials from the period of early Christian monasticism give indications of a similar view – or complex constellation of views – abroad in the early church, most of them inspired by Galatians 3. 28. It should not be assumed that the only view of gender transformation then canvassed was that of ascetic women 'becoming male' – although, in a complex range of alternative possibilities, this was indeed one dominant trope. I shall return to this topic in Chapter 6.

clue woven into the crooked human heart that ever reminds it of its relatedness and its source.[10]

But to say that 'desire is more fundamental than gender' is not thereby to make gender (once understood as 'differentiated embodied relationship') *insignificant*: it does indeed 'matter'. But what it has to say is that gender is not static, not fixed into the seemingly immovable stuckness of what secular theory gloomily calls 'the gender binary'. Rather, it is made redemptively labile – subject to endless reformulations one can scarcely imagine at the beginning of the spiritual journey. And this occurs precisely by its submission to something more fundamental: the interruptive desire of the trinitarian God for fallen creation. In the 'impossibility' of the prayer of contemplation, in which the Spirit cracks open the human heart to this new future, divine desire purgatively reformulates human desire. It follows that all the other problems of power, sex, and gender with which contemporary theory struggles so notably cannot be solved, I dare to say – whether by human political power, violent fiat, or even subversive deviousness or ritualized revolt – without such prior surrender to the divine.

This is clearly an audacious claim, but it is not one that is enunciated in a social or political vacuum. The method of *théologie totale*, as is now becoming clear, puts contemplation at is heart, but spirals out to acknowledge the complexity of the entanglement of the secular and spiritual realms for those who dare to practise it. For there is no escape from such messy entanglement. *Théologie totale*, as this chapter has shown, insists on the sweated-out significance of embodied (and thus gendered, and socially located) contemplation, not mere verbal play or abstract thought. It attends to the different *levels* and *forms* at which

---

[10] It follows that the basic view of sin in this systematics is of misdirected desire – desire missing its goal (*hamartanein* in the Greek). The implications of this view of sin will be given fuller attention in volumes II and III of this systematics.

doctrine may be purveyed, aware of the ways in which intellect, affect, and imagination are progressively magnetized by the contentful, cataphatic claims of a variety of mediums, yet how they are also constantly judged and purged by the apophatic act of contemplation. But just as importantly, *théologie totale* is keenly aware of the social locations and worldly power – or powerlessness – of those who undertake this ascetic task. The examination of such variables, as I must now go on to show, is a crucial part of its attempt to probe a 'total' theological picture.

Not that there is any fantasy of mastery here in such an attempt at 'totality': the submission of contemplation is, and remains, prior. Yet how, then, is such submission not just mere human *subjection*, a false consciousness wrapped in religious robes? How is it not yet another (subtle, but deluded) capitulation to worldly powers? To these questions I must now urgently attend, and so reveal the remaining methodological features of my 'unsystematic systematics'.

* * *

BIBLIOGRAPHIC NOTE

THE CATEGORY OF 'SYSTEMATIC THEOLOGY'

The term 'systematic theology' is a modern one and is generally thought to have been used for the first time by Bartholomaeus Keckermann (1571?–1608) in his *Systema SS Theologiae, tribus libris adornatum* (Hanoviae, Apud Guilielmum Antonium, 1602). Earlier, celebrated accounts of Christian faith given in an ordered manner come in a remarkable variety of genres, but include, as discussed in this chapter (and supplied here in English translation): Origen, *On First Principles*, trans. G. W. Butterworth (London: SPCK, 1936); John of Damascus, *On the Orthodox Faith*, in John of Damascus, *Writings*, trans. Frederic H. Chase (FC 37; New York: Fathers of the Church, 1958), 165–406; Peter Lombard, *The*

Sentences, trans. Giulio Silano (Toronto: Pontifical Institute of Medieval Studies, 2007–); Thomas Aquinas, *Summa Theologiae*, trans. various (60 vols.; Cambridge University Press, 2006); John Calvin, *Institutes of the Christian Religion*, ed. John T. McNeill and trans. Ford Lewis Battles (2 vols.; Louisville, KY: Westminster John Knox Press, 1960); Friedrich Schleiermacher, *The Christian Faith*, ed. H. R. Mackintosh and J. S. Stewart (2nd edn; Edinburgh: T&T Clark, 1928); Karl Barth, *Church Dogmatics* (Edinburgh: T&T Clark, 1956–75); Karl Rahner, *Foundations of Christian Faith: An Introduction to the Idea of Christianity* (London: DLT, 1978); and Hans Urs von Balthasar, *Glory of the Lord: A Theological Aesthetics* (8 vols.; San Francisco: Ignatius Press, 1982–9), *Theo-Drama: Theological Dramatic Theory* (5 vols.; San Francisco: Ignatius Press, 1988–98), and *Theo-Logic* (3 vols.; San Francisco: Ignatius Press, 2000–5).

SYSTEMATIC THEOLOGY AND GENDER

One must first remark on significant facts of omission. Some of the most eminent and influential systematicians of the twentieth century do not regard gender as worthy of any sustained comment or analysis, for example: Eberhard Jüngel, *God as the Mystery of the World: On the Foundation of the Theology of the Crucified One in the Dispute Between Theism and Atheism* (Edinburgh: T&T Clark, 1984); Wolfhart Pannenberg, *Systematic Theology* (3 vols.; Grand Rapids, MI: Eerdmans, 1991–8); Robert Jenson, *Systematic Theology* (2 vols.; Oxford University Press, 1997–9); Colin Gunton, *The One, the Three and the Many: God, Creation and the Culture of Modernity* (Cambridge University Press, 1993).

In contrast, Karl Barth devoted several sections of his *Church Dogmatics* to expounding a subordinationist view of female gender based on biblical proto-types for human nature. See especially: Karl Barth, *Church Dogmatics* (Edinburgh: T&T Clark, 1956–75), vol. iii/1, 203–6, 288–329; vol. iii/2, 285–324.

But it is the Protestant systematician Moltmann, and the Roman Catholic von Balthasar, who have made gender intrinsic to their very notions of *God*. See especially: Jürgen Moltmann, *The Trinity and the Kingdom: The Doctrine of God* (London: SCM Press, 1981), and Jürgen Moltmann and Elisabeth Moltmann-Wendel, *Humanity in God* (London: SCM Press, 1984); compare Hans Urs von Balthasar, *Theo-Drama*, vols. III and IV, and, 'Women

Priests?', in *New Elucidations* (San Francisco: Ignatius Press, 1986), 187–98.
Ironically, and despite their very different modes of applying gender to the
inner life of God, both these theologians smuggle similar 'Romantic' visions
of 'femininity' into their accounts. For a critique, see my essays 'The Woman
at the Altar: Cosmological Disturbance or Gender Fluidity?', *Anglican
Theological Review* 86 (2004), 75–93 (on von Balthasar), and 'The Trinity
and Gender Reconsidered', in Miroslav Volf and Michael Welker, eds., *God's
Life in Trinity* (Minneapolis: Fortress Press, 2006), 133–42 (on Moltmann).

L'HISTOIRE TOTALE AS BACKGROUND TO 'THÉOLOGIE TOTALE'

The term *'histoire totale'* ('total', or holistic, history) is associated with the
Annales School of French historians, so called following the journal *Annales
d'Histoire Économique et Sociale* (1929–), which remains its principal organ. It
was one of the founders of the journal, Lucien Febvre, who coined the term
'histoire totale' or *'histoire tout court'*. The approach of the school aimed to
uncover the thick textures in which historical events are couched, and in
particular they brought social scientific methods to bear in order to provide
fuller understandings of the contexts of history and its links with the present. A
celebrated example of this approach is Emmanuel le Roy Ladurie, *Montaillou:
Cathars and Catholics in a French Village, 1274–1324* (Harmondsworth:
Penguin, 1980). For a full treatment of this historiographical school see
André Burguière, *The Annales School: An Intellectual History* (Ithaca, NY:
Cornell University Press, 2009). It should be clear in my account of *théologie
totale*, however, that I do not share all the methodological presumptions of
histoire totale (which themselves have been controversial amongst historians).
In particular, I carefully resist any straightforward reduction of theological
categories or explanations to social science ones.

'ONTO-THEOLOGY' AND 'METAPHYSICS'

The now celebrated (but contentious) critique of classic Western 'metaphysics' mounted by Heidegger can be found in Martin Heidegger,
Identity and Difference (University of Chicago Press, 2002). Marion has
taken up the Heideggerian critique and attempted an ingenious solution
via 'apophatic', revelatory theology in Jean-Luc Marion, *God Without*

Being: Hors Texte (University of Chicago Press, 1995); he was later forced to admit that he had falsely included Thomas Aquinas in the 'onto-theological' charge: see Jean-Luc Marion, 'Thomas Aquinas and Onto-theology', in Michael Kessler and Christian Sheppard, eds., *Mystics: Presence and Aporia* (University of Chicago Press, 2003), 38–74. At the other end of the theological spectrum, the American 'liberal' tradition, strongly influenced by Kant, has continued to do a form of speculative metaphysics while insisting that its status can only be that of human 'imaginative construction', God-in-Godself being radically shrouded in 'mystery': see Gordon D. Kaufman, *God the Problem* (Cambridge, MA: Harvard University Press, 1972), and his later *In Face of Mystery: A Constructive Theology* (Cambridge, MA: Harvard University Press, 1993).

THEOLOGY AND 'HEGEMONY'

Antonio Gramsci first used the term 'hegemony' in 1926 in his *Notes on the Southern Question* (see Antonio Gramsci, *Selections from Political Writings 1921–26* (London: Lawrence & Wishart, 1978), 443); he continued to discuss the theme in his *Selections from the Prison Notebooks* (London: Lawrence & Wishart, 1971), blending themes from Nietzsche and Marx. For a secondary analysis, see Chantal Mouffe, 'Hegemony and Ideology in Gramsci', in Chantal Mouffe, ed., *Gramsci and Marxist Theory* (London: Routledge & Kegan Paul, 1979), 168–204. Theologians concerned about 'totalizing' approaches to state power have also been drawn in recent decades to the work of Michel Foucault and his account of how prisons and hospitals can patrol populations in the modern state: see especially Michel Foucault, *Discipline and Punish: The Birth of the Prison* (New York: Vintage, 1995), and Michel Foucault, *The Birth of the Clinic: An Archaeology of Medical Perception* (New York: Vintage, 1994).

Whilst classic 'liberation theology' drew controversially on socialist and Marxist analysis, as well as on biblical sources, to enunciate a 'preferential option for the poor' (see especially Gustavo Gutiérrez, *A Theology of Liberation: History, Politics, and Salvation* (rev. edn; London: SCM Press, 2001); and Juan Luis Segundo, *Liberation of Theology* (New York: Orbis, 1976)), more recent 'post-colonial' thought has cast the spotlight on personal identity and the problems of 'agency': see Gayatri Chakravorty Spivak, 'Can the Subaltern Speak?', in Cary Nelson and Larry Grossberg, eds., *Marxism and the Interpretation of Culture* (Urbana: University of Illinois Press, 1988), 271–313; and Donna Landry and Gerald MacLean, eds., *The Spivak Reader: Selected Works of Gayatri Chakravorty Spivak* (New York: Routledge, 1996). In this context of postmodern multiple contestations of power and identity, many theologians have been attracted to the ethical thought of Emmanuel Lévinas and his insistence that the 'face' of the 'other' makes an irreducible moral claim on our humanity, despite all 'differences': see Emmanuel Lévinas, *Otherwise than Being, or, Beyond Essence* (Pittsburgh: Duquesne University Press, 1998), and *Humanism of the Other* (Urbana: University of Illinois Press, 2003). Problems remain, however, as I argue in this chapter, if true recognition of the 'other' is blocked by an incapacity to *attend* to 'difference' in a disciplined, practised, manner.

THEOLOGY AND POST-FREUDIAN FEMINISMS

Post-Freudian feminisms in France require the reader to understand something of the work of Lacan, and his interpretation of Freud, as background to these feminists' critique: see Jacques Lacan, *Écrits: The First Complete Edition in English* (New York: W. W. Norton, 2006), and the excellently clear Malcolm Bowie, *Lacan: An Introduction* (Cambridge, MA: Harvard University Press, 1991). Juliet Mitchell and Jacqueline Rose, eds., *Feminine Sexuality: Jacques Lacan and the École Freudienne* (New York: W. W. Norton, 1985) also provides a useful way into Lacan's thought for the English reader. Notions of 'symbolic' and 'semiotic', with their associated connotations of 'masculinity' and 'femininity', and their connections to the physical body, are here carefully explained in ways which head off the common charge of 'gender essentialism'. Toril Moi, ed., *The Kristeva Reader* (New York: Columbia University Press, 1986), Margaret Whitford, ed., *The Irigaray Reader* (Oxford: Blackwell, 1991), and Susan Sellers, ed., *The Hélène Cixous Reader* (London: Routledge, 1994) provide useful compendia of three of the movement's most celebrated exponents. Grace Jantzen, *Becoming Divine: Towards a Feminist Philosophy of Religion* (Manchester University Press, 1998) mounts a sustained case, for the English-speaking reader, of the implications of Irigaray's thought for the discipline of philosophy of religion. I respond with a sympathetic, but ultimately critical, account of Irigaray's and Jantzen's philosophical projects in 'Feminism and Analytic Philosophy of Religion', in William Wainwright, ed., *The Oxford Handbook to Philosophy of Religion* (Oxford University Press, 2005), 494–525.

THEOLOGY AND NORTH AMERICAN GENDER THEORY

In contrast to the dominance of French feminisms in contemporary feminist theory of continental Europe, and the critique in this discussion of so-called 'phallocentrism', recent North American gender theory has been predominantly concerned with gay and lesbian rights, and with the problem of what Judith Butler has called 'heteronormativity' – the cultural imposition of 'heterosexuality' as the only acceptable sexual norm in society. According to Butler, only ritualized acts of dissent from such 'normativity' can begin to shift this imposition: see Judith Butler, *Gender Trouble: Feminism and the Subversion of Identity* (New York: Routledge, 1990); *Bodies that Matter: On the Discursive Limits of 'Sex'* (New York: Routledge, 1993); *Excitable Speech: A Politics of the Performative* (New York: Routledge, 1997); and *Undoing Gender* (New York: Routledge, 2004), the last book explicitly tackling the medical and cultural problems of sex changes and the phenomenon of 'intersexuality'. I have myself suggested that Butler's early work ironically parallels, in some regards, the 'gender fluidity' exemplified in some early Christian ascetic literature, while lacking the substantial eschatological hope evidenced there (see my *Powers and Submissions: Philosophy, Spirituality and Gender* (Oxford: Blackwell, 2002), ch. 9). As I argue further in this chapter and beyond, however, 'sexual identity' or 'orientation', when dislocated from a nexus of *final* spiritual and theological meanings, becomes curiously pedestalized and obsessional. Arguably, the current anxieties in this area can only be properly adjudicated in the context of a rich *theology* of desire more generally.

CHAPTER 2

Doing theology 'on Wigan Pier': why feminism and the social sciences matter to theology

In the last chapter I argued that current resistances to systematic theology can be answered precisely by acknowledging the force of their critiques – and then subtly shifting the vision of the systematic undertaking to enable a simultaneous response and rebuttal. The danger of a false reification of the divine, the danger of a false bid for totalizing power, the danger of a false suppression of material associated with the 'unconscious', gender, and desire: all these are real dangers for contemporary systematic theology, I conceded, and not ones that can be dealt with either by evasion or denial. But a theology founded in intentional practices of 'un-mastery', I claimed, is able to meet them precisely by its learned, and embodied, strategies of dispossession to the divine. And not only that; for as I now begin to work with the full set of methodological tools of a *théologie totale*, I can show that the root problem of fallen human desire is displayed in each of these notable contemporary criticisms of systematic theology, and can thus only be addressed by a trans-formative, indeed ascetical, approach to the theological task itself. Such a theology is indeed *in via* (as I put it in the Prelude): it is challenged to examine, and chasten, its own desires, and to draw all dimensions of the self transformatively into that quest.

The same tangled root of desire, I argued, underlies the current cultural fixations and debates on gender, exposing problems which finally can only adequately be addressed theologically, and by specific recourse to reflection on a trinitarian God. It is the 'interruptive', or purgative, work of the Holy Spirit, I claimed, drawing the believer progressively into the life of crucified and resurrected 'Sonship', that gives the key to gender's ultimate rootedness in *divine* desire. In short, from the perspective of a *théologie totale*, desire, asceticism, and God as Trinity belong together, all the way down.

But that still leaves various important methodological questions and problems unclarified or unanswered; and to these I turn in this second, and concluding, chapter on the method of my *théologie totale*. There are, to be sure, many sceptical challenges still waiting to be met and confronted. How, for instance, is the 'submission' of ascetical contemplation not simply another falsity – a self-deluding accession to worldly or abusive human powers? How, again, is this contemplation socially mediated and placed? What is the *texture* of its assent to God? Does it come with a simultaneous acceptance of existing political and social forces, and that without critique? Or is it capable of a critical discernment of what I have called the 'messy entanglements' of human and divine powers and submissions? And how is contemplation's distinctive silence not merely a *silencing* of those who may already be socially marginalized? Finally, what do my answers to these questions imply for theology's proper relation to the secular discourses of the social sciences, on the one hand, and to liberal, and especially feminist, traditions of justice-seeking, on the other? How can an appeal to Christian contemplation have any valency or purchase in such realms of discourse?

These are the questions I shall attend to in this chapter, in which I shall mount a complex argument for the indispensability of field-work observation for the systematic task of a *théologie totale*. With that I shall also make a case for a continuing, albeit critical, interaction with traditions of political liberalism and feminism. I shall proceed initially by a sort of pincer movement. First,

I shall look briefly at a notable current debate in postmodern theology about the relation between theology and the social sciences, and argue that without a critical and discerning use of the tools of social science, theology itself is 'beached' in an arid, and often drily disputatious, terrain, one eerily displaced from the turbulent seascape of actual lived religion. The recovery of a vital relation between systematic theology and such lived religion involves both unexpected gains and notable challenges; and here the second prong of my argument will link me back to a discussion of certain classical feminist concerns. If a close analysis of lived religion reveals that the purity of orthodox doctrine is not always what it seems once purveyed in the field, then it is the task of a *théologie totale* to clarify how it can deal with doctrine's manifestation in a variety of forms, genres, and social locations, fully acknowledging its *potential* for distorted and sinful application.

Feminist theology of an earlier generation, however, laboured with a certain notable restriction on its spiritual and theological efficacy – a certain stuckness in anger, hostility, and victimology. These traits need now to be faced and corrected; and the current fissure between postmodern gender theory, on the one hand (which tends to deny the possibility of a universal 'grand narrative' of freedom, responsibility, and rights), and this liberal, Enlightenment-spawned feminism, on the other (which seeks to sustain such a narrative), has to be negotiated *theologically* before a creative way through can be seen. A discussion of the problem of idolatry, already tackled preliminarily in the Prelude and Chapter 1, will here be brought to completion, with the (perhaps surprising) conclusion that feminist theology's abiding significance resides in its attention to this perennial spiritual temptation of idolatry. If, conversely, it itself fails to acknowledge the temptation, then it can dangerously fall prey to its own forms of idolatrous bewitchment.

Finally, at the end of this chapter, I shall be able to re-gather all the methodological strands from the foregoing discussion and to conclude with a succinct résumé of the distinctive hallmarks of a *théologie totale*.

But first let me move to tackle the question of systematic theology's proper relation to the social sciences. As already intimated, I shall here appeal – I trust illuminatingly – to a celebrated marine metaphor, but one with a proposed new eddy of evocation.

WHAT FUTURE FOR THE SOCIAL SCIENCES AND THEOLOGY ON DOVER BEACH?

The modernistic presumption that Christian faith is in an inexorable decline, subject to encroaching secular forces, has been expressed in watery metaphors at least since the publication of Matthew Arnold's oft-quoted poem *Dover Beach* (1867).[1] Arnold's 'melancholy, long withdrawing roar' of the 'sea of faith' was, as many have commented, but the poetic expression of the philosophical, scientific, and cultural impetuses of the Victorian period, which seemed inevitably to spell the end of a pre-modern religious enchantment. Christian faith was in decline, overtaken by the modernizing trends of science, industrial revolution, and critical 'rationality'. Northern Europe's disengagement with God was said to be virtually complete: this state of affairs was announced, and then charted, by the various sociologists' confident rehearsal of the 'secularization thesis'. The religious tide was not only going out, but – if such

---

[1] Arnold here likened the withdrawing tide to the retreat of Christian faith in his time: 'The Sea of Faith / Was once, too, at the full, and round earth's shore / Lay like the folds of a bright girdle furled. / But now I only hear / Its melancholy, long, withdrawing roar, / Retreating, to the breath / Of the night wind, down the vast edges drear / And naked shingles of the world.'

sociological predictions were to be believed – a quite *unique* 'miracle' was about to occur, transgressing every known regularity of nature. For according to the modern sociologists, the tide was not ever going to wash back again at all.

Some in Britain may have felt, at least in the later 1970s and early 1980s, that the plug had definitively been pulled on the 'sea of faith', and that theologians henceforth would be seeking to describe an increasingly *depopulated* beachscape of Christian commitment. In part they were not wrong: the precipitous decline in church membership and church attendance in Northern Europe (in stark contrast to the situation in North America, and throughout the southern hemisphere) has continued almost unabated since then. But in another way the sociological commentators were *completely* wrong. For their inverse 'miracle' did not occur after all. The religious tide turned all right; but it seeped back in across marshes, via backwaters and underground channels that few could have predicted – accompanied, on occasion, by an exciting flash flood of new enthusiasm or spiritual élan. It turned out that there was still plenty of 'religion' about, but a grave erosion (in now 'secularized' Britain) of commitment to ecclesiastical *institutions*, and especially to the established or denominational churches. New age 'spirituality' proved, however, attractive in a variety of forms, as did increasingly vibrant evangelicalism, some of it markedly fundamentalist and anti-intellectual in tone. Meanwhile, pockets of militant Islam sheltered disaffected youth in some worrying areas of Britain, and further encouraged the secularists' jibe that 'religion' was essentially violent and irrational, a mere sign of primitive backwardness.

But what has been on offer *theologically* during this same curious and paradoxical transition into 'postmodernity', when institutional Christianity's attraction seems to have almost washed away but various other forms of 'lived religion' have washed back in? And in particular, what has been the relation between these theological options and the now chastened sociology of religion which had earlier forecast only inexorable decline? It is here that a new variation on Arnold's classic marine metaphor may provide an illuminating ruse to offset my own systematic proposal.

THEOLOGICAL OPTIONS 'ON WIGAN PIER'?

Given that the tide is coming back in via some rather strange new waterways, it is 'Wigan Pier', let me suggest, rather than Dover Beach, with which theologians now have to do. For Wigan Pier – that modest canal jetty at least fifteen miles from any actual ocean tide[2] – now beckons theologians seductively, in a variety of forms and evocations, and it may be said to represent certain current theological choices that I precisely want to steer beyond.[3] Let me explain.

---

[2] The ruse that follows may need some initial explanation, especially for readers who are not British. A fuller account of the history of 'Wigan Pier' (Wigan is an industrial area in the north-west of England) can be found on the website of the Wigan Archaeological Society, which reports: 'A "pier", in this context, is a device for tipping the contents of coal trucks onto canal boats. There were once many such devices in the Wigan area. "Wigan Pier" is situated on the Leeds–Liverpool canal near the centre of the town ... The "joke" is thought to have originated in a music-hall act performed by George Formby Sr in which he talked of Wigan Pier in the same terms as the seaside pleasure piers in nearby Blackpool and Southport. George Orwell perpetuated the ... conception in his book *The Road to Wigan Pier*, in which he portrayed the dismal side of the town and ignored the positive aspects of life in a working class community ... [The original Wigan Pier was however demolished in 1929, before Orwell's book was even published.] ... Since then ... a replica tippler has been erected on the site of the old one and the whole area has become today's attractive cultural centre.'

[3] It should be stressed immediately that what follows is not in any way an exhaustive account of current theological options – far from it. Nor do the trends I describe line up precisely with any particular denominational template. But the three 'types' of theology I choose to highlight do represent distinctive contemporary responses to the issue of how social science and theology should relate today. The fact that I myself am regularly accused of belonging to these alternative camps – all three! – is a sign of their current dominance in the theological imagination.

First, there is the possibility today of a reactive return to a high, authoritarian ecclesiastical Christian 'orthodoxy', cut off from the real 'sea' of lived religion by hierarchical avoidance or denial. The errors of 'modernity' are here decried, and revelatory or magisterial authority strongly reasserted. To many, such an option attracts simply because of its overriding ethos of certainty: in an era of conflicting postmodern values it confronts the threat of moral relativism head-on. It also deals with contemporary questions of feminism and gender in a confidently high-handed and 'tradition-alist' manner. The deck looks nice and neat here, to be sure; but there is a notable repression, even a willed ignorance, of those features of *distorted* religion that investigative sociology can chart with such acumen (witness again the recent Roman Catholic sex scandals). This, we might say, is the 'Wigan Pier' of the original ironic vaudeville song. Since it has cut itself off from the messy detritus of the actual 'sea of faith', its exponents can enjoy a certain delusion about the ecclesiastical realities around them. Offerings from the secular sociologists can be largely ignored on the grounds that they themselves merely succumb to the moral relativism that is being resisted.[4]

The second possibility is arguably more exciting, and – in its own distinctive claims to authority – less institutional, more purely intellectual, in tone. Here is a theological option that uses post-modernism precisely against itself, and triumphs rhetorically by appeal to a new *theological* 'metanarrative'. If all false modern foundationalisms from secular philosophy are now decried, why

---

[4] Telling examples of this first kind of approach, and its particular resistance to moral relativism, can be found in the magisterial writings of John Paul II and Benedict XVI, but this option is not only Roman Catholic: various sophisticated forms of neoconservatism and neoscholasticism in Reformed and Lutheran circles also fall under this general 'type'. Refusal to attend to 'the field' can result in denial, however, about sexual aberrations and about pressing feminist questions.

not – it urges – choose a more classic theological option from the patristic or high medieval period, rather than kowtow to the 'false modesty' of a dying Enlightenment liberalism? Theological truth is here not so much rationally argued as pronounced by fiat. It 'overcomes' modern science, philosophy, and social science in one fell swoop, as manifestations of debased, but hidden, theological agendas which had their ultimate origins in later medieval suppressions of divine mystery. The particular argument with the modern sociology of Weber and Durkheim is, however, in this theological option, astute and canny: the secular reductionisms they espoused were themselves variations on weak theological alternatives, it is claimed, and hence sociology of religion, *tout court*, can be declared intellectually bankrupt.[5]

Despite the brilliant intellectual table-turnings of this theological strategy, however, and its heady reassertion of theological confidence within the secularized university, this second ploy can, in the wrong hands, rapidly turn into a different sort of 'Wigan Pier' escapism. Here is the new 'Pier' in contemporary Wigan, we might say: it represents a postmodern theme park 'option' worthy of a quick Sunday excursion off the M6 motorway. For the danger of this second theological alternative, thrilling as it is, is that it invites a nostalgia trip to another, pre-modern age which simultaneously decries the entire Enlightenment programme (forgetting the blood that was spilt to achieve it, and the profound political achievements it garnered). Moreover, in rejecting at the same time the whole

---

[5] I refer here of course to John Milbank's justly celebrated *Theology and Social Theory: Beyond Secular Reason* (Oxford: Blackwell, 1990; 2nd edn 2006): relevant discussions of classical sociology and of liberation theology can be found at 101–44 and 235–56 (2006 edn). It should be acknowledged that while *Theology and Social Theory* evidences no interest in, or sympathy for, feminist concerns, Milbank's more recent writing (e.g., *Being Reconciled: Ontology and Pardon* (London: Routledge, 2003)) has some occasional discussion of French postmodern feminism.

project of sociology of religion (this time on *intellectual* rather than moral grounds), it again undercuts the possibility of receiving complicating or embarrassing reports from the ecclesiastical trenches. Not least is this worrying where abuses to women and the underprivileged are concerned, especially given the stringently critical assault that this type of theology simultaneously makes on 'liberation theology' as yet another 'modern' option.

These first two forms of 'Wigan Pierism' obviously have certain shared interests in common in their resistance to secular 'modernity', despite their notable other differences of strategy and emphasis. A third option that presents itself is, however, altogether different. This is the form of liberal feminist theology which has survived the various mutations of feminist fashion in the later twentieth century, and can now be almost taken for granted in the (admittedly shrinking) liberal Protestant denominations of North America. Its influence has found its way powerfully into new liturgies as well as into theological imaginations and consciousnesses: the language of divine 'Fatherhood' has been banned or suppressed, and replaced either by sprinklings of complementary allusions to divine 'femininity', or – in the less Romantic formations of this type – by more anodyne descriptions of God as 'lover' or 'friend'.[6] In Britain and Northern Europe at large, too, its exponents are to be found amongst the middle-aged clerisy of the established churches (both amongst women and feminist-identified men), although its preserve and impact here is not nearly as strong as it has proved in North America. In its more radical, American, form, this feminist approach

---

[6] I refer here to Sallie McFague, *Models of God: Theology for an Ecological, Nuclear Age* (Philadelphia: Fortress Press, 1987): see 125–56, 157–80. I place McFague in a spectrum of other American feminist theological approaches in my survey essay, 'Feminist Theology', in James C. Livingstone and Francis Schüssler Fiorenza, eds., *Modern Christian Thought* (Minneapolis: Fortress Press, 2006), 417–42.

takes it for granted that classic Christianity is *inherently* 'patriarchal', and that – without necessary ideological correction – it will inevitably tend towards the suppression of the rights and dignity of women and of other marginalized people, including ethnic minorities and homosexuals and lesbians. Theological truth is thus often here reconceived as 'justice', over against creedal 'orthodoxy'; and in certain forms of post-Kantian American liberal theology, 'God' is freely reconceived to fit with pragmatist feminist goals. A freedom from restrictive biblical authority is announced in aid of this liberation of the imagination in the ongoing quest for 'equality'. All this bespeaks an ostensible spiritual confidence, and a stringent will to effect change over against tradition. Yet there often remains in this type of theology, nonetheless, a striking pessimism about the possibility of any lasting transformation of the institutional churches, and a marked cynicism about prayer as anything other than a delusive 'navel-gazing'.[7]

What sort of theological 'Wigan Pierism' is this third type? It is certainly a very different one from the first two types. One might say that it summons rather the evocations of Orwell's exposé of the grime and abuse suffered by the miners in his classic monograph *On the Road to Wigan Pier*. It insistently, and rightly, draws attention to questions of privilege, class, prejudice, and abuse, and their entanglement with theological projects. Insights and messages from the social sciences (and behind them, from Enlightenment traditions of philosophy and theology) are thus gratefully – but somewhat uncritically – embraced. The trouble is that this third theological programme (unlike Orwell's own rather different political agenda) seems to present no lasting way out of feminist anger and stuckness

---

[7] This charge is explicitly made in the feminist theological compendium volume of the Mudflower Collective, *God's Fierce Whimsy: Christian Feminism and Theological Education* (New York: Pilgrim Press, 1985), 25.

except by remaking God *in its own image* again. To this last point I shall shortly return.

I promised at the start of this chapter to deliver a pincer movement argument, and I am now in a position to clarify the first of these two moves I need to make in order to indicate the fuller systematic implications of a *théologie totale*. If we now ask how we might escape the mistakes of the various 'Wigan Pier' alternatives I have just outlined (with their different understandings of the relation of theology and the social sciences, both critical and uncritical), the answer must be this.

My thesis here is that the recovery of a creative *and* critical relation of theology to the social sciences is a vital one for a *théologie totale*. Provided the secular reductive pretensions of classic sociology of religion are undercut, sociology can continue to unearth 'in the field' both ecclesiastical embarrassments *and* hidden treasure for theology. This is because the wider realm of 'doctrine' has many levels, mediums of expression, and spheres of response – not merely those enshrined in the official creeds and re-enunciated by theologians and church leaders. *Théologie totale* aims to dig down the social tell of doctrine, even as it simultaneously purges and unifies the engaged theologian's faculties in response to that tell (see again the Prelude). To switch the metaphor back to the watery one beloved of recent theologians: the 'sea of faith' may indeed be murky, polluted, or marshy, existing more in underground streams than in overt ecclesiastical commitment. But its tide is by no means out for ever, and the 'messy entanglements' and detritus that we find in it deserve the closest theological attention. Only after I so attend am I in a position to assess; and without the aid of the social sciences there are many such realms of doctrinal enactment – rich, strange, debased, freshly creative – I cannot know about at all.

Thus the options presented by the 'Wigan Pier' alternatives just outlined turn out to be false ones, although each, to be sure, deserves a certain sympathetic initial hearing. The first alternative rightly seeks to extract itself from dependence on secular 'foundations', whether philosophical or sociological, and to resist moral relativism; but in the process it repressively ignores the complex actualities of the lives of its religious adherents. The second alternative rightly exposes the pretensions of a modern secular sociology that sought to explain religion *away*; but in the process it also averts its intellectual gaze from the entanglements of high doctrinal 'orthodoxy' with messy heterodox realities. The third option, quite differently, declares itself unashamedly 'modern' and has no fear of the hermeneutics of suspicion, as such: sociology can well be utilized to trace 'patriarchal' aberrations within the faith, to the point of asserting that those aberrations represent its natural and intrinsic identity. The remaining problem in this third option is a different one, then, from that of the other two. For here modern philosophy and social science, as such, seem to provide no reason for theological *hope* in the face of these exposés of failure, except to invite one to remake 'God' by almost arbitrary personal preference. God in Godself, on this third view, is radically unavailable, cut off behind a veil of Kantian nescience; we can 'make' God what we like, it is declared, but God cannot change *us*. Prayer is a delusion, a mere monologue projected into the atmosphere.[8]

---

[8] It was Immanuel Kant who put 'limits' (*Grenzen*) on what – as he argued – could be known of God speculatively in a 'scientific' metaphysics; prayer for him therefore becomes merely the 'sincere wish to please God in all our doings' (*Religion within the Bounds of Mere Reason* (orig. 1793; Cambridge University Press, 1998), 186). Much of the force of the 'liberal'

But as I have already argued in the Prelude and Chapter 1, a contemplative alternative to this liberal theological stuckness in the knowing subject is able to change the landscape – or rather the seascape – dramatically. Kantian nescience may, under these conditions of contemplative commitment, become 'dazzling darkness'; the 'limits' of knowledge may become limitless horizons of divine mystery. Indeed, from this perspective the modern 'death of God' may turn out in retrospective to have been an absolutely necessary purgation of false gods, the prelude to a contemplative rebirth.[9] Just as the 'onto-theological' challenge caused systematic theology to re-examine itself contemplatively (Chapter 1), so now does the axis between sociology and theology. A way between and beyond the three false choices above can be made with the aid of a contemplative *théologie totale*.

But before I explain this possibility further, I must next turn to the promised second pincer movement in my argument.

WHAT THEN OF THE RELATION OF POSTMODERN GENDER THEORY TO LIBERAL ENLIGHTENMENT THOUGHT AND FEMINIST THEOLOGY?

I have already examined the significance of contemporary gender theory for systematic theology in Chapter 1, and have argued strenuously that its secular presumptions must be transformed by an

---

type of theology under discussion here resides in a particular reading of Kant on this point, one that declares any claims to interact directly with God to be philosophically insupportable: see especially Gordon D. Kaufman, *In Face of Mystery: A Constructive Theology* (Cambridge, MA: Harvard University Press, 1993), 332–3, 356.

[9] This point is made with wonderful verve in Michael Buckley, 'Atheism and Contemplation', *Theological Studies* 40 (1979), 680–99, in which the modern anti-theological critiques of Feuerbach, Marx and Freud are compared with the early modern mystical purgations of John of the Cross's spiritual theology.

ascetical and contemplative approach to the central spiritual question of desire. Often today secular exponents of postmodern gender theory look askance at an earlier generation's 'feminist' concerns, regarding them as outdated both in their attitudes to gender and orientation (because 'essentialist' or 'heterosexist') and in their commitment to a 'liberal' Enlightenment universalism which appears to ignore, or even obliterate, 'difference'. The resultant standoff between secularized gender theory in the 'study of religion', on the one hand, and feminist theology of an earlier vintage in the churches, on the other, is a marked and uneasy feature of the contemporary theological terrain for those concerned about the fundamental flourishing of women. Meanwhile, those conservative theological critics who are sceptical of the whole debate about gender may, unfortunately, use a 'divide and rule' strategy in the face of this ideological disagreement; whereas – ironically – what conjoins both sides in the gender theory and feminist divide (a strong hermeneutics of suspicion about the 'patriarchal' ballast of the Christian tradition) is not always adequately accompanied by richly *theological* strategies of retrieval and transformation.

This problem – or rather, its potential solution – represents the second pincer in the question of theological method being addressed in this chapter. For clearly it intersects with, or is overlaid upon, the 'Wigan Pier' divides already described. Whereas the first type of 'Wigan Pierism' outlined above shows outright hostility to feminism, and the second displays only an occasional interest in postmodern gender theory (in contradistinction to classic egalitarian feminism), the third is, in contrast, notably committed to an older form of feminist theory and theology which exponents of postmodernity would now regard as outdated. Walking the decks of Wigan Pier is, alas, no holiday from the ideological gender wars.

My own thesis in the face of this divisive difficulty is that the classic (modern) feminist theological critique of Christianity still has to be taken with deep seriousness. But the answer to its critique is *neither* precipitously to abandon the spiritual riches of traditional Christian thought (in all its complexity and ambiguity), *nor* over-hastily to reject those crucial strands of Enlightenment philosophy on which modern liberal feminism was itself predicated. Appeals to human 'rights', 'justice', and 'equality' must go on *strategically*, I want to argue, even as those crucial Enlightenment notions are critically renegotiated and reparsed by a postmodern scholarship newly suspicious of flat, universalist claims. Rightly, this recent postmodern scholarship draws attention to the ways in which such universalism may actually cloak a Western imperialism. But what it also reveals is that the history of the modern rhetoric of 'rights' and 'equality' was itself crucially inflected by Christian tradition from the outset, and was not, as was claimed at the time, essentially an *escape* from dependence on Christian tradition and authority. The resulting discussion is a rich and subtle one. It is forced, first, to acknowledge the Jewish and Christian roots of contemporary 'rights' language, and at the same time to divest that (supposedly secular) language of covert bids for Western political power. This task is – to say the least – an exercise of historical, religious, and political sophistication, requiring distinctive spiritual strengths of self-knowledge and humility. It is not, then, a task best accom-plished by a *divestment* from religious practices and traditions, as is still assumed in dominant secular circles; on the contrary, it may be that contemplative religious practices of 'effacement' are precisely the enabling incubator for such reconsideration.

Perhaps we may now sum up the conclusions about the second of our 'pincer movements', thus. As we saw in Chapter 1, postmodern gender theory has rightly drawn attention to the centrality of questions of desire, but it becomes narcissistic and inward-looking if it fails to confront the wider and continuing problems of universal 'justice' and 'rights' for women, worldwide. A classic form of liberal feminism or feminist theology, in contrast, correctly keeps up the ongoing battle on behalf of oppressed and subjugated women, but has difficulties in resisting the dangers of a flat or idolatrous imposition of its own Western agendas, or – more personally – the traps of unresolved personal resentment and hatred. In both cases, as we now see, there are profound *spiritual* problems to be confronted: the necessary theological repair involves nothing less than an expansion of spiritual consciousness. Such a way invites us beyond the false binary choices we have here discussed.

I am now in a position to bring the different strands of my argument in this chapter together, and to end with a final enunci- ation of the distinctive marks of the method of *théologie totale*.

WHY ENLIGHTENMENT FEMINISM AND THE SOCIAL SCIENCES DO MATTER TO THEOLOGY

I have argued in this chapter that classic modern feminism (as distinct from postmodern gender theory, which was discussed in Chapter 1) still matters to theology, first, because it – or something very like it – is needed for continual vigilance about how doctrine is purveyed and has impacts 'in the field' on women's flourishing. Such factors are still often outright denied by officialdom in eccle- siastical circles. Yet doctrine always has an embedded texture, a set of subliminal cultural and societal associations and evocations, as well as its 'plain' meaning. Thus, often one must read between or under the lines to see what is going on doctrinally *in context*. The tools of the social sciences, when stripped of secularizing preten- sions, are vital for any such investigation, as will be demonstrated more concretely later in this volume (Chapters 3 and 4). In partic- ular, the doctrine of God as Trinity presents us with a supposed

charter of 'perfect relationship' – one that has often been represented, either explicitly or implicitly, as having strong implications
for societal and gendered relations (see Chapter 5). It is thus
incumbent on the theologian to tease out those associations and
implications, and to submit them to conscious and critical
assessment.

Secondly, the question of women's flourishing remains an urgent
theological concern in a world of profound inequalities of wealth
and privilege. For it is invariably vulnerable women (and children)
who are doubly subjected in conditions of political oppression and
poverty. It follows that a proper concern for women's rights is
equally a concern for *human rights* and for the dignity of human life
before God. To mask this problem by reference to the many other
factors that cause deprivation, marginalization, and oppression is a
danger inherent in the fashionable postmodern resistance to gender
'essentialism'. Social science investigation can help continue to
probe the relation of such varied oppressions to questions of 'powers
and submissions' between men and women in the family, and also in
conditions outside the family where vulnerable women may become
sexually enslaved or otherwise endangered.

Thirdly, we have seen that there is a dangerous temptation in
postmodern gender theory to suppress discussion of the *universality*
of the problem of the subjected 'other' (using arguments against a
supposedly hegemonic Western 'modernity' or 'justice' as a cloak
for relativism or parochialism). There is an added temptation in
secular gender theory to avoid discussing the issue of the *religiosity*
of the subjected 'other', as if it can be explained away in terms of
something else. But matters of religious power and religious allegiance are often entangled, both negatively and positively, with
conditions of subjection and political powerlessness. There are
profound paradoxes here which, again, social science investigations

can – in the right spirit – probe with insight, and to great theological advantage. Religious commitment and practice are not necessarily signs of a (double) subjugation. On the contrary, they may be a means of integrity, transformation, and empowerment. The wisdom to know the difference – between right and false alternatives – is, I submit, itself fostered in and through the contemplative act.

Fourthly, theology needs *both* to unearth the religious (Jewish and Christian) roots of Western 'human rights' talk, *and* at the same time to maintain a strategic insistence on the political and humanitarian importance of such talk – as a brokered bridgehead between those of many different religious convictions, or of none. This is a difficult and complex task, involving great spiritual and intellectual subtlety. But, as an increasing number of studies and projects now demonstrate, it is not an impossible one. Human 'rights'- and 'democracy'-talk does not have to be immunized against religion; indeed, it is fatal and self-defeating to attempt such an enforced secularizing project while claiming to aid the path towards democracy amongst populations of deep religious conviction.

So if, for all these reasons, the (pincer-related) disciplines of the social sciences and of feminism must continue to matter to theology, why is a contemplative *théologie totale* of special importance for such a nexus of concerns?

Here I have already argued, first, that what theology *in via* (*théologie totale*) most distinctively can contribute is an insistence on the ascetical practice of contemplation as a preparation for *radical* attention to the 'other'. The imposition of one's own perception of (women's) flourishing on the subjugated 'other' can itself become covertly imperialistic or even abusive; the ongoing task of the shattering of one's own idols – a personal and ecclesiastical task that never comes to an end – has to accompany any such attempt at the amelioration of women's lot worldwide. In short, the capacity to divest oneself of imperialistic impulses is not a mere matter of good intentions or rhetorical enunciation. It is, finally, a grace encountered in the patient waiting of prayer.

It follows that *théologie totale* must be acutely attentive, rather than the opposite, to the social and political contexts of theology. The idea of contemplation as an exercise of merely individual insight or self-cultivation must, as has been insisted in the Prelude, be rudely and firmly rejected. For it is a distortion of the intrinsically incarnational and social impulse of the practice: here, over time, is the mysterious interpenetration of all created life glimpsed and intuited, the 'groaning of all creation' straining towards its final goal. But this means that the feminist hermeneutics of suspicion, which itself remains a necessary discipline of social analysis *as well as* a vital theological means of resistance to patri- archal idolatry, must avoid crudely hostile and cynical forms, if charity and hope are to be maintained. Hence a *théologie totale* refuses to *reduce* doctrine to a mere effect of social, political, or patriarchal conditions. For once such a reductive hermeneutics of suspicion is allowed to triumph over the (eternal, divine) invitation to charity, forgiveness, and reconciliation, a new idolatry has also triumphed: that of anger stuck in victimology, and the implicit recreation of a 'God' made merely in my own image. *Théologie totale* protects its insistence on what I have called the 'ground bass' of divine revelation – the *cantus firmus* of charity and grace. But its assent to such is precisely *not* an assent to fallen political or eccle- siastical structures in need of reform or transformation.

What also follows is that the silence of contemplation is of a particular, *sui generis*, form: it is not the silence of *being silenced*. Rather, it is the voluntary silence of attention, transformation, mysterious interconnection, and (in violent, abusive, or oppressive contexts) rightful and divinely empowered *resistance*: it is a special 'power-in-vulnerability', as I have elsewhere called it.[10] Contemplation engenders courage to *give voice*, but in a changed, prophetic key. A certain worldly dignity – it is true – may necessarily be lost in the process, but not the fundamental spiritual integrity that the practice, over time, inculcates.

We can therefore conclude that non-reductive sociology, and especially non-reductive sociology of religion, has a vital role to play as handmaid to a *théologie totale*. God 'in the field' is found by lifting the decks on the grimy ills of 'Wigan Pier' *without getting stuck there*, not by fantasizing about a postmodern theme park 'Wigan Pier' of unreal nostalgia (for a lost past of neo-Gothic liturgical enchantment), nor by denying that the sea of faith is often awash with muck. But sociology of religion does not only expose ills and abuses; it can also turn up unexpected arenas of grace and faith: it can discover ways in which doctrine can be made newly alive by reference to its earthed manifestations, as well as ways in which doctrine is abused in its earthed distortions. That is why the feminist hermeneutics of suspicion, while never rendered otiose, can never represent the last word either.

A final, and major, objection to what I have argued here must be addressed in closing. It will not have escaped the reader's attention that I have made some very fulsome claims about contemplation and its implications in this and the last chapter. The immediate *secular* riposte might well be that it is inappropriate, and entirely question-begging, to bring the religious realm of practice into the sphere of political and public debate – that of government, of the university, and of international law. Further, the *non-Christian* religious response, in contrast, might be that my appeal to

---

[10] For a more extended discussion of this paradox, see my *Powers and Submissions: Philosophy, Spirituality and Gender* (Oxford: Blackwell, 2002), especially the prologue, xii–xx.

Christian contemplation is an insidious new 'hegemonic' move, replacing doctrinal supersessionism with a more covert supersessionism of practice. These objections – apparently polar opposites on the secular–religious divide – are both fuelled, however, by the presumption that religious 'practice' is precisely what engenders and mandates a sectarian *withdrawal* from public commitments and shared projects. On this view, 'religion' – and especially any sort of ramified belief and accompanying bodily practice – needs to be debarred from the public arena before a generic conversation about human rights can begin.

But it must be clear by now that this presumption is precisely what I have set out to question in this chapter. It is perfectly true that 'practices' of a religious sort *can* be utilized as statements of political demarcation, supersessionist avowal, declarations of hostility, or sheer refusals to join a cross-boundary discussion. But what I have argued here about authentic contemplation, in contrast, is that its very practice of gentle effacement allows communication with the 'other' at a depth not otherwise possible, indeed perhaps not even imaginable. To contemplate is to invite uncomfortable change, not to bludgeon the other with one's certainties. To ask its exponents then to *relinquish* their practice in order to join a common discussion is to vitiate precisely the subtle distinctiveness of its contribution. It is worth remembering here too that the separation of philosophical ideas and personal practice is a specifically modern invention, which we may do well now to reconsider. That such a reconsideration lands us in a trans-religious plane of multiple, rich, and conflicting beliefs is undeniable; but it does not thereby follow that withdrawal to a falsely generic secular space holds any intellectual or moral advantages.

Let me then recap the range of claims I have made so impenitently throughout the first section of this book about the particular practice of Christian contemplation in its graced vulnerability to the

Spirit. That these claims will remain contentious is undeniable; that they mark the very distinctiveness of my project cannot be gainsaid.

Christian contemplative practice, if it is working aright (purgatively, transformatively, and with its full social implications manifested) has the following dimensions which I have now urged in some detail.

Spiritually, it involves a progressive – and sometimes painful – incorporation into the life of God (the 'likeness' of the 'Son') via the 'interruption' of the Holy Spirit, as desire is gradually purified, and anger metabolized into the energy of love (the Prelude). In gender terms, it involves a rendering labile of gender to the workings of divine desire, a loosening of the restrictions of worldly presumptions about gender as selfhood expands into God and is thereby released for the same great work of love (Chapter 1).

Finally, in feminist and political terms, it involves an intensification of attention to the 'other' in her specific social conditions, a guarding even against the imposition of imperialistic (Western) *feminist* agendas (Chapter 2). Thus contemplation, in all these aspects, promotes a concern for the common good beyond the boundaries of narrow ecclesiastical or national interests: it fosters what the early Christian fathers called *leitourgia* ('liturgy', public service) in the best theological sense, as service to the world in humility and hope. Finally, as will have become clear from all these traits, contemplation keeps ethics, doctrine, and spiritual practice tightly wound together. The spiritual purgations of what Origen called '*ethikē*' (the tough, first stage of the spiritual ascent) are the conditions under which one's own ethical and political judgements are best made, and doctrine personally assimilated. But these purgations are also the conditions for seeing what is awry without falsely projecting one's own inner darkness onto the 'other' and perpetrating new political and theological idolatries.

CONCLUSION: THE METHODOLOGICAL HALLMARKS
OF THÉOLOGIE TOTALE

What then are the distinctive hallmarks of *théologie totale* which have emerged through the arguments of this whole first section of the book? Below are the methodological presumptions which will characterize the undertaking of my systematic theology as a whole. Since I am recapitulating here more complicated points which have already been rehearsed, I write in a certain shorthand.

1. *Privileging contemplation.* The practice of contemplation sustains the systematic theological enterprise, not because it is a man-made 'foundation' for it, but because it is the primary ascetical submission to the divine demanded by revelation, and the link to the creative source of life to which it continually returns. This practice is neither an élitist nor an arcane act, as might be feared: it is an undertaking of radical attention to the Real which is open to all who seek to foster it.

2. *Theology in via.* *Théologie totale* acknowledges the primacy of such contemplation for systematics, not as the quest for some sort of authenticating 'religious experience', but as an attentive openness of the whole self (intellect, will, memory, imagination, feeling, bodiliness) to the reality of God and of the creation. Through the 'interruption' of the Spirit, the authority of the revelatory Word is continually and freshly encountered and expounded – by a 'reason' which is itself in process of disclosure. It follows that *théologie totale* involves an ongoing journey of purgative transformation and change.

3. *The counterpoint of philosophy, science, and théologie totale.* Theology does not thereby claim to *subsume* or 'overcome' secular philosophy and science. So grace and nature remain in an important sense theoretically demarcated, even though there is no isolable 'pure nature' as such, and the grace of the Spirit 'blows where it

wills' – not at the theologian's behest.[11] Only *God* can 'take over' nature; that is not human theology's task. It is the Spirit's interruption that finally enables full human participation in God. It follows that secular philosophy and secular science will of course choose to retain their own spheres, and will remain in constant critical interaction with Christian theology: they cannot merely be trumped by theology's rhetorical fiat, although the invitation to enter into the realm of faith, or conversation with it, can ever be laid before them.[12] Theology's 'reason', however, in comparison to all secular reasons, is both purified and *expanded* by the dark purgation of contemplation. So theology's reason, at a profound level, is in ongoing contrapuntal relation to revelation and grace, and continues to be transformed by it. But – rather differently, and at another level – theology's reason also remains in contrapuntal discussion with secular philosophy and science; for it cannot rule out the possibility that here, too, it will need to learn something by which it may be changed (again, the Spirit 'blows where it wills'). There is a paradoxical double counterpoint here between secular reason, theology's reason, and that reason still *in via* to God.

4. *Orthodoxy as goal.* 'Orthodoxy' in *théologie totale* is understood as a project, the longed-for horizon of personal transformation in response to divine truth. Orthodoxy is no mere creedal correctness,

---

[11] I am here traversing contentious territory in the debates about how to interpret Thomas Aquinas on the relation of nature and grace. For a readable and discerning account of these debates within 'neo-Thomism' and in twentieth century reactions to it, see Fergus Kerr, *After Aquinas: Versions of Thomism* (Oxford: Blackwell, 2002), esp. 134–48.

[12] Such exercises in 'apologetics' may be seen as spin-offs from the systematic enterprise, rather than integrally part of it; they need not thereby succumb to the underlying metaphysical presumptions of secular philosophy and science, but enter into a critical probing of them. For an example of such an undertaking in (revised) 'natural theology', see my recent Gifford Lectures, 'Sacrifice Regained: Evolution, Cooperation and God', given at Aberdeen, 2012.

no *imposed* ecclesiastical regulation. At that horizon of true orthodoxy, theology, 'spirituality', and ethics are fully united. This
alternative approach to orthodoxy has classically brought dangers:
it has been suspiciously derided as monastic or intellectual élitism,
or resisted as spiritually threatening by ecclesiastical and political
'powers', and so pushed to the edges. The loss of the integrity it
offers, however, comes with severe spiritual cost.

5. *Théologie totale as socially located but not socially reduced.*
Théologie totale peels down through the layers of society where
doctrine is received. It applies the hermeneutics of suspicion, but
ultimately too the hermeneutics of charity and hope, to whatever it
finds there. It follows that the social sciences (when duly shorn of
secular reductive presumptions) are crucial adjuncts to theology's
purposes, if all the layers and contexts of society are to be attended
to. The 'messy entanglements' of doctrinal truth and social reality,
of buried treasure and ecclesiastical embarrassments, are to be freely
acknowledged and discerningly adjudicated.

6. *Théologie totale and the expansion of the classic systematic loci.*
Théologie totale attends to all the classical '*loci*' of systematic theology (God, Trinity, Christ, Spirit, anthropology, sin and salvation,
the church, the sacraments, the end times, etc.), but not necessarily
in the classic orderings. It declares itself free to superimpose treatments of one doctrine on another, or to conjoin the discussion of
different loci in fresh ways. Moreover, it adds new loci as needed, to
re-enliven the systematic tradition for contemporary concerns of
pressing significance. In particular, the treatment of the doctrine of
the human person is enriched by special attention to gender and to
sexuality; the treatment of sin and salvation is complexified by
special attention to race and class.

7. *Théologie totale and aesthetic expression. Théologie totale* is
founded in the bodily practices of contemplation, which court the

'unconscious' and summon into new attentiveness those dimensions of human response which go beyond the verbal or the propositional. *Théologie totale* thus attends to all the various mediums (in addition to academic theological exposition, churchly teaching, and preaching), through which religious truth is expressed aesthetically, whether wordlessly or as 'cultural production': it attends to art, to poetry, to music, and (combining all of these) to liturgy. Through these mediums the realm of the senses can be sharpened, intensified, and then purged and redirected; and through these mediums, also, dimensions of divine truth are evoked which can be found in no other way. Each volume of this systematics therefore has a 'semiotic' moment of aesthetic attention and analysis (in this volume I, it is art; in volume II, poetry; in volume III, music; in volume IV, in summation, liturgy).

8. *The overcoming of false divides.* *Théologie totale* resists many of the binary disjunctions which so exercise, and distract, contemporary practitioners of systematic theology. It resists the divides between belief and practice, between thought and affect, between academic and accessible writing, between Christian theology and 'religious studies', between academic theology and 'pastoral' theology, and between 'liberal' feminism and postmodern gender theory. And it resists these divides not because it aims to forge a compromise between them, but because its contemplative method claims to cut across them and to redirect creative energy beyond them. It is an implication of this method that we must no longer rend 'practical' or 'pastoral' theology apart from 'systematic theology' and 'philosophical theology'. For they have always – properly – belonged together; and any systematic theology worth having must prove how it works in the field, and – conversely – how what happens in the field both challenges and reinvigorates its systematic tasks. That is why each volume in this systematics touches down in such a

fieldwork context, one which in each case presses the doctrinal imagination in new and creative directions.

9. *Desire as the constellating theological category of* théologie totale. At the heart of this systematics, as we have seen, is an examination of the relation of divine and human desires. 'On Desiring God' is the central theme which unites this full systematic endeavour: the dependence of human desire on divine (unchanging, but vibrant) desire, as both its source and goal, is the fundamental axis of the *théologie totale* and the means of rethinking contemporary dilemmas about sexuality and gender, exploitation and deprivation, punishment and healing.

All in all, *théologie totale* is hard work. But it is not the hard work of a Pelagian 'works righteousness'. It is the *graced* work of contemplation and theology and ethics and politics – without division, without confusion. The greatest of these, the essential work of love, is fostered in contemplation.

And now, after these last two chapters, we have done quite enough splashing about in the methodological shallows of the sea of faith. It is time to swim in the tide of the Spirit itself – to probe back to the early church and to see how and why the doctrine of the Trinity arose in the first place.

* * *

BIBLIOGRAPHIC NOTE

DOVER BEACH AND THE FATE OF THE
'SECULARIZATION' THESIS

The metaphor of Dover Beach and Matthew Arnold's prognostication there of the erosion of faith ('Dover Beach', in Kenneth and Miriam Allott, eds., *The Poems of Matthew Arnold* (London: Longman, 1979), 253–7) has come to have particular symbolic significance within British, and especially Cambridge-based, theological discussion: see Nicholas Lash, 'Doing Theology on Dover Beach', in *Theology on Dover Beach* (London: DLT, 1979), 3–23; and by way of riposte (and acceptance of the changed, postmodern seascape), Don Cupitt, *The Sea of Faith* (London: BBC Books, 1984). Max Weber's original account of the rational secularization of modernity (see Max Weber, *The Protestant Ethic and the Spirit of Capitalism* (orig. 1905; Oxford: Blackwell, 2002)) is now only sustained by a few stalwarts (see Steve Bruce, *God is Dead: Secularization in the West* (Oxford: Blackwell, 2002), and Steve Bruce, ed., *Religion and Modernization: Sociologists and Historians Debate the Secularization Thesis* (Oxford: Clarendon Press, 1992)). For the most part, sociologists now focus on the 'failure' of the secularization thesis in its classic form, and on the complexity and geographical differences of current religious traits worldwide: the stark collapse of church attendance in established churches and denominations in Northern Europe does not, for instance, signal any lack of interest in 'spirituality', so-called, or in 'new religious movements'; and this hybrid state of affairs coexists alongside the rise of Christian 'fundamentalisms' in various forms, especially in North America. The emergence of a militant Islam in the Middle East and beyond mirrors these developments, and gives a specific flavour to the anti-religious polemics of atheistical secularism. Recommended studies of these various, and paradoxical, dimensions of the post-'secularization' debate include: Charles Taylor, *A Secular Age* (Cambridge, MA: Harvard University Press, 2007); David Martin, *On Secularisation: Towards a Revised General Theory* (Aldershot: Ashgate, 2005); W. H. Swatos and D. V. Olson, eds., *The Secularization Debate* (Lanham, MD: Rowman & Littlefield, 2000); Rodney Stark and Roger Finke, *Acts of Faith: Exploring the Human Side of Religion* (Berkeley: University of California Press, 2000); Eileen Barker, *The New Religious Movements: A Practical*

Introduction (London: HMSO, 1989); Paul Heelas and Linda Woodhead, with Benjamin Seel, Bronislaw Szerszynski, and Karin Tusting, *The Spiritual Revolution: Why Religion is Giving Way to Spirituality* (Oxford: Blackwell, 2005); Gabriel Almond, R. Scott Appleby, and Emmanuel Sivan, *Strong Religion: The Rise of Fundamentalisms around the World* (University of Chicago Press, 2003); Grace Davie, *Religion in Britain since 1945: Believing without Belonging* (Oxford: Blackwell, 1994); Grace Davie, *Religion in Modern Europe: A Memory Mutates* (Oxford University Press, 2000); Peter Berger, Grace Davie, and Effie Fokas, *Religious America, Secular Europe? A Theme and Variations* (Aldershot: Ashgate, 2008); Bryan S. Turner, ed., *The New Blackwell Companion to the Sociology of Religion* (Oxford: Wiley–Blackwell, 2010); John Micklethwait and Alan Wooldridge, *God is Back: How the Global Revival of Faith is Changing the World* (London: Allen Lane, 2009); Anthony McRoy, *From Rushdie to 7/7: The Radicalisation of Islam in Britain* (London: Social Affairs Unit, 2006); Roger Eatwell and Matthew J. Goodwin, eds., *The New Extremism in 21st Century Britain* (London: Routledge, 2010); Shamit Saggar, *Pariah Politics: Understanding Western Radical Islamism and What Should Be Done* (Oxford University Press, 2009); and William Cavanaugh, *The Myth of Religious Violence: Secular Ideology and the Roots of Modern Conflict* (Oxford University Press, 2009).

'WIGAN PIER' OPTIONS: NEOCONSERVATISM, RADICAL
ORTHODOXY AND LIBERAL FEMINISM/WOMANISM

My use of the Wigan Pier 'ruse' may be pursued further in George Orwell, *The Road to Wigan Pier* (orig., 1937; Harmondsworth: Penguin, 2001), and George Orwell, *Orwell's England: The Road to Wigan Pier in the Context of Essays, Reviews, Letters and Poems Selected from the Complete Works of George Orwell*, ed. Peter Davison (Harmondsworth: Penguin, 2001).

My typology of three divergent theological forms of 'Wigan Pierism' in this chapter is intentionally provocative and to some extent stereo-typical. However, I see the first, neoconservative, type (whether Catholic or Protestant) as well represented in the standard offerings of quality journals such as *First Things, Pro Ecclesia, Communio,* and *Nova et Vetera;* and in recent compendium volumes such as Colin Gunton and Christoph Schwöbel, eds., *Persons Divine and Human: King's College Essays in*

Theological Anthropology (Edinburgh: T&T Clark, 1991); Paul J. Griffiths and Reinhard Hütter, eds., *Reason and the Reasons of Faith* (New York: Continuum, 2005); and Thomas-Joseph White, ed., *The Analogy of Being: Invention of the Anti-Christ or Wisdom of God* (Grand Rapids, MI: Eerdmans, 2010). The second type of 'Wigan Pierism' is somewhat connected but comes with the particular commitments of 'Radical Orthodoxy' – its specific riposte to the 'false modesty' of liberal Christianity and its call to 'overcome' secular philosophy with theology: see John Milbank, *Theology and Social Theory: Beyond Secular Reason* (orig. 1990; 2nd edn; Oxford: Blackwell, 2006); and two special issues of journals devoted to the initial assessment of Milbank's movement: *New Blackfriars* 73/861 (1992), and *Modern Theology* 8/4 (1992). John Milbank, Catherine Pickstock, and Graham Ward, eds., *Radical Orthodoxy: A New Theology* (London: Routledge, 1999) filled out Milbank's original call to purge theology of its implicit sociological reductionism into a much broader theological agenda: see Simon Oliver and John Milbank, eds., *The Radical Orthodoxy Reader* (London: Routledge, 2009) for an excellently clear account of the ongoing movement; and Laurence P. Hemming, ed., *Radical Orthodoxy? A Catholic Enquiry* (Aldershot: Ashgate, 2000), and Wayne J. Hankey and Douglas Hedley, eds., *Deconstructing Radical Orthodoxy: Postmodern Theology, Rhetoric and Truth* (Aldershot: Ashgate, 2005) for more nuanced and critical assessments. My third type of 'Wigan Pierism' is entirely different from the first two, and has its roots in classic modern feminist theology. For a sympathetic but critical introduction to feminist theology of the 1970s and 1980s, see again Sarah Coakley, 'Feminist Theology', in James C. Livingstone and Francis Schüssler Fiorenza, eds., *Modern Christian Thought* (2nd edn; Minneapolis: Fortress Press, 2006), 417–42. Emilie Townes, *Womanist Justice, Womanist Hope* (Atlanta, GA: Scholars Press, 1993), and Emilie Townes, *In a Blaze of Glory: Womanist Spirituality as Social Witness* (Nashville, KY: Abingdon Press, 1995) supply insight into 'womanism' as it developed into a distinctive theological witness; and Katie G. Cannon, Beverly W. Harrison, Carter Heyward, Ada Maria Isasi-Diaz, Bess B. Johnson, Mary D. Pellauer, and Nancy D. Richardson (the Mudflower collective), *God's Fierce Whimsy: Christian Feminism and Theological Education* (New York: Pilgrim Press, 1995) develop arguments for a distinctive pedagogy suitable for inculcating feminist and womanist goals.

THEOLOGICAL 'BOUNDARIES': KANTIAN NESCIENCE
OR DARK PURGATION?

What is underlyingly at stake in this section of my argument is a thorny exegetical problem at the heart of Kant's First Critique (see Immanuel Kant, *Critique of Pure Reason*, trans. Paul Guyer and Allen W. Wood (Cambridge University Press, 1998): is the crucial distinction that Kant sets up here between 'appearances' and 'things in themselves' the creation of two ontological worlds (one of which by definition we cannot know), or merely two ways of looking at the same world? For the latter, intriguing, interpretation of Kant's 'transcendenal idealism', see Henry Allison, *Kant's Transcendental Idealism* (2nd edn; New Haven: Yale University Press, 2004); for the former, see Rae Langton, *Kantian Humility: Our Ignorance of Things in Themselves* (Oxford University Press, 1998). Much hangs on this interpretative issue for the continuing possibility of any theological metaphysics post-Kant; does Kant altogether *rule out* the possibility of any metaphysical speculation about the 'noumenal' realm, as being beyond the 'limits' of human knowledge? Or is he himself inexorably still lured in that direction, despite protestations to the contrary? The suggestion I raise briefly in the body of this chapter is that the kind of 'self-censoring' Kant enjoins on us at the end of the First Critique *appears* to amount to pure *nescience* beyond the epistemological 'limits' he describes; but it may actually have a more subtle, disciplined spiritual dimension to it – a sensibility about what we would now call the divine 'apophatic'. However, what is seemingly lost altogether in Kant's modern notion of epistemic darkness is the Dionysian mystical idea of 'dazzling darkness': if Kant's epistemological project simply reminds us of our limitations, a mystical theologian such as John of the Cross can claim that Dionysian darkness can cleanse and purge us from idolatry while also preparing us for divine union: see John of the Cross, *The Collected Works of St John of the Cross* (Washington, DC: Institute of Carmelite Studies, 1991).

POSTMODERNISM AND FEMINISMS: POSTMODERNISM
AND THE POLITICS OF RIGHTS

Readers unfamiliar with the ongoing debates between classic modern forms of feminism (devoted to women's 'rights' and 'equality' in the workplace) and the rather different interests of postmodern gender theory may (beyond the material already covered in Chapter 1 above) find the following illuminating: Joan W. Scott, 'Deconstructing Equality-Versus-Difference: Or, the Uses of Poststructuralist Theory for Feminism', *Feminist Studies* 14 (1988), 33–50; Rosemarie Tong, *Feminist Thought: A More Comprehensive Introduction* (3rd edn; Boulder, CO: Westview Press, 2009); Susan James and Gisela Bock, eds., *Beyond Equality and Difference: Citizenship, Feminist Politics, and Female Subjectivity* (London: Routledge, 1992); Linda J. Nicholson, ed., *Feminism/ Postmodernism* (New York: Routledge, 1990); Margaret Ferguson and Jennifer Wicke, eds., *Feminism and Postmodernism* (Durham, NC: Duke University Press, 1994); Seyla Benhabib, Judith Butler, Drucilla Cornell, and Nancy Fraser, *Feminist Contentions: A Philosophical Exchange* (New York: Routledge, 1995). Martha C. Nussbaum has crossed swords notoriously with Judith Butler (see Chapter 1) on Butler's form of postmodern gender subversion (see Martha C. Nussbaum, 'The Professor of Parody', *New Republic*, 22 February 1999, 37–45), arguing strenuously that the classic modern goals of feminism have still to reach the Third World: see Martha C. Nussbaum, *Women and Human Development: The Capabilities Approach* (Cambridge University Press, 2000). In this she is much influenced by Amartya Sen, *The Idea of Justice* (London: Allen Lane, 2009).

Outside the sphere of feminism specifically, contemporary political theory is equally split about whether the modern, 'liberal', Enlightenment project is still philosophically tenable, and if so what it can do to accommodate a world of plural religious commitments (and none): for an astute analysis of this dilemma, see Richard J. Bernstein, *The New Constellation: The Ethical–Political Horizons of Modernity/Postmodernity* (Cambridge: Polity, 1991). John Rawls, *A Theory of Justice* (Cambridge, MA: Belknap Press, 1971) remains prominently influential in some arenas of public life in North America, and his broadly Kantian tradition has been extended at Harvard by others (see, e.g., Michael J. Sandel, *Liberalism and the Limits of Justice* (Cambridge University Press, 1982); Michael J. Sandel, *Justice: What's the Right Thing to Do?* (London: Allen Lane, 2009); Thomas Scanlon, *What We Owe to Each Other* (Cambridge, MA: Belknap Press, 1998)), and also sympathetically critiqued by others who wish to do better justice to the issues of justice and religious adherence: see Paul J. Weithman, *Religion and the Obligations of Citizenship* (Cambridge University Press, 2002); Ronald F. Thiemann, *Religion in Public Life: A Dilemma for Democracy* (Washington, DC: Georgetown University Press,

1996); Michael Walzer, *Politics and Passion: Towards a More Egalitarian Liberalism* (New Haven, CT: Yale University Press, 2004); Francis Schüssler Fiorenza, *Rights at Risk: Confronting the Cultural, Ethical and Religious Challenges* (London: Continuum, 2007).

However, in the same time span there has also been a powerful and influential critique of secular 'rights' language by theologians influenced by Barth or Thomas Aquinas (or both) and sceptical about the capacity of 'liberal' approaches to accommodate divine authority or the building of moral character: see Alasdair MacIntyre, *After Virtue: A Study in Moral Theory* (2nd edn; London: Duckworth, 1994), and Kelvin Knight, ed., *The MacIntyre Reader* (Cambridge: Polity, 1998); and Stanley Hauerwas, *A Community of Character: Toward a Constructive Christian Ethic* (University of Notre Dame Press, 1981); *The Peaceable Kingdom: A Primer in Christian Ethics* (University of Notre Dame Press, 1983); *Resident Aliens: Life in the Christian Colony: A Provocative Christian Assessment of Culture and Ministry for People Who Know that Something is Wrong* (Nashville, KY: Abingdon Press, 1989); *After Christendom: How the Church is to Behave if Freedom, Justice and a Christian Nation are Bad Ideas* (Nashville, KY: Abingdon Press, 1991). Luke Bretherton's *Christianity and Contemporary Politics: The Conditions and Possibilities of Faithful Witness* (Oxford: Wiley–Blackwell, 2010) provides a clear introduction to these debates and presses beyond them to suggest modes of Christian political activism even within a religiously plural and 'secular' society.

POWERS AND SUBMISSIONS: FEMINIST FREEDOMS AND THE DANGER OF NEW IDOLATRIES

In my own theological account (*Powers and Submissions: Philosophy, Spirituality and Gender* (Oxford: Blackwell, 2002)) of how authentic feminist freedom must be undergirded by divine grace and power rather than set in competitive opposition to it, I confront a perennial point of division in feminist writing. Two other monographs which, however, follow a similar trajectory in the feminist study of religion, tracing the distinctive power of submission to the divine, are: R. Marie Griffith, *God's Daughters: Evangelical Women and the Power of Submission* (Berkeley: University of California Press, 1997), and Saba Mahmood, *Politics of Piety: The Islamic Revival and the Feminist Subject* (Princeton University Press, 2005). My suggestion that even 'liberal' feminist theology can be subject to the spiritual dangers of idolatry is inspired not only by the work of John of the Cross (*Collected Works*, esp. 336–7), but also by other classic biblical and theological reflections on the seductions of idols: see especially the intriguing study by Moshe Halbertal and Avishai Margalit, *Idolatry* (Cambridge, MA: Harvard University Press, 1992); and two of the most significant treatments of visual idolatry: the *Acta* of Nicaea II (787), in Norman Tanner, ed., *Decrees of the Ecumenical Councils* (London: Sheed & Ward, 1990), vol. I, 131–59; and John Calvin, *Institutes of the Christian Religion*, trans. Ford Lewis Battles (Louisville, KY: Westminster John Knox Press, 1960), book I, chs. 11–12.

CHAPTER 3

Praying the Trinity: a neglected patristic tradition

In this chapter I shall be asking at one level the most fundamental question about the doctrine of the Trinity possible: why was this doctrine needed at all, and why was God theorized as 'triune' in the first place? At another level I shall be probing some connected issues which traditional textbook accounts are more coy about exploring. I shall be asking how questions of spiritual power, desire, and gender were from the outset entangled in this nexus of doctrinal decision. But, as the Prelude has shown, this entanglement will not be read simplistically, as if the emergence of trinitarian 'orthodoxy' was by definition nothing but a repressive powerplay, and 'heresy' the neglected theological Cinderella intrinsically worthy of new contemporary adulation. The spiritual and theological discernment required here is more complicated than such a stark opposition would suggest.

By the end of the chapter, however, a bold and paradoxical conclusion will emerge from the conjoining of my two levels of analysis. This conclusion is worth stating anticipatorily at the outset, lest the complexity of the biblical and historical materials to be covered obscures the undergirding thesis.

I shall be arguing that the conciliar negotiation of trinitarian orthodoxy in the fourth century, by which the Christian God came normatively to be spoken of as three 'persons' in one 'substance', actually brought with it a profound theological and spiritual danger, even given its extraordinary theological achievement. For it came with the potential, at least, to an ironic *unorthodoxy* – in the form of the temptation to re-relegate the Spirit to an effective remaining subordination, even despite the rhetoric of full equality with the other two persons. Covert issues of spiritual power and gender were deeply involved in this temptation, as I shall show. The overzealous achievement of orthodoxy, especially when politically enforced, could simultaneously undo itself. It follows, then, that the issues which I claim have often remained buried in this nexus of decision now need new excavation.

But how could this temptation to resubordinate the Spirit come about in the first place? Such a tendency arose partly and originally, I shall argue, from an intrinsic ambiguity in the biblical resources for the later, developed, trinitarian thinking. For the 'ordering' of the language of Father, Son, and Spirit is varied in the biblical witness; and when the picture evoked by John's gospel, especially, comes to dominate,[1] the Spirit almost inevitably becomes – in effect – the secondary communicator of an already privileged dyad of Father and Son. That the Council of Nicaea (325 CE) devoted its attention to the 'substantial' (*homoousian*) equality of the Son with the Father – before any official creedal clarifications were made about the Spirit – merely intensified this tendency, and witnessed to a certain privileged scriptural status that the Prologue to the Gospel

---

[1] The notion of 'ordering' here is of course ambiguous: one might be pointing to the 'order' of human experiences of God, or the 'order' within the divine ontology. Since the Bible itself is not yet 'trinitarian' in the later sense of developed Christian 'orthodoxy', these two levels of reflection remain fluid and interchangeable. But in John's gospel there is no doubt that from the outset it is the Father–Son dyad that dominates. The representation of Christ as God's eternal 'Word' in the Prologue (John 1. 1–18), and as in unique and unbroken relationship to the Father throughout his earthly life, contrasts with the announcement made by Jesus much later in the gospel, in his Farewell Discourses, of the Spirit coming to *replace* him and to remind the disciples of his teaching, after he has 'gone away' (John 14. 15–17, 26; 15. 26–7; 16. 7–15). The Spirit's role here is to 'glorify' the Son by (secondarily) passing on his teaching and 'declaring' it to the disciples (John 16. 14).

of John, with its celebrated Logos christology, had arrived at even before Nicaea.

However, this primary scriptural factor, significant as it was, was not the only reason for the effective subordinationist tendency in relation to the Spirit, as I shall be arguing here at some length. Rather, an 'alternative' vision of a Spirit-*leading* approach to the trinitarian life of God (such as is found in nascent form in Paul's theology and in some parts of Luke)[2] was to run the gauntlet of centralized ecclesiastical opposition in the early Christian centuries, on at least two scores. First, it could lead to 'sectarian' or purist tendencies on the part of those seeking a life of special abandonment to the Spirit, and such prophetic tendencies the centralizing church at Rome increasingly frowned upon from the second century onwards. Secondly, a special commitment to deep prayer in the Spirit (whether 'charismatic' or 'contemplative') came with the concomitant danger of the intensification of erotic power and a problematic entanglement of human spiritual and sexual desires. Paul had of course already confronted this second difficulty in the Corinthian church;[3] but the issue did not go away. There was continuing concern about forms of prayer which ostensibly released the pray-er from rational means of control. Both these latter factors

---

[2] See especially Rom. 8. 9–30, already alluded to in Chapter 1, and discussed in detail below; and the logic of the annunciation story in Luke (Luke 1. 26–38), in which, in the realm of historical narrative, the Spirit is the initiatory *means* of Christ's conception. In dubbing this approach 'Spirit-leading', I am again speaking at the level of the 'economy' of salvation; I shall return in Chapter 7 to the implications for 'processions' in the Godhead itself.

[3] See especially 1 Cor. 11. 2–16. Significantly, the earliest patristic treatises 'On prayer' (Tertullian's and Origen's texts *De oratione* are the main cases in point), while primarily devoted to an exposition of the Lord's Prayer, continually return to this problematic Pauline passage and its attendant issues of gender, power, and sexual attractiveness: see Origen, *De oratione*, 2.2; Tertullian, *De oratione*, 20–2; and the whole of Tertullian's connected treatise *De virginibus velandis* (*On the veiling of virgins*). The early church definitely found it necessary to discourse on issues of sexual attraction when it reflected on the nature of prayer.

(the sectarian tendency, and the question of sexual order) also had important implications for the status of women in the church. Were women of spiritual gifts to be accorded roles of leadership alongside men, or could this only be allowed, in an era of increasing ecclesiastical institutionalization, if in some way their sexual attractiveness to men was neutralized?

What seems, then, like an initially rather arbitrary choice of alternative biblical patterns for thinking about the Trinity turns out to come with extraordinarily weighty political and gendered ballast for church life, even within the vital early patristic period in which normative patterns for trinitarian expression were still unfixed. But such complicating ballast merely took on new forms after Nicaea, with the accompanying Constantinian settlement which made Christianity the established religion of the empire, and the vicissitudes of the later Arian controversy which finally gave way to the new trinitarian orthodoxy. That this period also marked the rise of the monastic movement allowed the potentially élitist 'Spirit-leading' approach to the Trinity to take on a new form, and in time to cause its own difficulty in ranging a form of monastic, spiritual power over against hierarchical, episcopal power – the latter now of course institutionally sustained by the empire.

Needless to say, this complicated story of the entanglement of political, sexual, and spiritual forces is not the one usually told in textbook accounts of the development of the doctrine of God as Trinity. But nor is it reducible, on the other hand, to the rather tired (Weberian) sociological account of the supposed perennial tension between 'institution' and 'charisma'. It is distinctive to a *théologie totale*, however, with its interest in doctrinal 'earthing', and its non-reductive appreciation of the sociological dimensions of Christian teaching, to excavate these points of connection afresh.

But further, there is more than merely historical significance encoded in this approach to the Trinity, as will become apparent. For there are also continuing, contemporary reasons why the 'alternative', Spirit-leading approach to the Trinity has systematic importance. In an age of scepticism about the intrinsic authority of any creedal formulae, a primary stress on the Spirit – as I shall attempt to demonstrate – is able to answer the basic 'Why three?' question much more effectively than other approaches. For this first attention to the Spirit links trinitarian thought directly to its true matrix in prayer and worship, and so defuses the misleading expectation that the problem of the Trinity can be 'solved' by mere cognitive ratiocination. And further, such a primary stress on the Spirit can also reveal, and then seek to address, why the question of God as Trinity has always been implicitly linked to disturbing questions about desire, power, and gender. These issues, as is clear, are as pressing today, if not more so, as they were in the patristic era. By the end of this chapter it will be possible to see why those constituencies of the church which did stress this problematic nexus, and were actively engaged in prayer of a deep sort (whether contemplative or charismatic), were regularly pressed to the edges of the emerging 'church' type of Christianity (that is, Christianity in its institutionalized and eventually 'established' form). That leaves us with a conundrum: if the most fruitful *spiritual* contexts for a vibrant trinitarianism tend to be marginalized institutionally, how can the churches today regenerate themselves doctrinally, and especially in relation to the deeply connected issues of prayer and desire? Here I must insist once more that my approach does not make foreclosing presumptions about 'orthodoxy' and 'heresy' either in the traditional sense of straightforward doctrinal truth versus error, or in the reverse mode of some recent reactions for the sake of retrieving and valorizing 'gnostic' and other repressed traditions of the early centuries. Nor is my position one of anti-'heretical' or pro-'heretical' traditions *as such*, but rather one of probing the spiritual, social, and gendered accompaniments to notable theological variations in the doctrine of God in the early patristic period.

In short, the paradox this chapter seeks to demonstrate can now be more precisely re-expressed as follows. One sort of trinitarian 'orthodoxy' (in the sense I outlined at the end of the last chapter: orthodoxy as transformative spiritual *process*) constantly risks the charge against it of 'unorthodoxy', and thus often exists on the edges of the settled, institutionalized, 'church' type; for it has seen, through deepened practices of prayer, that doctrinal rectitude does not live on a flat or uncomplicated plane, any more than an accompanying erotic maturation does. In contrast, another sort of 'orthodoxy', which is primarily concerned to protect and sustain ecclesiastical and political order, and which associates doctrinal rectitude with creedal assent as well as churchly obedience, runs the risk of an effective subordination or taming of the Spirit, even as the creed it proclaims explicitly denies this.

Such is the broad outline of the argument I shall now unfold in detail.

THE MODERN SCEPTICAL CHALLENGE TO THE RATIONALITY OF THE HISTORICAL DEVELOPMENT OF THE TRINITY

Let me first grasp the modern, anti-trinitarian nettle. Perhaps the most celebrated critique of the Trinity in the modern period comes from Friedrich Schleiermacher, who famously averred at the end of his own systematic theology (the *Glaubenslehre* of 1821) that the Trinity was not 'direct to consciousness', that is, that it could not in any obvious sense be verified experientially. The doctrine was thus subject to the criticism that it had unnecessarily multiplied hypotheses: perhaps the Son and Spirit did not need to be regarded as ontologically distinguishable 'persons' (*hypostases*) alongside the 'Father' after all. Schleiermacher's discussion of the Trinity is often misunderstood; in fact he did not intend to 'relegate it to an appendix' as is so often charged, but rather to place it, in a less obviously ontologized form, as the final 'coping stone' (*Schlussstein* is his own chosen word) at the end of his systematic project, holding it all together. He remained, however, sceptical about the particular way that the patristic period had come to insist on the 'hypostatic' distinction of the 'persons', regarding this as logically question-begging and unscriptural. This charge, as Schleiermacher was well aware, had been anticipated long before him by the persecuted Socinians of the seventeenth and eighteenth centuries.

In the later twentieth century, the Socinian and Schleiermacherian critique was taken up again with fresh verve in the English-speaking world by the liberal Anglican theologian Maurice Wiles.[4] It is Wiles's deconstructive account that I choose to focus on in this chapter, because it represents possibly the most fearless and sustained attack on the rationality of the development of the 'orthodox' doctrine of the Trinity in the contemporary period. It also builds more or less consciously on the Socinian and Schleiermacherian critiques while imparting to them a more detailed historical analysis. By facing Wiles's attack explicitly, I shall not only have to unearth some revealing but questionable methodological presumptions with which

---

[4] Geoffrey Lampe's *God as Spirit* (Oxford: Clarendon Press, 1977) was a parallel critique, with a similar aim to question the necessity of 'hypostasizing' the Spirit in the first place: God simply *is* Spirit on Lampe's analysis. I focus on Wiles here, however, because I think that his argument, if successful, is more devastating for the whole project of trinitarian thinking, and explicitly extends both Arian and Socinian traditions.

he himself operates, but also indicate, more crucially, the vital textual evidences about the *Spirit* in the earliest church which I believe have been ignored in his – and indeed many others' – analyses.

In his justly famous article of 1957, 'Some Reflections on the Origins of the Doctrine of the Trinity',[5] Wiles set out to foil attempts to give a rational defence to the doctrine of the Trinity based on liturgical evidences or personal experience. His conclusion was that once the triadic baptismal formula for Christian baptism became fixed, quite early in the church's life (as witnessed by its appearance on Jesus's lips at the end of Matthew's gospel: Matthew 28. 19), it exercised a strongly authoritative – but ultimately 'arbitrary' – clamp on more properly critical reflection. Attempts in the modern period, then, to provide *ex post facto* justifications for the doctrine of the Trinity out of the church's early 'experience' were in Wiles's view fatally flawed: we find in the ante-Nicene fathers, he showed, neither any consistent allocation of different *activities* to the three persons, nor (the epistemological correlate of this) any distinctive set of human *experiences* associated with each of the three. And indeed – for here Wiles produced his theological *coup de grâce* – to look for such would, from the perspective of the achieved fourth-century orthodoxy taught by the Cappadocian fathers, be intrinsically suspect in any case. As had been arduously argued by those late fourth-century expositors of the new trinitarianism, to insist that the three 'persons' were 'of one substance' with each other was to rule out having any distinctive 'experiences' of any one of them *alone*: this would merely 'divide the persons'. That same *homoousian* principle would also debar the possibility that one could prove the number of the 'persons' on the basis of counting

[5] Maurice F. Wiles, 'Some Reflections on the Origins of the Doctrine of the Trinity', *Journal of Theological Studies* 8 (1957), 92–106; reprinted in his *Working Papers in Doctrine* (London: SCM Press, 1976), 1–17.

up their different sorts of activities, since it was now agreed that only 'internal relations' could distinguish the divine hypostases, if tritheism was to be avoided; and in their experiential effects, equally, all three 'persons' should be found to work together cooperatively. To have an 'experience' of any one of the 'persons' was, by definition, also to experience the other two simultaneously.

The logic of Wiles's argument revealed the inherently circular nature of this problem, as was more starkly spelled out in his slightly later book, *The Making of Christian Doctrine*.[6] Looking back, Wiles argues here, we see in the third century, in reaction to the heresy called 'Sabellianism',[7] an emphasis first on the *distinctness* of Father and Son (and it seems that, on Wiles's view, the distinctness of the Spirit was here merely unthinkingly duplicated alongside the Son's); whereas in contrast, in the fourth century, and in reaction to Arianism,[8] the *unity* of Father and Son became the obsessive concern of the orthodox. Developed trinitarianism thus unfolded in two distinct, but problematically related, phases, which Wiles seeks now to expose: 'there is a danger', he writes, 'that the arguments used in the second stage of the inquiry may be logically incompatible with those in the first, and that that inconsistency may remain wholly undetected'.[9]

This point does not only score, according to Wiles, against the divinity of the Son; indeed, as my discussion will seek to highlight

---

[6] Maurice F. Wiles, *The Making of Christian Doctrine: A Study in the Early Development of Christian Doctrine* (Cambridge University Press, 1967), esp. ch. 6.

[7] This was the heresy that represented the Son and Spirit as merely aspects or 'modes' of the Father's operations. As Tertullian charged in response to one such 'modalist', however, this led to an intolerable logical difficulty: if the Son was not 'personally' distinguished from the Father, then the Father too would be crucified on the Cross, along with his Son: see Tertullian's *Adversus Praxean*, 10.

[8] Arius and his followers in various ways subordinated the Son to the Father: according to Arius, the Son was divine but only 'so to speak', in a secondary sense.

[9] Wiles, *Making of Christian Doctrine*, 124.

further, it is the question of the 'hypostatic' status of the *Spirit* which is structurally more pressing for the maintenance of a credible trinitarianism in a sceptical milieu. According to Wiles, this question of the Spirit's personal distinctness (as opposed to the Spirit's divinity) was never adequately or rationally faced at all in the early centuries. Binitarianism would have been more logical, he thinks (accounting for divine transcendence on the one hand, and immanence or incarnation on the other); or, if one wanted to 'hypostatize' other divine attributes, why stop at the 'Spirit' of God, he asks? Wiles's argument about the mesmeric hold of the triadic baptismal formula is here undergirded by a more general thesis about the operation of what is often called the 'law of prayer' (the *lex orandi*) on the development of early doctrine. Wiles sees the effect of this *lex orandi* as primarily 'conservative' and soporific, a sort of dogmatic slumbering of the patristic period, inviting both gnostic-tending traits in christology and a profound lack of critical thinking in pneumatology – a failure to grasp that the Spirit's 'hypostatic' existence was demanded neither by experience nor reason.[10] In other words, the church was duped all along by its own authority and tradition. From the perspective of a post-Enlightenment 'autonomy', with its intrinsic suspicion of religious authoritarianism, however, these fatal illogicalities emerge: the dismantling of trinitarianism can thus begin.

There was something deeply refreshing about the critical clarity of Wiles's approach when it was first published. It provided a release from the characteristically dogmatic tilt of most of the older textbooks, the judging of the moves of the earlier centuries as either false starts or unclarified approximations to later orthodoxy, as if the entire process was obvious from the outset. And indeed, surely

---

[10] See ibid., ch. 4.

much of Wiles's critique still remains apposite: the conservative tug of liturgical tradition, the force of clerical authority, and the impact of Scripture *as an assumed unity* all shielded doctrinal debate from certain critical questions which are taken for granted in the modern period; this enabled, for instance, that strange swing between the third and fourth centuries which Wiles so perceptively highlights. But there are central elements in Wiles's thesis with which I must now take issue; and they focus on the question which he himself shows is critical for the maintenance of any trinitarianism. That is: 'But why *three*?' Why indeed 'hypostatize' the Spirit at all? This is where I must press back to the New Testament, to an analysis of a view of the Trinity which Wiles does not even consider, but which might, I suggest, provide the beginnings of an answer to his critical questioning.

We shall have to take care, however, not to succumb ourselves in the process to a question-begging philosophical presumption that animates Wiles's whole endeavour, as may already have become apparent. For him, the 'evidences' and 'experiences' gleaned from the Bible and early patristic writings are required to provide *demonstrative* force in favour of a threefold God, if he is to allow himself to accept the authoritative conciliar view of the Trinity. As he himself puts it unembarrassedly, the activity of God witnessed to there must be so 'unquestionably threefold' as to '*force*' one to postulate a trinitarian nature.[11] But as will already have become clear from my treatment of the problems of philosophical 'foundationalism' in the Prelude above, this kind of demand represents a sort of modernist hunting of the snark that few would now engage in; a more subtle understanding of the relation between prayer, liturgy, scriptural reflection, and rational engagement is required if our sceptical

[11] Wiles, 'Some Reflections', in *Working Papers*, 3, my emphasis.

questioning is to find a satisfactory answer. That is not to say, however, that there need be any return to mere authoritarian creedal bludgeoning, as Wiles evidently fears.

STARTING WITH THE HOLY SPIRIT: A PRAYER-BASED MODEL OF THE TRINITY

The model of the Trinity which Wiles completely misses in his analysis might be termed 'incorporative', or 'reflexive', for in it the Holy Spirit is perceived as the primary means of incorporation into the trinitarian life of God, and as constantly and 'reflexively' at work in believers in the circle of response to the Father's call. This is to be contrasted with what might be called the 'linear' revelatory model, in which primary focus is given to the Father–Son relationship, and the Holy Spirit becomes the secondary purveyor of that relationship to the church.[12] As already noted, the latter model is represented with great power in John's gospel, and given further validation by being stretched out along the narrative of the church year in the book of Acts.[13] In the incorporative model, in contrast, the Holy Spirit is construed not simply as extending the revelation of Christ, nor even merely as enabling Christ's recognition, but as actually catching up the created realm into the life of God (making

---

[12] As already stressed above, these two models remain at this point in discussion at the level of the 'economy': speculation about what this apparent choice means for God-in-Godself will be reserved for Chapter 7 below. And as I shall shortly acknowledge, the distinction between the two models is not necessarily absolute: the two *can* be conjoined in practice (because the 'linear' model is not lacking in its own perception of 'incorporation'); and it might even be argued the two models in a sense presume each other, given their close contiguity and entanglement within the texts of the New Testament. The problem however, is that when all the focus is on the 'linear' type, the subtlety of what the Spirit does as primary instigator of transformative participation in the God is often completely lost.

[13] Here Christ first ascends to heaven (Acts 1. 1–11), and then the Spirit comes at Pentecost (Acts 2. 1–41).

it 'conformed to the likeness of his Son', to use Paul's memorable phrase in Romans 8. 29).

Thus, whereas a linear-inspired model draws implicitly on Acts' distinction between Ascension and Pentecost, and also on John's prediction of the 'other comforter' *replacing* Christ (John 14. 16), this 'incorporative' one owes its first allegiance to Paul, and supremely to Romans 8, with its description of the cooperative action of the praying Christian with the energizing promptings of the Holy Spirit. On this view, what the 'Trinity' *is* is the graced ways of God with creation, alluring and conforming that creation into the life of the 'Son'. ('When we cry "Abba, Father", it is the Spirit bearing witness with our spirit that we are children of God' (Romans 8. 15–16).) But note that the priority here, logically and experientially speaking, is given to the *Spirit*: the 'Spirit' is that which, while being nothing less than 'God', cannot quite be reduced to a metaphorical naming of the Father's outreach. It is not that the pray-er is having a conversation with some distant and undifferentiated deity, and then is being asked (rather arbitrarily) to 'hypostatize' that conversation (or 'relationship') into a 'person' (the Spirit); but rather, that there is something, admittedly obscure, about the sustained activity of prayer that makes one want to claim that it is personally and divinely activated from within, and yet that that activation (the 'Spirit') is not quite *reducible* to that from which it flows (the 'Father').

To say this is admittedly already to build on Paul, to go somewhat beyond him into explicitly trinitarian language; and we cannot therefore say that his position leads inexorably towards an 'orthodox' trinitarianism: that would be misleading and anachronistic. And yet there are seminal insights here. For instance, it is the perception of many Christians who pray either contemplatively or charismatically (in both cases there is a willed suspension of one's own agenda, a deliberate waiting on the divine) that the dialogue of prayer is strictly speaking not a simple communication between an individual and a divine monad, but rather a movement of divine reflexivity, a sort of answering of God to God in and through the one who prays (see again Romans 8. 26–7). Here, if I am right, is the only valid *experientially based* pressure towards hypostatizing the Spirit (if that, with Wiles, is what one is looking for). Yet even to call it this – to call it a human (let alone a 'religious') 'experi-ence' – is to risk a serious misunderstanding; for the whole point is that it is a delicate ceding to something precisely not done by oneself. It is the sense (admittedly obscure) of an irreducibly dy-polar divine *activity* – a call and response of divine desire – into which the pray-er is drawn and incorporated.[14]

The 'Son', we note further, is on this model released from what we may call a narrow 'extrinsicism'. The term 'Son' connotes not just the past earthly Jesus, nor even yet the risen person of 'Christ' (if that is individualistically conceived), but rather the divine life of Christ to which the whole creation, animate and inanimate, is tending, and into which it is being progressively transformed (Romans 8. 19–25). Moreover, one must underscore once more that any 'experience' claimed of the Spirit here (and 'experience', note, is not Paul's word) is not that of some different quality, or emotional tonality, from the (simultaneously experienced) 'Father' and 'Son'. It is not that different *sorts* of discrete 'experience' attend the three entities. (Perhaps, indeed, this is why Paul notoriously slides between 'God', 'Christ', and 'Spirit' in straining to express the

---

[14] It important to stress that the Spirit 'comes to our aid' according to Paul in Romans 8 through our own longing: this is not a violent assault or unwanted imposition (as charged by the radical feminist Mary Daly, commenting on the cognate passage Gal. 4. 4, thus: 'we do not wish to be redeemed by a god, to be adopted as sons, or to have the spirit of a god's son artificially injected into our hearts, crying "father"' – Mary Daly, *Pure Lust* (Boston, MA: Beacon, 1984), 9).

almost inexpressible in Romans 8. 9–11.) Rather, the pray-er's total perception of *God* is here found to be ineluctably trifaceted. The 'Father' is both 'source' and ultimate object of divine desire; the 'Spirit' is that (irreducibly distinct) enabler and incorporator of that desire in creation – that which *makes* the creation divine; the 'Son' *is* that divine and perfected creation.[15]

It is worth mentioning, too, that there are other remarkable features of Paul's accounts of prayer in Romans 8 which have special relevance for the themes in this chapter, and which will in due course be taken up further. First, as I have just noted, the life of 'Sonship' on Paul's rendition here is not only not restricted to Jesus's human (male) life, but nor even to the mystical 'body of Christ' which is the church; it is in this passage expanded even further to include the full cosmological implications of the incarnation, the whole creation 'groaning' to its final christological telos in God (Romans 8. 18–21). What this underscores is the extraordinary ripple effect of prayer in the Spirit – its inexorably social and even cosmic significance as an act of cooperation with, and incorporation into, the still extending life of the incarnation. It gives the lie, by implication, to any falsely 'privatized' or 'subjectivized' associations of prayer with mere self-cultivation which may have accrued in the modern period. And if prayer has social and cosmic significance, note, it certainly also has political import (see Romans 12. 14; 13. 1–7). Secondly, the use of the 'birth-pangs' metaphor by Paul for this whole unfolding event of cosmic gestation 'genders' the picture of prayer in a striking way, figuring the entire Christic event as the groanings of a woman in labour (Romans 8. 22–3); it possibly also explains why Paul flip-flops between 'children of God (*tekna*)' and

---

[15] At the end of this book I shall come back to discuss the distinctly unique sense in which one must talk of the 'Father' as 'source' in the Godhead, according to the argument that unfolds throughout the book: see Chapter 7.

'sonship' in his language of 'adoption' into Christ (Romans 8. 14–17). It is as if prayer in the Spirit both takes up and transforms the usual societal implications of gender, and renders them both labile and cosmic.[16] Finally, since Paul acknowledges openly that 'we do not know how to pray' (*sc.* 'what to ask for': Romans 8. 26), and so we have to yield to the Spirit's 'sighs too deep for words', it follows that prayer at its deepest is God's, not ours, and takes the pray-er beyond any normal human language or rationality of control.

All these features of Paul's vision of prayer in the Spirit were to cause ecclesiastical trouble later, as we shall see. But let us return now to Wiles's basic challenge about the number of the trinitarian 'persons'. In answering it, we shall in due course be forced back inexorably to these other issues.

THE TRINITY AND THE 'LAW OF PRAYER' IN EARLIEST CHRISTIANITY

We must now confront the most intriguing question about the early patristic period's discussion of the Trinity, and that is this: why was this prayer-based argument for the Spirit's 'hypostatic' (or distinct) existence not wielded by the early fathers, especially granted the suggestive basis for this in Romans 8? Wiles – and many other commentators – would seem to imply a silence here; but is it really so? What happened to the patristic interpretation of Romans 8? Of course, the early fathers certainly did not face the critical question of the Spirit's distinctness in precisely the sceptical fashion of the modern theologian, and it would be anachronistic to expect them to do so. Nonetheless, could it be that the textbooks' characteristic

---

[16] See again also, of course, Gal. 3. 28, much contested in its meanings but at the very least implying some sort of transcendence in Christ over normal societal understandings of gender.

forced march from Nicaea to Constantinople[17] has failed to engage the fathers at the moments when they *do* comment on such an alternative trinitarian approach, one not dominated by the 'linear' economy, but giving experiential priority to the Spirit in prayer?

There are several gaps in Wiles's argument here, despite his laudable attempt to take some account of the *lex orandi* (the 'law of prayer'). First, and most importantly, Wiles does not seek to probe back into the New Testament era, to argue why the triadic baptismal formula gained the hold it did in the first place. This is a question at least worth asking. Thereafter, according to him, the 'Second century writers show comparatively little interest in the Spirit'; these were, he says, 'dormant years' for pneumatology.[18] In what follows, I shall fundamentally question this viewpoint and suggest a rather different story. I shall argue that the earliest Christian period (up to and including the second and early third centuries) was characterized by a normative association of the 'Spirit' with charismatic gifts, and especially prophecy. To say this is to accept that the full potential of Romans 8, and the subtleties here of a *simultaneous* experience of 'Father', 'Son', and 'Spirit', was not immediately grasped. But the emphasis we find in this period on the ecstatic quality of experience of the Spirit is nonetheless in line with what I have called the 'prayer-based' approach. Far from leading to a dormant pneumatology in the second century, an idle and unthinking repetition of the baptismal formula, this emphasis was to produce at least one phenomenon, 'Montanism',[19] deemed

[17] It was at the second 'ecumenical' (worldwide) Council of Constantinople in 381 CE that the 'Niceno-Constantinopolitan' creed (now known as the Nicene Creed) was ratified, and the full divinity of the Holy Spirit officially confirmed against the so-called 'Spirit-fighters'.

[18] Wiles, *Making of Christian Doctrine*, 79, 80.

[19] 'The New Prophecy', or 'Montanism' (the latter an appellation used by those opposed to it, and in modern textbooks), was a prophetic, Spirit-centred movement which started in Phrygia in the second century and later spread westwards through the empire, being

unacceptably dangerous to ecclesiastical stability. In other words, the charismatic connotations of a doctrine of the Spirit granted this kind of priority and authority could, if not carefully checked and contained, lead to what Rome saw as sectarian 'aberration'. Hence – or so I shall speculate – we find a nervousness, subsequently, about making explicit any view of the Trinity not firmly reined back into the rationality of the Logos.

The potential of the Romans 8 approach did continue to emerge, however, albeit more commonly in tracts 'On prayer' (and later in early monastic texts on the same theme) than in strictly doctrinal treatises. The logic of public, eucharistic worship from the third century might also be said to point – if only implicitly – to the model I am adumbrating, as I shall indicate. But the fourth-century Cappadocians' account of the Trinity (although having some important features in common with the same model), seems to present for the most part a variant more affected by a 'linear' and hierarchical perception of the divine persons, despite occasional appeals by them to Romans 8 (and to the cognate Galatians 4. 6), and despite Gregory of Nyssa's profoundly contemplative and apophatic account of the approach to God. My thesis, then, is not the rather hackneyed one that the East produced an incorporative (or 'mystical') form of trinitarianism that the West never really appreciated (as some modern Orthodox writers would have us believe). For there are, as I shall show, a number of Western writers

particularly vibrant in North Africa. In its original form it was led by Montanus and by two women, Priscilla and Maximilla. While not actually heretical in any clear doctrinal sense, it was treated with suspicion by Rome, and eventually condemned there (according to Tertullian, himself a convert to Montanist teaching) by Pope Zephyrinus at the beginning of the third century. As is the case with the term 'Gnosticism' (see note 26 below), the most recent scholarship rightly tends to question homogenized accounts of this multifaceted rigorist and prophetic movement, and instead probes the sources we have about it for signs of contested authority in a period of rapid change and diversification within early Christianity. These caveats notwithstanding, I shall continue to use the shorthand 'Montanism' in what follows.

who evidence a tendency towards this type of approach, even if rather implicitly. Instead, I wish to argue that giving *priority* to the Spirit (in contemplation, prophecy, charismatic ecstasy) leads, if not to outright sectarian rejection of the Trinity, to a form of trinitarian reflection that has tended to sit somewhat uneasily within what is called the (sociological) 'church' type, that is, within 'established', hierarchical, or politically mandated forms of Christianity. We might call this kind of trinitarian thinking, perhaps (wielding admittedly contentious terminology coined by Ernst Troeltsch), a 'mystic' variant *within* the 'church' type.[20] If this is broadly right, so to line up different forms of pneumatology with different forms of social organization, we should not be surprised to find the *earliest* church – that is, during its persecuted phase – often manifesting a classically 'sectarian' pneumatology, that is, one allowing the work-ings of the Spirit not just an ecstatic effect but particular activities and 'experiences' actually distinctive to it. For 'sectarian' thinking, unlike settled 'church'-type theology, is most naturally found in conditions of marginalization and rigorist demands. Let me briefly now survey the evidence for this thesis.

What, first, lay behind the initial construction of the triadic baptismal formula (Matthew 28. 19)? Wiles does not explain this. The obvious answer is the example of Jesus's own baptism (Mark 1. 9–11 and parallels), with its conjunction of the Father's voice, the Son's baptismal calling, and the Spirit's descent. But this is perhaps not the whole story. It is worth also recalling the testimony of Acts,

---

[20] See Ernst Troeltsch, *The Social Teaching of the Christian Churches* (orig. 1913; London: Allen & Unwin, 1931) for his modification and extension of Weber's sociological 'church'–'sect' distinction to include a third 'type', the 'mystic'. While I utilize and complexify this Troeltschian typology afresh in this chapter to illuminate the various types of trinitarianism in the patristic era, this is not something that Troeltsch himself does; he only discourses on the 'mystic' type when he arrives at the early modern period. I discuss the sociological theory underlying Troeltsch's approach in more critical detail in Chapter 4 below.

which refers in its early chapters to a baptism simply 'in the name of Jesus Christ', but promises as a specific mark of that baptism the 'gift of the Holy Spirit' (Acts 2. 38). The confusing story in Acts 8 about evangelization in Samaria, which suggests some delay between baptism and reception of the Holy Spirit, probably does, as is often argued, reflect some untidiness in the earliest church which Luke is attempting to paper over: to record legitimation by the Jerusalem authorities of apparently freelance evangelism (Acts 8. 14–17) is doubtless part of Luke's theological schema of smooth ecclesiastical expansion.[21] But this is not to say that there are *no* germs of historical truth here about the origins of the baptismal formula. Speculatively, we might suggest that Acts 19. 1–6 (the story of Paul at Ephesus) contains some insight into why the more primitive baptismal formula became expanded into the triadic one. Rivalry with John's baptism (mentioned already in Acts 1. 5) may have caused the early community to draw attention to the *special* gifts of the 'Holy Spirit' (tongues and prophecy) which marked out baptism in Jesus's name as superior (Acts 19. 1–6). If, then, despite all the theological overlay, there is a germ of historical truth here in Acts, it was dramatic charismatic gifts – involving the ecstatic capacity – which were the hallmark of some of the earliest Christian baptisms. Acts associates the Spirit with manifest 'signs and wonders' (Acts 2. 43), whereas Paul's association of the Spirit with baptism is, as we have seen, more concerned with the incorporation into the effects of Christ's death and resurrection (Romans 6. 3–11; 8. 9–11). Nonetheless, we propose here, albeit speculatively, a possible reason why the 'Holy Spirit' quickly became part of the baptismal formula (Matthew 28. 19), and one based precisely

---

[21] So Ernst Käsemann argued in a famous article: 'The Disciples of John the Baptist at Ephesus', in *Essays on New Testament Themes* (London: SCM, 1964), 136–48.

in *distinctive* experiential effects, the ecstatic quality of the reception of the divine.

To say this, of course, is to meet Wiles's charge of 'arbitrariness' only part way; for an 'experience of the Spirit', however distinctive, would not necessarily lead to 'hypostasization', any more than dramatic promptings of the Spirit in the Hebrew Scriptures did. Admittedly, there were already in the Jewish background significant nudgings towards divine 'hypostasizations' of this sort; but these quasi-hypostases seem not to have been consistent in their numbers or forms. The further move required to answer Wiles, then, as we have seen, is a more conscious explication of the trifaceted logic of Romans 8; and that appears not to be immediately forthcoming in the earliest patristic evidence. There is indeed, as Wiles shows, confusion in the early years about the allocation of attributes to Son and Holy Spirit. But what is also distinctive of the early 'Apostolic' fathers is a continuing association of the Holy Spirit with ecstatic, visionary, and prophetic activity; and this fact Wiles passes over. The highly popular *Shepherd of Hermas*, for instance, is rife with these prophetic and visionary claims, and also contains an extended and profound reflection on the transformative potential of the indwelling Spirit. The *Epistle of Barnabas*, too, gives examples of prophecies 'in the Spirit' (*Barnabas*, 9); and the *Didachē* provides guidelines on how to distinguish good and bad wandering prophets according to similar presumptions (*Didachē*, 11–13). Even the more philosophical apologist Justin, who notoriously obscures the function of the Holy Spirit, and even subordinates the Spirit to the angels at one point (*First Apology*, 6.1–2), continues to term the Spirit 'prophetic'. Perhaps in retrospect, then, we may see Justin's *First Apology* (written not long before the outbreak of Montanism) as a revealing example of an implicitly trinitarian decision. Was the church to follow Justin's rationality-based theology, centred on the Word and rapprochement with

Greek philosophy, and explicitly subordinate the Spirit? Or was it to be true to the older heritage of the primacy of the Spirit's prophetic function?

'MONTANISM' AND BEYOND: THE THREAT OF SECTARIAN 'HERESY'

The sectarian climax to which this older prophetic tradition was to move is revealingly described later in Eusebius' *Ecclesiastical History* (v.17). The Montanist prophet, it was said, 'spoke in ecstasy', moving from 'voluntary ignorance' (perhaps a deliberate emptying of the mind?) to 'involuntary madness of soul'. Granting experiential priority to the Spirit in this abandoned way is seen by critical patristic commentators to have both political and sexual implications: political, because it could lead to challenging ecclesiastical authority with a higher, and still unfolding, revelation ('more than Christ'); and sexual, because (scandalously, as Hippolytus reports)[22] this ecstasy released 'wretched women' into positions of power and authority, women who claimed to find the notion of 'Christ' so expanded and transformed that they even had visions of him *as* a woman.[23] This is good evidence, then, of the unmanageable sectarian *potential* of Paul's 'incorporative' vision: the transformative view of the Spirit might expand the reference of the redeemed life of 'Sonship' even beyond what the church could predict or control. It is striking indeed that, from this early period, 'ecstasy' becomes a word with a tendency to negative evocations for

---

[22] Hippolytus, *Refutation of all Heresies*, 8.12.

[23] 'Christ came to me in the likeness of a woman, clad in a bright robe, and He planted wisdom in me and revealed that this place [*sc.* Pepuza in Phrygia] is holy, and that here Jerusalem comes down from heaven' – a saying attributed to the Montanist leader Priscilla in Epiphanius, *Panarion Omnium Haeresium*, 49.1. It is also not a coincidence, surely, that Montanism's opponents went on to malign its male leader Montanus for 'effeminate' behaviours and appearance: see Jerome, *Epistulae*, xli.4, in which Montanus is called a 'semi man'.

the emerging 'mainstream' of Christianity, in stark contrast to the much later (early sixth-century) work of the pseudo-Dionysius, with his explicit, positive, appeal to 'ecstasy' via 'mystical contemplation'. And even then Dionysius was to come under continuing suspicion for his very evident use of neo-Platonic philosophical sources to express this trope.

What happened to our 'alternative' view of the Trinity after the immediate crisis of early Montanism? Was it merely discredited, or could it in time be assimilated into a 'church'-type trinitarianism? The twin cases of the near contemporary theologians Irenaeus and Tertullian,[24] often treated side by side in textbook accounts of developing trinitarianism (as so-called 'economic' trinitarians still implicitly subordinating Son and Spirit to the Father)[25] are, I believe, illuminatingly different when examined in the light of my thesis. Although both initially appear to subscribe to what I have called the 'linear' type of trinitarian thinking, it would be a mistake to assimilate them too quickly into this one shared category. In fact, at this point my theory has to garner some new complications.

Irenaeus' rich soteriological theory of 'recapitulation' (by which Christ undoes the effects of sin by replaying the role of Adam without his downfall) is enunciated against the backcloth of deep concern not so much about Montanism but about other 'heretical' groups antagonistic to the 'flesh' and incarnation.[26] Irenaeus' theory

---

[24] Irenaeus (125–200) is writing in Lyons, Gaul, at the end of the second century, Tertullian (*c.* 160–*c.* 230) only a little later in Carthage, North Africa.

[25] The term 'economic trinitarianism' is often used by writers of textbooks to describe early (pre-Nicaean) patristic authors who have not yet developed the notion of an eternal and equal coexistence of the Father, Son and Holy Spirit, but rather concentrate on what I have called the 'linear' production of Son and Spirit for the purposes of salvation history.

[26] It is misleading to unify these different groups into one category, 'Gnosticism', since our varying independent textual evidences indicate a wide plethora of views and types of community: see Karen L. King, *What is Gnosticism?* (Cambridge, MA: Harvard University Press, 2003).

in response to these groups is however sometimes discussed in modern textbooks in isolation from his emerging trinitarianism; and this is distinctly misleading. For Irenaeus' understanding of salvation is deeply Pauline, based on the incorporation thesis of the 'first Adam' and the 'last' (see Romans 5. 15–19; 1 Corinthians 15. 22). It should not surprise us, therefore, to find Irenaeus' treatment in book 5 of his *Against Heresies* focusing on the incorporative outreach of the Spirit as that which *enables* the transformative process of 'recapitulation':

> These things, therefore, He recapitulated in Himself: by uniting man to the Spirit and causing the Spirit to dwell in man, He is Himself made the head of the Spirit, and given the Spirit to be the head of man: for through him [*sc.* the Spirit] we see, and hear, and speak. (*Adv. haer.*, 5.20.2)

It seems, then, that here we have something *akin* to our 'alternative' approach to the Trinity manifested in, and assimilated by, an emergent 'church'-type author, Irenaeus, who otherwise might be more easily characterized as 'linear' in his approach to the Trinity. Does he thus represent a 'mixed type', perhaps befitting (if our Troeltschian sociological patterning has any value) an authoritative bishop countering 'heresy', yet in an era of continuing persecution of his own church? Such an hypothesis might be supported by another feature of the text. Although Irenaeus undoubtedly signals 'incorporation' of some sort here, his argument lacks the 'reflexive' and 'ecstatic' subtlety of the Romans 8 approach: he makes no appeal to Spirit-infused *prayer* as such, and the overtones of the language of 'head' over 'Spirit' reintroduce a 'linear' or hierarchical sensibility. This suggests in turn that Irenaeus' approach is 'mixed' in more than one way: at least some of the groups Irenaeus countered allowed significant leadership roles to women, and accorded high value to women's testimony from the circle of

Jesus.[27] But the fact that Irenaeus richly draws on, and extends, the Pauline theme of 'incorporation' does not here lead to precisely the same set of associations met with elsewhere: the enablement of forms of women's leadership, for instance. We have to face the fact that what I have called an 'incorporative' approach *may* be mediated exegetically in ways which implicitly signal the consolidation of male gendered authority rather than any 'ecstatic' release from such. And this complicates our picture, as will be seen when we come to the cases of Athanasius and the Cappadocians.

The same charge of 'mixedness' might apply, but in a reverse way, to Tertullian, Irenaeus' younger contemporary in North Africa, who is often seen as simply extending and refining Irenaeus' 'economic' trinitarianism. Such an analysis is doubtless correct in some ways, but again there is another and different side to Tertullian, arising out of his own adoption of Montanism in later career, and so pointing back to the earlier tradition of associating the Spirit with particular, prophetic activities. (In his Montanist phase, Tertullian is even willing to give credence to female prophets, a considerable achievement granted

---

[27] It is well known that some early Christian groups dubbed 'heretical' by thinkers such as Irenaeus and Hippolytus also accorded roles of leadership to women: on this see, classically, Elaine Pagels, *The Gnostic Gospels* (New York: Random House, 1982). Amongst the 'gnostic' texts found in the Nag Hammadi library recovered from the sands of Egypt, there is also plenty of evidence of interest in the Holy Spirit, some of it highly speculative cosmologically and implying an *exclusive* form of 'incorporation' into the divine: see, e.g., *The Secret Revelation of John*, ed. Karen L. King (Cambridge, MA: Harvard University Press, 2005), 23.4–5: 'Those upon whom the Spirit of Life descends, having been yoked with the power, they will be saved and become perfect. And they will be worthy to be purified there from all evil and the enticements of wickedness.' In some contrast, the followers of the rigorist, anti-Judaistic teaching of Marcion in Rome (which also, interestingly, produced some women leaders), were not interested in any spiritual 'incorporation' which would involve *bodily* transformation or expression. Tertullian, who is one of our main sources for Marcion's teaching, largely ignores Romans 8 in his *Adv. Marc.*, leaving it unclear what Marcion would have made of Rom. 8. 14–30; but we can safely assume that he would not have supported Paul's concern for bodily 'groaning' in the Spirit. I am grateful to Karen King and Judith Lieu for illuminating discussion about the fate of the 'Romans 8' model in various 'gnostic' interpretations.

the concern about female seductiveness which is otherwise character-istic of his writings, including his *On Prayer*;[28] but it is significant that the woman prophetess whose insights he particularly reveres in his *De anima* is post-menopausal, and thus rendered – for him – sexually unproblematic. Much more important in her case, then, are the special *philosophical* insights granted her by the Spirit.)[29] Whereas Irenaeus has what I have dubbed a 'mixed' incorporative *Pauline* streak in his trinitarianism, Tertullian's chiding of Praxeas for 'putting the Paraclete to flight' (*Adv. Prax.*, 1.1) is, as I read him, a rather different argument that specific prophetic manifestations must be defended. This approach is more reminiscent of the book of Acts than of Paul: the Spirit is a *distinct* 'third stage' (*Adv. Prax.*, 9). Tertullian's treatise *On Baptism* is written before his Montanist conversion, but even here the careful treatment of the theology of the Holy Spirit (*De baptismo*, 6–8) is not easily dismissed – contra Wiles – as an unthinking duplication of the distinct status granted to the Son: 'Will God not be allowed', writes Tertullian, 'in the case of His own instrument [*sc.* the Holy Spirit] to strike the note of *spiritual elevation* by means of holy hands?' (*De baptismo*, 8, my emphasis).

In other words, Tertullian's pneumatology represents on my reading a throwback to the earlier tradition of granting the Spirit *specific* tasks and effects; and in his own Montanist phase he is able to defuse the charges made against earlier (behaviourally ecstatic) Montanists by careful insistence that the main admired prophetess of his acquaintance is both philosophically sophisticated in Stoic terms and – as Peter Brown has quipped – conveniently geriatric.[30]

---

[28] See again note 3 above, and especially *De virginibus velandis*, 2.

[29] See *De anima*, 9.4.

[30] Peter Brown, *The Body and Society: Men, Women, and Sexual Renunciation in Early Christianity* (London: Faber & Faber, 1988), 79: 'Tertullian's view of the ideal leadership of the Church was a Spirit-filled gerontocracy'.

For Tertullian, women *are* released into positions of authority by the Spirit, but their sexual dangers need to be carefully circumscribed and defused at the same time.

ORIGEN, CONTEMPLATIVE ÉLITISM, AND THE ROMANS 8 MODEL

If my thesis is correct – that early 'Montanists' gave the Spirit a bad name, and that this discouraged explicit or apologetic use of a trinitarianism giving experiential priority to the Spirit – then Origen, writing not long afterwards, represents a most interesting test case for the theory, although also a new manifestation of it. In Origen we confront perhaps the most significant and subtle rendition of Romans 8 in the early centuries. Unlike Tertullian, Origen's trinitarianism – though still seemingly subordinationist (this time according to a Middle Platonist model of descending levels of divinity) – avoids for the most part the allocation of special *activities* to the Spirit. However, a close reading of Origen's *On Prayer* (*De oratione*) reveals not only a clearly 'incorporative' rendition of the Trinity in the Pauline mode, but a fascinating, and newly enunciated, apprehension of the entanglement of this theme with issues of (what would now be called) sex and gender. Much hangs for my thesis on close attention to this nexus; so it is worth probing the evidences of Origen's *De oratione* rather closely.

We recall that Paul's analysis of prayer in Romans 8 notably involves: (i) a certain loss of control to the *leading* experiential force of the Spirit; (ii) an entry into a realm beyond words; and (iii) the striking use of a (female) 'birth-pangs' metaphor to describe the yearning of creation for its 'glorious liberty'. After Montanism, it was not hard to see why any or all of these features could look less than attractive to an emerging mainstream Roman 'orthodoxy', at least as a first basis for trinitarian reflection. The danger of ecstatic prophecy, when loosed from the primary control of an extrinsic Logos, was one matter; the releasing of women into positions of authority and prominence was a second one. But there was a third danger, with which it seems Origen is primarily concerned (much more than he is with Montanism); and that is the potential, in any form of prayer that deliberately gives away rational mastery to the Spirit, of possible confusion between loss of control to that Spirit and loss of *sexual* control. The issue is one already familiar in different forms, as we have seen, in Paul and Tertullian; but it is dealt with by Origen in a particularly distinctive way, crucial for our thesis of the 'entanglement' of deep prayer, trinitarian conceptuality, and issues of sex and gender. Not the least of the important developments here is Origen's newly creative marriage of biblical themes with the Platonic notion of 'eros'.

I would like to draw attention to the following four features of Origen's *De oratione* in connection with these themes.

First, the treatise starts (1) with an insistence on the priority and primacy of the Holy Spirit in understanding the nature and purpose of prayer; and it stresses the capacity of the grace of God to take us beyond the 'worthless' 'reasoning of mortals' to a sphere of unutterable mysteries (see 2 Corinthians 12), where 'spiritual prayer' occurs in the 'heart' (11.5). Already, then, there is the explicit willingness to allow that the Spirit – though from the start a 'fellow worker' with the Father and Son – escorts the pray-er to a realm beyond the normal constraints of human rationality. Second, the exegesis of Romans 8 is central to the argument from the start, and citations are reiterated more than once; it is through prayer, and being '*mingled* with the Spirit', that we become 'partakers of the Word of God' (x.2). Third, this form of prayer is repeatedly, and strikingly, compared to sexual intercourse and procreation, for example: 'Just as it is not possible to beget children without a woman and without receiving the power that serves to beget children, so no one may obtain . . . requests . . . unless he has prayed with such and such a disposition' (VIII.I). Hannah, on this view, becomes the supreme type of the pray-er who overcomes sterility through the Spirit (II.5, etc.). But, fourthly and finally, an equally careful disjunction, according to Origen, must be made between the sexual and procreative theme in its *metaphorical* force, and in its normal human physiological functioning. Thus Tatiana, the woman to whom (along with Ambrose) this work is addressed, can be trusted with this approach because she is 'most manly' (*andreiotatē*) and has gone beyond 'womanish things' (*gynēkaia*) – in the manner of Sarah (Genesis 18. 11) (II.2). And knowing how to 'pray as we ought' (Romans 8. 26) is *paralleled* with an appropriately 'passionless', 'deliberate', and 'holy' performance of the 'mysteries of marriage' (II.2), lest 'Satan rejoice over you' 'through lack of *self-control*' (II.2). Unsurprisingly, Origen's daring treatment of Romans 8 also occasions an immediate reminder (with reference to 1 Timothy 2 and 1 Corinthians 11) that women should always wear modest apparel and cover their heads at prayer, lest their distracting presence lead to the same loss of (male) sexual control (II.2). Later in the text, too, Origen advises against praying at all in a room in which sexual intercourse has taken place (XXXI.4). The intrinsic connections between prayer and eroticism, it seems, are too close to be avoided, but also too dangerous to be allowed free rein.

This nexus of associations – between the Spirit, prayer, loss of control, and the dangers of women's attractiveness and sexual susceptibility – is further illuminated by themes from Origen's later works on the *Song of Songs*, and from his apologetic treatise, the *Contra Celsum*. On the one hand, the *Commentary* and the *Homilies* on the *Song of Songs* elaborate the biblical text as an allegorical account of the soul's most intimate advance to God through Christ's (the Bridegroom's) 'erotic' embrace. But as in the *De oratione*, the same paradox is enunciated: Origen stresses both the indispensability of the sexual metaphor, and also its grave dangers to those not yet morally prepared through a process of spiritual maturation.[31] It is therefore appropriate only to the highest stage of the 'mystical' ascent. It applies to the 'inner' 'spiritual senses', and never to the 'outer' physical senses.[32] While there is greater emphasis on the Word as 'Bridegroom' than on the Spirit in the *Commentary on the Song*, some reference to the Spirit, consistent with that in the *De oratione*, is also alluringly present, allowing us – I would argue – to read the *Commentary* as another vision of trinitarian 'incorporation' into the life of Sonship.[33] The contrast with a slightly later passage in the *Contra Celsum*, VII.2–7, on the other hand, reveals the dangers Origen sees in the *wrong* sort of 'ecstatic' behaviour and sexual abandonment to 'daemon' spirits. Here he castigates the Pythian oracular 'priestesses' who receive impure spirits through their (physical) 'private parts' rather than through 'invisible pores' (VII.3), and through 'ecstasy' and 'frenzy' rather

---

[31] For the importance of spiritual and erotic maturity for a right reading of the *Song*, see *Commentarium in Canticum Canticorum*, Prologue, 2.39–40. For Origen, Christian maturation happens in three stages of ascent: the 'ethical', the 'physical' (the capacity to see the physical world as it is, and as a whole), and the 'epoptic' (the contemplative). Meditation on the *Song* is appropriate to the 'epoptic' stage, in which Christ's erotic embrace is sought: see ibid., Prologue, 3.3; 3.5–7; 3.21–3 for the three stages.

[32] See ibid., Prologue, 3.15–16; I, 4.16–19.

[33] For the Spirit in the *Commentarium in Canticum Canticorum*, see ibid., Prologue, 2.46–8; III, 1.4–13. We also find the motif of pneumatological incorporation, in somewhat different mode, in another of Origen's later works, the *Exhortatio ad Martyrium*, where readiness for martyrdom is represented as a 'giv[ing] place to the Spirit', so that one may 'welcome the great encouragement of Christ's sufferings' and thus become one with the very life of the Trinity (*Exhortatio ad Martyrium*, 39). Here the 'incorporative' motif is specifically linked to Christic *suffering*; but this too, of course, has echoes of Romans 8 (verse 17).

than through the 'superior' illumination of the Holy Spirit (VII.4). The contrast is revealing and instructive.

The conclusions I wish to draw from this important material in Origen are the following. First, the 'erotic' thematization of incorporation into the Trinity that I have here examined deserves greater attention, I suggest, in the textbook accounts of Origen's doctrine of the Trinity than it currently enjoys. Most often, Origen's treatment of the Trinity in his earlier *De principiis* is taken to be the 'systematic' or normative one, and hence a false impression is gleaned: for here Origen is certainly found to be guarded about the ecstatic dimensions of engagement with the Spirit. The significance of the divine 'reason' in Christians is carefully stressed in the first discussion of the Spirit in that work (*De princ.*, 1.3.4–6); and later, in the rather different treatment in book 2 (7.2–4), Origen argues that 'all rational creatures receive a share in Him [*sc.* the Spirit]' (2.7.2), but that there is a danger of confusion with 'common spirits' which 'excite dissensions of no small extent among brethren' (2.7.3). My suggestion, then, is that the cautious and subordinating notes struck here are quite different from the rich prayer-based, 'erotic' themes of the later *De oratione* and the *Commentary on the Song*. These different strands of trinitarian thought need to be assessed together, then, as well as in alignment with the theme of participatory 'Sonship' in Origen's *Commentary on John*, his *Commentary on Romans*, and other related commentary materials. Something important is at stake here, both spiritually and morally, which links Origen's trinitarianism creatively with his theory of mystical ascent and his allegorical reading of Scripture.

Secondly, the crucial role of the Spirit in the *De oratione* – as initiator in prayer and guide to 'inaccessible' divine realms – gives the lie to oft-repeated platitudes about Origen's 'subordination' of the Spirit, and should again cause us to return to the pneumatology and trinitarianism of the *De principiis* with somewhat new eyes. Is this 'incorporative', Spirit-leading, 'eroticized' vision of the Trinity simply in inconsistent *tension* with the controlled linear 'ordering' of Father, Son, and Spirit in the *De principiis* (where the Spirit is *third*, safely aligned with the publicly attested rationality of the Logos (1.3))? Or is it – as I find much more plausible – that there is one vision of the Trinity which Origen presents for the spiritually mature (the contemplative *epoptics*), and another – a safer version, one might say – for those not yet so high on the spiritual slopes? If this is so (as I believe to be the case), we then have identified an important point of application relating to Origen's understanding of 'orthodoxy' as a demanding spiritual *process*, and one of potentially continuing systematic import.

Lastly, and not at all least: the gender implications of the material I have discussed may be obvious, but perhaps need underscoring nonetheless. According to the approach of the *De oratione* and the commentary on the *Song*, men (in ceding control to the Spirit and submitting to the Bridegroom's embrace) take on an implicitly 'feminine' role spiritually which is, however, debarred to *women* unless in some sense they eschew their initial 'womanishness' and become 'manly' (in order, yet further, to become 'feminine' to the Word as well).[34] Even then they may remain subject to the charge

---

[34] Here, of course, Origen is using gender terms in what would now be called 'stereotypical' mode. But this does not mean for him that gender is prescriptively understood in a *fixed* sense; indeed, both men and women are for Origen, in their slightly different ways, set on the course of a malleable transformation and ascent to God. Still, there is no denying the greater degree of opprobrium associated with women's sexualized bodies, especially prior to any such spiritualized ascent. The Greek fragments that have come down to us from Origen's homilies on 1 Corinthians (where questions of gender and ecstasy come up) are also relevant here: for an astute analysis, see Judith Kovics, 'Servant of Christ and Steward of the Mysteries of God: The Purpose of a Pauline Letter according to Origen's *Homilies on 1 Corinthians*', in Paul M. Blowers, Angela Russell Christman, David Hunter, and Robin Darling Young, eds., *In Dominico Eloquio: Essays on Patristic Exegesis in Honor of Robert Louis Wilken* (Grand Rapids, MI: Eerdmans, 2002), 147–71.

of distracting men from their true spiritual goal; and their more permeable orifices are dangerous openings for 'daemon' spirits. Still, the *epoptic* heights are by no means debarred to them, as is clear from the dedication of the *De oratione* to (the mature) Tatiana as well as to Ambrose. It is just that a demanding and complicated renegotiation of gender (and yet simultaneously a release from societally mandated roles) is clearly something inherent to the spiritual transformations required of those introduced to the higher flights of contemplative ascent. This theme, with all its ambiguity for women, will return to entice us in Chapter 6.

THE 'PRAYER-BASED' MODEL AND THE WATERSHED OF THE ARIAN CONTROVERSY

How then are we to assess the significance of Origen's 'incorporative' approach in its social and ecclesiastical impact? We might speculate, again, that the mixed feelings evidenced in the two strands of Origen's trinitarian thought are a classic case of the ambivalence of a 'mystic' type operating within the boundaries of the 'church' (in the sociological sense). A purer 'sectarian' type would allow distinctive experiences to attend the reception of the Holy Spirit, and encourage them; a purer 'church' type might have less vibrant a sense of the contemplative model of incorporation and its mature transformative possibilities for union with Christ. The spiritual élitism signalled by the latter alternative was indeed to cause some difficulties once the church became the church of the empire, and thus inevitably became newly condoning of half-hearted commitment.

This reflection raises an issue which up to now has remained moot. We have been focusing so far on the particular views of prayer and the Spirit evidenced in a number of important and distinctive theologians of the earliest centuries, including – in some cases – in their theologies of public baptism. But we have not so far considered the case of *eucharistic* prayer, often of course presided over by the local bishop himself. What does our knowledge about the various shapes of liturgical prayer in the earliest centuries suggest by way of an implicit pneumatology in this public ecclesial context, and in particular of a theology of 'incorporation'? It is hard to make convincing generalizations here on the basis of varied, fragmented, and complex evidences. But at least from the time that Hippolytus witnesses to an *epiclēsis* (formal 'calling in') of the Spirit at the eucharist in the third century at Rome, there is at least an implicit signal that some sort of incorporative trinitarianism of the sort I have been outlining undergirded the logic of the eucharistic act. For the Holy Spirit was invoked as a transformative factor either on the people of God as Christ's body (as in Hippolytus), or later, as in Cyril of Jerusalem, on the eucharistic *elements* themselves, understood as Christ's body and blood. In an unofficial or implicit fashion, then, or so one might argue, what I have called the 'mystic'/church vision of the Trinity haunted the celebration of the eucharistic mysteries from relatively early years: the *lex orandi* as 'incorporation' was ever on offer to the faithful. But we have already seen in the subtly different cases of Irenaeus, Tertullian, and Origen that mere appeal to such a vague implicit logic could not, as such, either predict or clarify some of the finer tuning of their pneumatologies (whether subordinationist or not), their views of episcopal and spiritual authority, or their accompanying attitudes to gender. Nor, alas, could it – per se – solve the ferocious trinitarian debates that were to erupt in the Arian controversy, when both sides were to appeal to the 'law of prayer', especially to the public prayer of baptism and eucharist, in defence of their positions and their subordinationist – or non-subordinationist – accounts of the 'divinity' of Son and Spirit. The very fact that this standoff could happen as it did underscores the complexity of the aligned patternings of social, political, and theological factors which were at stake, and the seismic shifting in the relations of such factors as Christianity became imperially supported.[35] At the heart of this complex of realignments, moreover, was an irreducible theological problem which we have so far only hinted at: how was the approach to God as Trinity (and especially God as Spirit) which in the biblical witness and early centuries had been thought of mainly at the level of the 'economy' (God's ways with us on earth) now to be thematized eternally and 'ontologically' (as God immanent in Godself)? How would the ecstatic, 'incorporative', model of the Spirit, let alone the 'linear' and 'hierarchical' model (with its seemingly implicit subordination of the Spirit) be convincingly wrenched into the new requirements of absolute ontological equality *in* the Godhead?

To this more contorted period of dispute we must thus now turn. Only a selective treatment of key moments and figures is here possible, at the end of this already long and complicated chapter. However, the most important and paradoxical message is the one anticipatorily enunciated at the start of the chapter, and which relates intimately to the new conditions of imperial establishment. As the Arian controversy came finally to its end, with the Cappadocian insistence on *homoousian* equality for the Spirit alongside Father and Son, the more demanding incorporative rendition of the Spirit à la Romans 8 which we witnessed in Origen came to sit somewhat uneasily alongside obedient assent to the new achieved orthodoxy of 'three persons in one substance'. And here was the

---

[35] George H. Williams's classic study, 'Christology and Church–State Relations in the Fourth Century', *Church History* 20/3 (1951), 3–33, and 20/4 (1951), 3–26, remains outstandingly prescient and illuminating in making these connections.

irony: despite the blood spilt in the later fourth century over the struggle for the Spirit's equality, that formal creedal equality was bought with a certain price now that the church was no longer persecuted. To sign on propositionally to the Spirit's equality, to continue to worship liturgically in a way which bespoke an incorporation in the rather vague sense the eucharist had long suggested, was not in itself a guarantee of grasping the *full* implications of the Romans 8 nexus as Paul and some earlier writers had perceived it. It was the monastic movement, par excellence, which was to keep that subtle alternative – that radical insistence on the Spirit's primary ecstatic power to transform and perfect – most vibrantly alive; and with that came new potential for tensions between different social groupings in the church.

A key transitional figure in this story is of course Athanasius, the late fourth-century bishop of Alexandria and great defender of emerging Nicene orthodoxy. With the vicissitudes of the fortunes of the Arian and Nicene parties (succeeding emperors coming and going in their allegiance), Athanasius was forced to go into exile no fewer than five times in his career as a bishop, as the hopes for his theological position waned and waxed. In the course of these exiles, Athanasius came under the strong influence of the new monastic movement of the Egyptian desert, and under the particular spell of Antony the Great, whose *Life* he subsequently wrote.[36] This special Antonine influence is, on my reading, enormously significant for an important change in Athanasius' theology that occurs in the later part of his career. Athanasius' pneumatology is muted, if

---

[36] It is often argued that Athanasius has in this work massaged the figure of Antony into a cultured Alexandrian philosopher and *savant*, when really he must have been nothing more than an unlettered rustic. Recent scholarship has begun to resist that hypothesis and shows that Antony most likely did have some philosophical cognizance, and particularly some acquaintance with the thought of Origen: see Samuel Rubenson, *The Letters of St Anthony: Monasticism and the Making of a Saint* (Lund University Press, 1990).

not non-existent, in his earlier writings; but after the intense contact with the desert monks, and in particular with the thinking of Antony and his immediate followers, a turn to the vibrancy of a Romans 8 approach – of an incorporative 'adoption' into Sonship by the Spirit – becomes a marked theme in his thought, just at the moment that he also affirms the Spirit's ontological *equality* in the Godhead.

Athanasius' use of Romans 8 in his mature work on the Spirit's divinity thus marks a watershed. Whereas his early work *On the Incarnation* significantly mentions the Spirit not at all in its exposition of an incorporative *Christology* (the comparison with Irenaeus is revealing), the later *Letters to Serapion*, in contrast, insist that 'The Father does all things through the Word *in the Holy Spirit*' (1.28, my emphasis). Interestingly, we find this work almost obsessively appealing to Romans 8 (and its parallel passage Galatians 4. 6). Commenting on Romans 8. 29, for instance, Athanasius writes: 'It is through the Spirit that we are partakers of God ... the fact of our being called partakers of God shows that the unction and seal that is in us belongs, not to the nature of things originate, but to the nature of the Son who, through the Spirit who is in him, joins us to the Father' (*Letters to Serapion*, 1.24). Earlier too, in one striking passage in *Against the Arians* (2.59), Athanasius had anticipated this move by commenting on Galatians 4. 6: 'Accordingly this passage ... proves, that we are not sons by nature, but [by] the Son who is in us; ... in receiving the grace of the Spirit, we are said thenceforth to be begotten also'. It seems that something of the full force of the Romans 8 approach has now been recovered here.

Yet it remains hard to assess quite what Athanasius is doing with this 'incorporative' theme, since the context is a very different one from that of either Irenaeus or Origen: what is now at stake, of course, is whether the Spirit should be granted completely equal *divinity* with the Father and Son, as was not presumed by these forebears. From a modern critical perspective, a scholar like Wiles would object, no doubt, that Athanasius is thus not even here concentrating on establishing the problematic 'personal' *distinctness* of the Spirit; it is Athanasius' opponents, the Tropici,[37] with their rejection of the Spirit's fully divine status, whom he is countering. He has therefore seemingly taken the 'hypostatic' distinctness of the Spirit for granted, even though in principle he could have argued for it on the basis of his preferred Pauline passages. Moreover, the production of these arguments about the Spirit at a comparatively late stage in Athanasius' theological career, and for the purposes of seeing off a new heresy, might again cause someone like Wiles to wonder whether they are truly distinctive of his output: why was the Spirit ignored, indeed mentioned only fleetingly in the doxology of the *On the Incarnation*?

My hypothesis about monastic influence might be important here, for amongst the monks could be found circles which carefully maintained the distinctive, and demanding, Origenistic/Romans 8 approach to prayer.[38] And, possibly under their influence, there is a reflexive subtlety about Athanasius' late doctrine of the Spirit which even his successors the Cappadocians do not emulate consistently. Athanasius is true to the Pauline passages to which he constantly adverts; it is not that the Spirit simply 'enlightens' or 'sanctifies', but is transformatively present in all that we do. We pray therefore, he says, '*in the Triad* . . . for inasmuch as we partake of the Spirit, we

---

[37] The Tropici were an Alexandrian-based group of the so-called 'Spirit-fighters', those who denied the full divinity of the Spirit.

[38] This is notably true of the letters of Antony himself: see the analysis in my essay, 'Prayer, Politics and the Trinity: Vying Models of Authority in Third–Fourth-Century Debates on Prayer and "Orthodoxy"', *Scottish Journal of Theology* 66 (2013), forthcoming.

have the grace of the Word and, in the Word, the love of the Father'
(*Ad Ser.*, 3.6, my emphasis).

In comparison with this rich Athanasian theology of pneumatological 'adoption', the tendency of the earlier Cappadocian view of
incorporation into the Trinity (as I already intimated at the start of
the chapter) seems to me characteristically more explicitly 'linear',
and even at times distinctly 'hierarchical' (despite, of course, *homoousian* protestations to the contrary). For Basil, for instance (*On the
Holy Spirit*, 9.23), even 'drawing near' to the Paraclete is not
possible unless one is already cleansed from sin; from there the
Holy Spirit 'like the sun, will by the aid of thy purified eye show
thee in Himself the image of the invisible, and in the blessed
spectacle of the image, thou shalt behold the unspeakable beauty
of the archetype' (9.23). The metaphors are distinctly neo-Platonic
in this famous passage of Basil's: this is a step-by-step process of
'enlightenment', with the Spirit as first point of entry into higher
things. Whereas Athanasius brought Son and Spirit together 'in the
Triad', Basil seems to redistinguish them, specifically allocating
'enlightenment' and 'sanctification' to the third in the economy.[39]

Gregory of Nazianzus and Gregory of Nyssa (the two other
'Cappadocian' fathers) are subtly different in their trinitarianisms
from Basil, neither of them being happy with the allocation of
'sanctifying power' to the Spirit alone. For Nyssen, the invocation
of the Holy Spirit is *for* the cleansing of sin (*The Lord's prayer*, 3),
rather than that cleansing being a prerequisite for engagement by
the Spirit. But the 'order' of appropriation to the persons of the

---

[39] It is an irony that this text of Basil's is the most celebrated of the attempts to make
theological sense of the 'equality' of the Spirit from the perspective of the church's *lex
orandi*; yet ultimately an undergirding neo-Platonic metaphysic seems to remain the
primary philosophical inspiration. This is yet another indication that the *lex orandi* appeal
can have multiple outcomes, and also that the rhetoric of 'equality' may have very varied
ecclesiastical outworkings.

Trinity is again very clear in some passages now attributed to Nyssen: 'It is impossible for a man, if he has not been previously enlightened by the Spirit, to arrive at a conception of the Son'. So too, 'Just as he who grasps one end of a chain pulls both along with it and the other end also to himself, so he who draws the Spirit ... through the Spirit draws both the Son and the Father along with it'.[40] Other discussions, however, especially in Gregory's famous response to his opponent Eunomius, show him struggling to find the right way of positioning the Spirit in God's internal/eternal life in such a way that no such remaining 'hierarchalization' could even be suggested.[41] Further, what Gregory's later *Life of Moses* makes memorably clear, and with deepened spiritual insight, is that human spiritual advance towards intimacy with God as Trinity ultimately leads to an unnerving 'darkness' – the 'darkness of incomprehensibility' – rather than the 'enlightenment' that may have characterized an earlier stage of the ascent. The linked question of the significance of this darkness in terms of Gregory's *sexual* metaphors as applied to the ascent to God is an important one, also connected to his distinctive trinitarianism, and to which I shall return in some detail in Chapter 6. Here we find gender messages at least as interesting as those in Origen, but arguably more creative in their implications for ascetic women and their status in the church. Further, Gregory has all the convictions of an apophatic thinker that trinitarian doctrine does not strictly speaking *describe* God; yet, as we have seen, his incorporative vision of the Trinity is

---

[40] This passage comes from a letter previously attributed to Basil (Letter 38, in *The Letters of St Basil*, 1, 206–7), which might explain this trope. However, intensive comparative analysis of Greek style suggests that this is, after all, Nyssen's work, but probably from the period when he is most under his brother Basil's influence.

[41] The effort is not without paradoxical strain, since the Origenist tradition is still vibrant for the Cappadocians spiritually; and at the same time they are struggling to incorporate hallowed language previously applied to the 'economic' level into the new vision of the tripersonal 'ontological' Trinity.

nonetheless often – especially in his polemical doctrinal writings of the middle period of his career – shot through with metaphors of a descending divine outreach and a human responsive 'ascent'.

Of course, the irony is that Origen's treatment of prayer in the *De oratione* was in one sense equally affected by a rhetoric of Platonic 'ascent'; indeed, that is why, according to Origen, it is not proper to pray *to* Spirit or Son, but rather in and through them to the Father. But what I tried to show in my earlier analysis of Origen's text is that his faithfulness to Paul's account of the Spirit in Romans 8, combined with his Platonic understanding of 'erotic' ascent and purgation through prayer, resulted in a particularly rich theory of prayer and contemplation as an incorporative participation within the very life of the Trinity: one does not *start* with the Spirit here only later to 'advance' to Son and Father. Origen's theory, too, was one that spanned a whole lifetime of moral and spiritual preparation for union and ascetic struggles in prayer for perfection; perhaps this was why his approach proved so attractive to Antony and his followers, and later to a celebrated second-generation monastic author such as Evagrius of Pontus, who took up the Romans 8 incorporative model of prayer again with special verve and insight, following in Origen's footsteps in writing his own treatise 'On prayer'.[42] When the

---

[42] For the appeal to Romans 8 in Evagrius' *De oratione*, see especially no. 63: 'The Holy Spirit, out of compassion for our weakness, comes to us even when we are impure. And if only He finds our intellect truly praying to Him, He enters it and puts to flight the whole array of thoughts and ideas circling within it, and He arouses it to a longing for spiritual prayer' (in G. E. H. Palmer, Philip Sherrad, and Kallistos Ware, eds., *The Philokalia* (London, Faber & Faber, 1969), vol. 1, 63); it should be added that the influence of Origen's *De oratione* is clear throughout this Evagrian text). It is, of course, a unique irony – central to the consciously paradoxical story told in this chapter – that Origen could *both* be the source for the richest theory of non-hierarchical 'incorporative' trinitarianism *and* the one subsequently (and anachronistically) scapegoated by the institutionally 'orthodox' *for* his hierarchical subordinationism. If the argument of this chapter has proved its weight, however, this paradox will at least seem theoretically explicable: after all, to blame the one who spiritually threatens you for a fault which is

so-called 'Origenist' crisis broke out in the last months of the fourth century, the sudden hostility evidenced by the then bishop of Alexandria, Theophilus, against certain 'Origenist' monks of high reputation in the Nitrian desert, may well then be better explained as a tension between episcopal authority under its new imperial protection, on the one hand, and an impressive monastic spiritual élitism with sectarian potential, on the other, than it is by the anachronistic charges of doctrinal error that were levied at the time. Why else would Origen's *De oratione* be so central to the debates, one might wonder? It seems that Theophilus himself had had long reverence for the monks and even believed that their ascetic feats of prayer could lead to perfection in this life. If so, it seems more likely that he would have wished to harness and domesticate their envied spiritual power than merely to humiliate them on grounds of implied doctrinal subordinationism, as was the trumped charge. Once again, the reception history of Romans 8, via Origen, was having a contentious outcome: monastic spiritual authority, vested in prayer, found itself in political tension with episcopal administrative jurisdiction.[43] The issue of the Spirit, power, and prayer was still a vibrant one. It had merely taken on new forms under the aegis of imperial Christianity.

CONCLUSIONS

Let me try now to pull together the threads of this complicated chapter. What does the patristic evidence we have surveyed indicate for our own contemporary theological concerns?

more your own is not an uncommon phenomenon in the framework of social science. Here I give it *theological* instantiation.

[43] As mentioned at the start of this chapter, I do not want to leave the impression that I am hypothesizing a straightforward Weberian disjunction between 'charisma' and 'institution' here. The evidences suggest a more complicated scenario in which Theophilus himself revered, but simultaneously wished to coopt and control, a form of monastic spiritual élitism. On this, see again my 'Prayer, Politics and the Trinity'.

I have attempted to illuminate what I have called an 'alternative' approach to the Trinity which gives strong priority to the Spirit in prayer, and which the modern textbooks have often obscured or ignored. We have now seen, however, that this alternative tradition takes a number of forms: a type granting *specific* experiential effects to the Spirit, and manifesting a sectarian tendency which even – as an accompanying feature – granted positions of relative power to some women; a type fumbling towards expression of the *simultaneous* experience of Father, Son, and Spirit in a reflexive divine 'incorporative' act which makes Christians participative of divine 'Sonship'; and a more hierarchical perception of 'incorporation', in which the Spirit is the point of entry in a movement of progressive 'ascent'. Both the latter types I would dub 'mystic/church' in Troeltschian sociological terms; and both, as we shall have reason to explore in a later chapters, make significant use of erotic metaphors in relation to God. Although to place the Cappadocians solely in the third category would be to demean their subtlety (I shall return to this issue in due course), it is nevertheless not hard to see how that third variation would prove the more enduring of the incorporative understandings of the Trinity for an established, hierarchically ordered church. For here the linear vision of God presented to us serves to mirror something of the ordered arrangement of the institutional church itself, even as subordinationism in the Godhead was officially (and of course creedally) denied.

But it has been shown, therefore, *pace* Wiles, that pneumatology was by no means 'dormant' in the early Christian centuries, but was rather a disputed and sometimes embarrassing issue with political and gendered dimensions. Likewise in subsequent generations, whenever leading authority was given to 'experiences of the Spirit', suspicions of heresy often followed (as in the Messalian-tinged *Macarian homilies*, for instance, or – much later – in the contentious case of Symeon the New Theologian).[44] It is perfectly true, as Wiles charged, that the fathers we have discussed in this chapter nowhere seemed to make *explicit* the prayer-based logic of this need to keep the Spirit 'distinct' (and unthinking conservatism and respect for authority surely did play some part in their theological thinking). But our brief survey of the use of Romans 8 indicates that in some authors this argument was at least *implicit*. Finally, as our evidence has already clearly shown, it would be misleading to say that only the Greek-speaking Christian East endorsed this prayer-based trinitarian logic; Augustine himself (contrary to some common, but misleading, stereotypes about 'Western' trinitarianism) shows signs of it, especially in his late work. He appeals interestingly to Romans 8 in his letter to the widow Proba on prayer (Letter 130); and moments in the last book of the *De trinitate*, especially, show the same characteristically 'incorporative' logic, a rhetoric of divine desire proceeding from the Father by means of the Holy Spirit, and so 'inflaming' us with love (*De trinitate*, xv.17.31, for instance).[45] Later Western mystical theologians rediscovered this model periodically, especially in a rich phase of 'indwelling Trinity' motifs in the later medieval mystics (such as Eckhart, Ruusbroec, Julian of Norwich). John of the Cross's *Spiritual canticle* provides a memorably beautiful instantiation of the type. Opening his text with an immediate allusion to Romans 8, John later speaks more explicitly of the Holy Spirit's action on the 'feminized' soul, which 'raises the soul most sublimely

[44] For the purported 'Messalianism' of Macarius, see Marcus Plested, *The Macarian Legacy: The Place of Macarius-Symeon in the Eastern Christian Tradition* (Oxford University Press, 2004), esp. 16–27; and on the conflict in which Symeon the New Theologian became embroiled as a result of his high claims for the 'purification' of the Holy Spirit, see Basil Krivocheine, *In the Light of Christ: St Symeon, the New Theologian – Life, Spirituality, Doctrine* (Crestwood, NY: St Vladimir's Press, 1986), esp. 45–9.

[45] I shall return to a comparative analysis of the trinitarian theologies of Gregory of Nyssa and Augustine in more detail in Chapter 6.

with that his divine breath . . . that she may breathe in God the same breath of love that the Father breathes in the Son and the Son in the Father' (*Spiritual canticle*, 39.3.4).

If then the 'incorporative' model whose history we have traced had important implications not only for moral and spiritual maturity and doctrinal understanding but also for political and ecclesial pressures to transformation and reform, how might this same model manifest itself creatively in a contemporary milieu? In my next 'foraging raid' into the tradition, I shall test my thesis by turning to a very different context, and to the contemporary Christian scene in which, simultaneously and paradoxically, we find practising 'church'-type Christians showing no apparent interest in the Trinity, and sectarian-tending charismatics apparently revivifying pneumatology and even trinitarianism too. How such a contemporary study might complement our patristic trinitarian reflections, further our project of a *théologie totale*, and complexify the Troeltschian social patternings I have so far essayed, I shall duly reveal in the next chapter. Without this apparent sidestep into the contemporary pastoral 'field', our trinitarian proposals would look very different and be much impoverished. Or so I hope now to show.

* * *

BIBLIOGRAPHIC NOTE

ORIGINAL SOURCES

By far the most important source materials behind this chapter are the original sources themselves: the New Testament, and the relevant works of the patristic period (and beyond) which I cite in my exposition. In what follows, I provide both the extrabiblical original texts and the English translations I have utilized in this chapter.

Antony of Egypt, *The Letters of St Antony the Great*, trans. Derwas J. Chitty (Oxford: SLG Press, 1975); Antony of Egypt, *Lettres: Version Géorgienne et Fragments Copts*, ed. Gérard Garitte (CSCO 148–9; Louvain: L. Durbecq, 1955).

Athanasius, *On the Incarnation*, ed. John Behr (PPS 3; Crestwood, NY: St Vladimir's Seminary Press, 1998); Athanasius, *Sur l'incarnation du Verbe*, ed. Charles Kannengiesser (SC 199; 2nd edn; Paris: Cerf, 2001); Athanasius, *Against the Arians*, in Philip Schaff, ed., *Nicene and Post-Nicene Fathers* (Grand Rapids, MI: Eerdmans, 1980), 2nd series, vol. IV, 303–431; Athanasius, *Orationes contra Arianos*, in Martin Tetz, ed., *Athanasius Werke* (Berlin: De Gruyter, 1924–), vol. I/1/2–3, 109–381; Athanasius, *The Life of Antony and the Letter to Marcellinus*, ed. Robert C. Gregg (CWS; New York: Paulist Press, 1980); Athanasius, *Vie d'Antoine*, ed. G. J. M. Bartelink (SC 400; Paris: Cerf, 1994); Athanasius, *The Letters of Saint Athanasius Concerning the Holy Spirit*, ed. C. R. B. Shapland (New York: Philosophical Library, 1951); Mark DelCogliano and Andrew Radde-Gallwitz, trans., *Works on the Holy Spirit: Athanasius and Didymus the Blind* (PPS 43; Crestwood, NY: St Vladimir's Seminary Press, 2012); Athanasius, *Lettres à Serapion sur la divinité du Saint Esprit*, ed. J. Lebon (SC 15; Paris: Cerf, 1947).

Augustine, *Letters*, ed. Roland Teske, John Rotelle, and Boniface Ramsey (New York: New City Press, 2001–5); Augustine, *Epistulae CI–CXXXIX*, ed. Klaus Daur (CCSL 31B; Turnhout: Brepols, 2009); Augustine, *The Trinity*, trans. Edmund Hill (New York: New City Press, 1991); Augustine, *De Trinitate Libri* XV, ed. W. J. Mountain (CCSL 50–50A; Turnhout: Brepols, 1968).

Basil of Caesarea, *On the Holy Spirit*, trans. Stephen Hildebrand (PPS 42; Crestwood, NY: St Vladimir's Seminary Press, 2011); Basil of Caesarea, *Sur le Saint-Esprit*, ed. Benoît Pruche (SC 17bis; Paris: Cerf, 1968); Basil,

Letters, trans. Roy J. Defarrari (LCL 190, 215, 243, 270; London: Heinemann, 1926–30); Basil, *Lettres*, ed. Yves Courtonne (Paris: Les Belles Lettres, 1957–66).

Eusebius of Caesarea, *Ecclesiastical History*, trans. Kirsopp Lake (LCL 153, 265; Cambridge, MA: Harvard University Press, 1980).

Evagrius Ponticus, 'On Prayer', in G. E. H. Palmer, Philip Sherrard, and Kallistos Ware, trans. and eds., *The Philokalia: The Complete Text Compiled by St Nikodimos of the Holy Mountain and St Makarios of Corinth* (London: Faber & Faber, 1979), vol. 1, 55–71; *Philokalia tōn hierōn nēptikōn* (Athens: A. and E. Papadēmētriou, 1957–76); *The Praktikos: Chapters on Prayer*, trans. John Eudes Bamberger (CSC 4; Spencer, MA: Cistercian Publications, 1970); Evagrius Ponticus, *Traité pratique, ou, le Moine*, ed. Antoine and Claire Guillaumont (SC 170–1; Paris: Cerf, 1971).

Gregory of Nyssa, *The Lord's Prayer; The Beatitudes*, trans. Hilda C. Graef (ACW 18; London: Longmans & Green, 1954); Gregory of Nyssa, *De Oratione Dominica, De Beatitudinibus*, ed. John F. Callahan (GNO vii/2; Leiden: Brill, 1992); Gregory of Nyssa, 'An Answer to Ablabius: That We should not Think of Saying there are Three Gods', in E. R. Hardy, ed., *Christology of the Later Fathers* (London: SCM Press, 1954), 256–67; Gregory of Nyssa, *Ad Ablabium*, in F. Müller, ed., *Opera Dogmatica Minora, Pars I* (GNO iii/1; Leiden: Brill, 1958), 35–67; Gregory of Nyssa, 'An Address on Religious Instruction', in E. R. Hardy, ed., *Christology of the Later Fathers* (London: SCM Press, 1954), 268–325; Gregory of Nyssa, *Oratio Catechetica*, ed. E. Mühlenberg (GNO iii/4; Leiden: Brill, 1996); Gregory of Nyssa, *The Life of Moses*, trans. Abraham J. Malherbe and Everett Ferguson (CWS; New York: Paulist Press, 1978); Gregory of Nyssa, *De Vita Moysis*, ed. H. Musurillo (GNO vii/1; Leiden: Brill, 1991); Gregory of Nyssa, *Homilies on the Song of Songs*, trans. and ed. Richard A. Norris (Greek text and English trans.) (Atlanta, GA: Society of Biblical Literature, 2012).

Hippolytus, *Philosophoumena, or, The Refutation of all Heresies*, trans. F. Legge (TCL; London: SPCK, 1921); Hippolytus, *Refutatio Omnium Haeresium*, ed. Miroslav Marcovich (PTS 25; Berlin: De Gruyter, 1986).

Irenaeus of Lyons, *St Irenaeus against the Heresies*, trans. Dominic J. Unger and John J. Dillon (ACW 55, 64, 65; New York: Paulist Press, 1992–); Irenaeus of Lyons, *Contre les hérésies*, ed. A. Rousseau, L. Doutreleau, C. Mercier, and B. Hemmerdinger (SC 100, 152, 153, 210, 211, 263, 264, 293, 294; Paris: Cerf, 1965–82).

Jerome, *The Letters of St Jerome*, trans. Charles Christopher Mierow (ACW 33; New York: Newman Press, 1961); Jerome, *Epistulae*, ed. Isidore Hilburg (CSEL 54–6; Vienna: F. Tempsky, 1910–18).

John of the Cross, *Spiritual Canticle*, in Kieran Kavanaugh and Otilio Rodriguez, trans., *The Collected Works of St John of the Cross* (Washington, DC: Institute of Carmelite Studies, 1991), 469–630; John of the Cross, *Cántico Espiritual*, in Silverio de Santa Teresa, ed., *Obras de San Juan de la Cruz*, vol. III (Burgo: El Monte Carmelo, 1930).

Origen, *Commentary on the Gospel According to John*, trans. Ronald E. Heine (FC 80, 89; Washington, DC: Catholic University of America Press, 1989–93); Origen, *Commentaire sur saint Jean*, ed. C. Blanc (SC 120, 157, 222, 290, 385; Paris: Cerf, 1964–92); Origen, *Commentary on the Epistle to the Romans*, trans. Thomas P. Scheck (FC 103, 104; Washington, DC: Catholic University of America Press, 2001–2); Origen, *Commentaire sur l'Épître aux Romains*, ed. Michel Fédou and Luc Brésard (SC 532, 539; Paris: Cerf, 2009–10); Origen, *Der Römerbriefkommentar des Origenes: Kritische Ausgabe der Übersetzung Rufins*, ed. Caroline P. Hammond Bammel (Freiburg: Herder, 1990); Origen, *On First Principles*, trans. G. W. Butterworth (New York: Harper & Row, 1966); Origen, *Traité des principes*, ed. Henri Crouzel and Manlio Simonetti (SC 252, 253, 268, 269, 312; Paris: Cerf, 1978–84); Origen, *An Exhortation to Martyrdom* and *Treatise on Prayer*, in Rowan E. Greer, trans., *Origen* (CWS; New York: Paulist Press, 1979), 41–79 and 81–170; Origen, *Exhortatio ad Martyrium, Contra Celsum, De Oratione*, ed. P. Koetschau, Origenes Werke 1–2 (Leipzig: Hinrichs, 1899–1955); Origen, *The Song of Songs: Commentary and Homilies*, trans. R. P. Lawson (ACW 26; New York: Newman Press, 1956); Origen, *Commentaire sur le Cantique des cantiques*, ed. Luc Brésard and Henri Crouzel (SC 375–6; Paris: Cerf, 1991–2); Claude Jenkins, 'Origen on 1 Corinthians' (surviving Greek fragments), *Journal of Theological Studies* 9 (1908), 232–47, 353–72, 500–14, and *Journal of Theological Studies* 10 (1908), 29–51; Origen, *Contra Celsum*, trans. Henry Chadwick (Cambridge University Press, 1953); Origen, *Contre Celse*, ed. Marcel Borret (SC 132, 136, 147, 150; Paris: Cerf, 1967–9).

Pseudo-Macarius, *The Fifty Spiritual Homilies; and, The Great Letter*, trans. George Maloney (CWS; New York: Paulist Press, 1992); Pseudo-Macarius, *Die 50 geistlichen Homilien des Makarios*, ed. Hermann Dörries, Erich Klostermann, and Mathias Kroeger (PTS 4; Berlin: De Gruyter, 1964).

Symeon the New Theologian, *The Discourses*, trans. C. J. Catanzaro (CWS; New York: Paulist Press, 1980); Symeon the New Theologian, *Catéchèses*, ed. Basile Krivochine and Joseph Paramelle (SC 96; Paris: Cerf, 2006).

Tertullian, *Tertullian's Tract on the Prayer*, ed. and trans. Ernest Evans (London: SPCK, 1953); Tertullian, *Concerning Baptism*, in *Tertullian's Treatises*, trans. Alexander Souter (London: SPCK, 1919); Tertullian, *Traité du baptême*, ed. R. F. Refoulé and M. Drouzy (SC 35; Paris: Cerf, 2002); Tertullian, *On the Soul*, in *Apologetical Works*, trans. Rudolph Arbesmann, Sr, Emily Joseph Daly, and Edwin A. Quain (FC 10; (Washington, DC: Catholic University of America Press, 1977); Tertullian, *De anima*, ed. J. H. Waszink, in *Opera Montanistica* (CCSL 2; Turnhout: Brepols, 1954), 779–869; Tertullian, *Tertullian against Praxeas*, trans. Alexander Souter (TCL; London: SPCK, 1920); Tertullian, *Q. Septimii Florentis Tertulliani Adversus Praxean Liber*, ed. Ernest Evans (London: SPCK, 1948); Tertullian, *On the Veiling of Virgins*, in Geoffrey D. Dunn, ed., *Tertullian* (London: Routledge, 2004), 135–61; Tertullian, *Le Voile des vierges*, ed. Eva Schulz-Flügel (SC 424; Paris: Cerf, 1997).

Two compendia of Gnostic texts which usefully provide a wide range of relevant materials are Bentley Layton, ed., *The Gnostic Scriptures: A New Translation* (London: SCM Press, 1987); and Marvin Meyer, ed., *The Nag Hammadi Scriptures: The International Edition* (New York: HarperOne, 2007).

SELECT EXEGETICAL STUDIES

I can here only note a few of the best of the classic and contemporary scholarly renditions of the early history of the doctrine of the Trinity which have particularly helped me to clarify my thesis, even when I take issue with them. (Note that the bibliographic note to the Prelude already discussed some of the most important recent revisionary accounts of the Trinity from a *systematic* perspective; here, in contrast, I point to a few close *textual* and *theoretical* analyses of the early development of the doctrine of the Trinity.)

For my work on the New Testament, and Romans in particular, I have found Stanley K. Stowers's *A Re-Reading of Romans* (New Haven, CT: Yale University Press, 1994) particularly generative in its probing behind the lens of Augustine's and Luther's later readings; but Stowers says strangely little on Romans 8. James D. G. Dunn, *Romans 1–8* (Dallas, TX: Word Books, 1988), and Jean-Noël Aletti, 'Romans 8: The Incarnation and its Redemptive Impact', in Stephen T. Davis, Daniel Kendall, and Gerald O'Collins, eds., *The Incarnation: An Interdisciplinary Symposium on the Incarnation of the Son of God* (Oxford University Press, 2002), 93–115, both focus on the prayer material in Romans 8, as does Gordon Fee, *God's Empowering Presence: The Holy Spirit in the Letters of Paul* (Peabody, MA: Hendrickson, 1994). Franz Dünzl, *A Brief History of the Doctrine of the Trinity in the Early Church* (London: Continuum, 2007) is a useful overview of the patristic material, though one which repeats the received view that there was relatively little reflection on the Holy Spirit in the early patristic years (ibid., 117). But see his impressive and copious more recent study, *Pneuma: Funktionen des theologischen Begriffs in frühchristlicher Literatur* (Munster: Aschendorff, 2000). With this, compare the studies in James J. Buckley and David S. Yeago, eds., *Knowing the Triune God: The Work of the Spirit in the Practices of the Church* (Grand Rapids, MI: Eerdmans, 2001), and D. Vincent Twomey and Jane E. Rutherford, eds., *The Holy Spirit in the Fathers of the Church* (Dublin: Four Courts Press, 2010). One of the most insightful and exciting recent accounts of the later patristic development of the doctrine of the Trinity is to be found in Lewis Ayres, *Nicaea and its Legacy: An Approach to Fourth-Century Trinitarian Theology* (Oxford University Press, 2004) – also discussed in the bibliographic notes to the Prelude and to Chapter 6; Ayres's analysis also provides a genealogy of swings of fashion in textbook accounts of the doctrine of the Trinity in the modern period. Patristic work of the later twentieth century has been enormously enriched by the *ressourcement* movement in French Catholicism, and the work of Jean Daniélou, Henri Crouzel, and Han Urs von Balthasar on the Greek Fathers – especially of those authors previously somewhat neglected (Origen, Gregory of Nyssa, Maximus the Confessor). This movement has brought commentary work by the Fathers much more intimately into the discussion of doctrinal or philosophical development. Lorenzo Perrone's recent work on Origen continues this trajectory: *La preghiera secondo Origene: l'impossibilità donata* (Brescia: Morcelliana, 2011). In some contrast to Ayres's style, Khaled Anatolios's *Retrieving Nicaea: The Development and Meaning of Trinitarian Doctrine* (Grand Rapids, MI: Baker Academic, 2011) presents the story of doctrinal development through the Nicene crisis as one of intrinsic and unfolding doctrinal consistency; this dogmatic tour de force is well worth comparing with David M. Gwynn, *Athanasius of Alexandria: Bishop, Theologian, Ascetic, Father* (Oxford University Press, 2012), and with the older Rowan Williams, *Arius: Heresy and Tradition* (2nd edn; London: SCM Press, 2001), both of whom stress the contingencies and local contexts of the debates, and the number of factors – philosophical, exegetical, and political – which entered into it. Also commended is Rowan Williams, 'Baptism and the Arian Controversy', in Michel R. Barnes and Daniel H. Williams, eds., *Arianism after Arius: Essays on the Development of the Fourth-Century Trinitarian Conflicts* (Edinburgh: T&T Clark, 1995), 149–80, which stresses how both Arian and Nicene parties could appeal to the '*lex orandi*' for their positions. John Behr is particularly careful and accurate on the Cappadocian accounts of the Trinity: *The Nicene Faith* (2 vols.; Crestwood, NY: St Vladimir's Seminary Press, 2004). Recent compendia that contain many useful and relevant articles are: Peter C. Phan, ed., *The Cambridge Companion to The Trinity* (Cambridge University Press, 2011); Roy Hammerling, *A History of Prayer: The First to the Fifteenth Century* (Leiden: Brill, 2008); and Gilles Emery, OP, and Matthew Levering, eds., *The Oxford Handbook of The Trinity* (Oxford University Press, 2011).

Normative accounts of early Christian doctrine ('patristics') contrast notably with the recent outpouring of work on late antique 'heresy' (see again the bibliographic note to the Prelude), and this can lead to unfortunate ideological warfare. One of the best recent introductory volumes on Christianity in late antiquity (Susan Ashbrook Harvey and David G. Hunter, eds., *The Oxford Handbook of Early Christian Studies* (Oxford University Press, 2008)) provides excellent, nuanced sections on 'Identities', 'Regions', and 'Structures and Authorities', thus illustrating the diversity and contested nature of early Christianity without neglecting theological themes. David Brakke, *The Gnostics: Myth, Ritual and Diversity in Early Christianity* (Cambridge, MA: Harvard University Press, 2010) is a careful and discerning study which surveys other recent assessments of 'Gnosticism' and their significance.

WOMEN, GENDER, AND EARLY CHRISTIANITY

Elizabeth A. Clark surveys the turns in fashion which have successively allowed women's studies, feminist theology, and gender studies to interact with late antique studies in 'The Lady Vanishes: Dilemmas of a Feminist

Historian after the "Linguistic Turn"', *Church History* 67 (1998), 1–31. This article also supplies a fine survey of some of the best recent work on women and gender in early Christianity; here I draw attention only to a few such studies of different genres, which have served as an important backcloth to the current chapter: Ross Shepard Kraemer, *Her Share of the Blessings: Women's Religions among Pagans, Jews, and Christians in the Greco-Roman World* (Oxford University Press, 1992); Anne Jensen, *God's Self-Confident Daughters: Early Christianity and the Liberation of Women* (Louisville, KY: Westminster John Knox Press, 1996); Christine Trevett, *Montanism: Gender, Authority and the New Prophecy* (Cambridge University Press, 1996); Margaret Y. MacDonald, *Early Christian Women and Pagan Opinion: The Power of the Hysterical Woman* (Cambridge University Press, 1996); Kate Cooper, *The Virgin and the Bride: Idealized Womanhood in Late Antiquity* (Cambridge, MA: Harvard University Press, 1996); Karen King, 'Prophetic Power and Women's Authority: The Case of the *Gospel of Mary (Magdalene)*', in Beverly Kienzle and Pamela Walker, eds., *Women Preachers and Prophets through Two Millennia of Christianity* (Berkeley: University of California Press, 1998), 21–41; Mary Keller, *The Hammer and the Flute: Women, Power, and Spirit Possession* (Baltimore, MD: Johns Hopkins University Press, 2002); Laura Salah Nasrallah, *An Ecstasy of Folly: Prophecy and Authority in Early Christianity* (Cambridge, MA: Harvard University Press for Harvard Theological Studies, 2003).

We return again to this theme in relation to Gregory of Nyssa and Augustine in Chapter 6.

CHAPTER 4

The charismatic constituency: embarrassment or riches?

In the last chapter I outlined a complex thesis about prayer and the Trinity in the early church. I suggested, first, that there is a neglected, 'alternative' approach to the Trinity in this period, rooted textually in Romans 8 and manifested personally in the sustained activities of ecstatic or wordless prayer. But I also went on to suggest a set of sociopolitical associations with this 'alternative approach' which may account for the relative neglect of it – not just in the modern textbooks, but even amongst many of the early fathers themselves. The reason seemed to lie in this model's potential, at least, for being charged with schism and subversion. If the prioritizing of the Spirit that it involved was given completely free rein, then sectarian revolt and tension with political authorities (such as in the case of the Montanist crisis) could ensue, and with them the splitting loose of the Spirit from what was later called *homoousian* equality and interaction with the Father and the Son: the Spirit was then granted *specific*, isolable effects and emotional tonalities. Hence, if my thesis is correct, it helps to explain the continuing anti-trinitarian tendency of many 'sectarian' forms of Christianity.

But if, on the other hand, the prayer-based model of the Trinity was maintained within the dominant 'church'-type form of Christianity, especially as it became formally established in the empire, then another danger ensued. The subtlety of this model's perception of the interactive operations of Spirit with Father in and through the 'Christo-morphic' pray-er (see again Romans 8. 15–17) was easy to miss or suppress; its particular insights into the incorporative and reflexive flow of divine desire in prayer were all too easily flattened out into a more conventional statement of what I called the 'linear economy' of much orthodox trinitarianism. Here, in contrast, there was a covert relegating of the Spirit to the safer position of the 'third' – subordinate in effect, if not in theological rhetoric.

We are talking, then, about a very elusive balancing act in this type of trinitarianism that prioritizes the Spirit in prayer. The 'orthodoxy' it espouses is one of a progressive, but radical, assimilation of the doctrine by the believer; it requires an *authentic*, and personally demanding, understanding of the equality of the three 'persons' in prayer and contemplation. And yet it is a perception of the Trinity that nonetheless keeps threatening to slide in one direction or another. Either it slides towards a charismatic dissolution of the doctrine of the Trinity (or, perhaps, as later, towards the supposedly 'tritheistic' solutions of an eschatological exegete like Joachim of Fiore):[1] such approaches give the Spirit something distinctive and *new* to do, but may appear subversive of existing church order. Or else, on the other hand, there may be a contrary tendency, under the *guise* of *homoousian* orthodoxy, towards a covert subordinationism and re-'hierarchalization' of the persons, the Spirit more safely tamed and regulated by a dominant emphasis on Father and Son, with a creeping, but enervating, loss of the vibrancy of prayer.

---

[1] Joachim's visual representation of overlapping, but distinct, realms of 'Father', 'Son', and 'Spirit' along the span of Christian history is discussed in the next chapter: see Fig. 34 and commentary.

I hinted in the last chapter, too, at significant gender and sexual 'subtexts' in this nexus of themes, and that issue I shall take up again in detail in Chapter 6. On the one hand, the sectarian alternative appeared occasionally to grant women, as in Montanist circles, brief moments of public empowerment or leadership (at least until a takeover by male leadership put paid to that).[2] On the other hand, the structured hierarchy of the linear model – as I shall investigate more powerfully in visual form in the next chapter – could combine naturally at the symbolic level with other biblically sanctioned forms of subordination: the church's subordination to Christ, woman's subordination to man, children's or slaves' subordination to the *pater familias*. In the middle, however, was this occasionally glimpsed prayer-based insight of the contemplative, often combined, not insignificantly, I stressed, with highly charged erotic language for God. (It is Origen and Gregory of Nyssa, after all, who are founding writers of Christian 'mystical' commentaries on the *Song of Songs*.) To say that this 'mystical' type of trinitarianism confronts issues of what is now called 'sexuality' is not of course to laud it for being somehow proto-feminist in a modern sense. On the contrary, as we have already seen, and shall examine further, it more commonly in the pre-modern era manifests a tragic sense of *disjunction* between desire for God on the one hand, and actual sexual relations with real-life women on the other (which were of course often shunned by ascetic men in the patristic period). But at least it begins to approach the heart of the contemporary

---

[2] At least until something like Weberian 'routinization' put paid to that: see Max Weber, *The Theory of Social and Economic Organization*, trans. A. R. Henderson and Talcott Parsons (London: Hodge, 1947), 334–54. However, note that I am not signing on to Weber's sociological theory *in toto* and especially not in its reductive dimensions: in the section that follows, I continue to use the word 'religious' in a way beloved of secularization theorists, despite the fact that it has thereby come to be associated with reductive explanations which I am explicitly countering.

Christian dilemmas about sex and gender – what I have called the 'messy entanglement' of sexual desire and desire for God. Here lies the root of the problem, and simultaneously, if I am right, the potential source of its solution. So much by way of recapitulation.

But before I proceed further with this argument, and apply it with a new twist directly to the contemporary scene, I must first meet a potential objection. This requires a very short return to the 'throat-clearing' matters of methodology, and in particular to the current status of 'typologies' in the sociology of religion.[3] My use of such is perhaps in need of some further clarification before I further extend its application in this chapter, not least because Ernst Troeltsch's standing as a *theological* sociologist is almost always misunderstood, and I have already appealed to his work in significant ways. My own view is that there is a remaining – and largely untapped – importance in the sociological insights he bequeathed to theology.

A BRIEF RETURN TO SOCIOLOGICAL METHOD: TROELTSCH'S TYPOLOGY OF 'CHURCH', 'SECT', AND 'MYSTIC'

My central thesis in the last chapter already involved an application of Weber's and Troeltsch's sociological distinction between 'church' and 'sect' to the evidences of emerging trinitarianism in the early church. As I noted there, this twofold Weberian typology of 'church' and 'sect' was embellished further by Troeltsch, who towards the end of his great *Social Teaching of the Christian Churches* (originally published in 1913) added a third 'type': 'mysticism'. This type was not clearly *sociological* in the same way as the other two, as is often pointed out by his critics; and it may even have been a

---

[3] See again Chapters 1 and 2.

manifestation of an autobiographical need on Troeltsch's part, as begins to emerge in the closing pages of his magisterial survey of Christian tradition. For Troeltsch was increasingly finding himself to be a misfit in the German Lutheran 'church'-type organization of his own day, even as he saw the political and social necessity of its continuing existence; he was, as he thought of himself, an 'individualist/intellectualist' – a free-thinker with 'mystic' and doctrinally subversive tendencies.

If we look at Troeltsch's typology with fresh eyes for a moment now, it will provide a good entrée to this chapter's material, and also a defence of his method's continuing importance – not so much against the false theological charge that it is 'reductive' (an issue already tackled in Chapter 2), but against the more common sociologist's claim that it is inept or outmoded. Much of the sociologists' criticism of Troeltsch in fact resides in the comment that his typology best fits the Christian medieval and early modern periods which originally inspired it, and has to be stretched or modified (and some would say even abandoned) when applied to the contemporary scene. It is one of my tasks in this chapter to test that hypothesis, and to see how, and why, I myself might need to massage or correct Troeltsch's insights, while still insisting on the typology's continuing relevance and insight: it can, and does, illuminate our *theological* choices, and shows how they tend to relate to particular social contexts. At the same time, and equally, I want to see if I must adjust or expand my own historical speculations about the prayer-based model of the Trinity when I take the evidences of contemporary Christian spiritual commitment into account. And this is where Troeltsch can indeed continue to help us.

What I am interested in here is looking again for significant social connections and *patternings* in doctrinal and spiritual expression. These are the issues that Troeltsch pressed with such originality, and which are still somewhat rarely attended to in theological discussion. That is: what forms of pneumatology, what forms of implicit or explicit trinitarianism, what 'thought styles' (to use a term of Mary Douglas's),[4] tend to cohere with particular types of ecclesiastical organization, political context, social structure, and indeed, class affiliation? And what types of such doctrine and organization go along with more or less enabling roles for women (or are associated with distinctive views on sex or gender)? As soon as we ask these questions we see the necessity for fieldwork (yes even bizarrely, it might be said, fieldwork on the Trinity, that most ramified of doctrines). But recall my earlier insistence that such fieldwork must always play an important, indeed central, part in the method of a *théologie totale*. If I am right, such fieldwork can almost always be relied upon to expose riches (buried treasures), as well as embarrassments (every kind of doctrinal heterodoxy). I am aware, however, of the methodological complexities of such a programme, and I will say a brief word about these before I recount the details of my own fieldwork adventures.

Weber was one of the first to utilize the *sociological* category of the 'sect', and characterized it as a 'restricted association' of religiously qualified and committed people.[5] Troeltsch then built on his friend Weber's distinction between church and sect, and amplified and enriched it, applying it with particular illumination to the Christian medieval synthesis of church and state, and 'sectarian'

---

[4] See Mary Douglas, 'Thought Style Exemplified: The Idea of the Self', in *Risk and Blame: Essays in Cultural Theory* (London: Routledge, 1992), 211–34, and also Douglas's short book, *Thought Styles: Critical Essays on Good Taste* (London: SAGE, 1996). Douglas's late work on cultural typologies might be said to extend Troeltsch's work both creatively and critically. I am much indebted to the late Mary Douglas for her friendship and inspiration in extending my argument in this chapter.

[5] See Max Weber, *The Sociology of Religion* (orig. 1922; Boston, MA: Beacon, 1993), 65. Note that Herbert Spencer and others had long reflected on 'sects' before Weber and Troeltsch (I am grateful to the late David Nicholls for illuminating discussions on this topic).

reactions to it.[6] He characterized the 'church' (in this sociological sense) as a type of organization that is essentially 'conservative', which 'accepts the secular order' and 'dominates the masses'; 'in principle, therefore', says Troeltsch 'it is universal'. But it 'utilizes the state and the ruling classes, and weaves these elements into its own life'. In contrast, the sects are 'comparatively small groups', usually operating in reaction to the (sometimes lax) church, 'aspiring towards inward perfection, and aiming at a direct personal fellowship between the members'. They 'renounce the idea of dominating the world', and indeed their attitude to the world, says Troeltsch, can range from indifference through tolerance to actual hostility. They tend to draw on the lower classes, or 'at least those elements in Society which are opposed to the State and Society'. Members join of their own free will, and through 'conscious conversion'. They are not usually born into the group, as is the case for the church. The sects tend to be eschatological in outlook, firmly scriptural, and less than enthusiastic about sacramentalism. But they also, at least in some circumstances, enable significant positions of leadership for women.[7]

Troeltsch freely acknowledges (and this is particularly important to underscore afresh) that this set of broad-stroke dualities and distinctions in his typology of church and sect is purely heuristic; in practice, he says, these two types 'may often impinge on one another'. But, he claims, 'both types are a logical result of the Gospel, and only conjointly do they exhaust the whole range of its sociological influence'. Troeltsch is thus, I insist again, not

---

[6] Ernst Troeltsch, *The Social Teaching of the Christian Churches* (2 vols.; London: George Allen & Unwin, 1931). The treatment of the relevant medieval material begins at vol. I, 201. The characterizations of 'church', 'sect', and 'mystic' given here all come from the section 'Sect-Type and Church-Type Contrasted', vol. I, 331–43; see also vol. II, 993–4.

[7] See e.g. ibid., vol. II, 809–10, 'The Sex Ethic', for such remarks on gender.

attempting to *explain away* these 'types' of Christianity as mere manifestations of social, political, gender, or class pressure; his primary intent is that of descriptive, observational insight, conjoined with his interesting theological insistence that the 'Gospel' *needs* these complementary expressions.

When he came later to describe eighteenth- and nineteenth-century German Lutheran movements, Troeltsch thought he needed to provide a third type, 'mysticism' (which admittedly is of slightly dubious parity with the other two, and perhaps plays a role somewhat overlapping with Weber's rich notion of 'charisma').[8] However, Troeltsch himself characterized 'mysticism' as a radical religious 'individualism' (and hence the apparent oddity of calling it another form of 'collectivity'). He saw it as tending to resist control by authorities, and as thus representing a certain threat to organized religious forms. It is remainingly attractive, however, he says, to intellectuals of his own day, including himself. Significantly, Troeltsch did not apply the 'mystic' type back to the early church;[9] my own suggestion in the last chapter that we do this acknowledges and accepts the common criticism of Troeltsch that the so-called sociological 'type' of 'mysticism' is more illuminatingly descriptive of certain types of *persons* than of social collectivities, and hence can be found within both of the other types – as a slightly subversive variation founded in profound spiritual commitment, but in turn having significant social effects on those

---

[8] For Troeltsch's initial discussion of the 'mystic' type, see ibid., vol. II, 691–4, 729–45. From the start, however, Troeltsch saw his 'mystic' type as individualistic, whereas Weber's notion of 'charisma' was overtly social in its effects. Arguably Troeltsch should have said more about the social effects (albeit somewhat indirect) of his third 'type': although the 'mystic' is in one sense an 'individualist', s/he undoubtedly also has social *effects*, whether within the church, the sect, or overlapping to the world.

[9] But nor does he apply the chuch–sect typology, *tout court*, until somewhat later in the story. Frankly, Troeltsch did his thinking on the job: the theory quite clearly expanded as he read and wrote, and this is partly why I feel a freedom to extend and tidy his own latent insights futher here.

around it. This seems to me to be a legitimate extension or interpretation of Troeltsch's (somewhat confused) intentions for this 'type', and to allow us to retroject its application to earlier phases in church history than Troeltsch himself did.

Another contemporary way of reading Troeltsch on the 'mystic' type, however (which I myself largely eschew), is to see its characterization as a prescient prediction of a type now called by sociologists the 'cult'. This category is often invoked to illuminate the plethora of contemporary 'new religious movements', which are also profoundly 'individualistic' in ethos; and if the sociologist of religion Meredith McGuire is right, cults are akin to sects in being in a negative relationship to society, but unlike sects in their 'pluralism', that is, in their acceptance of other coexistent cults.[10] My own suggestion, taking these different perspectives into account, is to read Troeltsch in contrast as providing in the 'mystic' type an extra 'woof' to place over the 'warp' of his 'church'–'sect' distinction, but to modify and critique Troeltsch's sole stress on 'individualism' in relation to it. Then it does seem to begin to provide real theological illumination. On this reading the 'mystic' type does indeed represent certain personal and intellectual predilections, but also a great commitment to personalized religious *depth*-within-community; and granted that this 'type' may have developed in various new directions in the contemporary period, what is clear is that it can be found in more than one sociological location as a particular form of intensification of it in terms of spiritual commitment and practice. Hence arose my suggestion in the last chapter that one may find 'mystic'–'church' as well as 'mystic'–'sectarian' forms of religious expression.[11] Such a 'warp' and 'woof'

---

[10] See Meredith B. McGuire, *Religion: The Social Context* (Belmont, CA: Wadsworth, 2002), 185–94.

[11] I believe this rendition to be in tune with at least what Troeltsch is able to clarify by the time he reaches the end of the *Social Teaching*.

understanding of the 'mystic' type's cross-boundary social location makes it, then, very different from McGuire's account of the contemporary 'cult'. The 'mystic' type does not withdraw, but more commonly disturbs and galvanizes the more settled social patterns of its surroundings, whatever they be.

Why is the continuing usefulness of Troeltsch's typological analysis so much disputed? Perhaps the main problems with it in North American scholarship, in particular, come from trying to stretch it to apply to circumstances in which, unlike in medieval Europe or in the established churches of modern Europe, no *one* 'church' dominates society, and thus cannot be identified with it. Hence H. Richard Niebuhr, albeit much influenced by Troeltsch, had to concoct the 'denomination' type to account for the growth and pluralistic acceptance of varieties of Protestantism in the United States, a country after all committed to the separation of church and state.[12] Troeltsch's typology is admittedly also of doubtful, perhaps negligible, helpfulness in *extra*-Christian circumstances, and even within Christianity has to be continually adjusted to account for rapid societal and religious changes (witness the late Bryan Wilson's constant changes of mind about the number of different sorts of 'sectarianisms' needed to do justice to contemporary British forms of religion).[13] But arguably a typology such as Troeltsch's possesses just such a plasticity to social change: it can be illuminatingly configured and reconfigured in a number of ways. Thus, as was already hinted by Troeltsch himself, and had been urged by others too (for instance Joachim Wach, with his sociological

[12] See H. Richard Niebuhr, *The Social Sources of Denominationalism* (New York: Meridian, 1929), 135–64. Niebuhr had earlier written his doctoral thesis on Troeltsch, and Troeltsch continued to exercise significant intellectual influence on him.
[13] See Bryan R. Wilson, *The Social Dimensions of Sectarianism: Sects and New Religious Movements* (Oxford: Clarendon Press, 1990), esp. 46–51.

concept of *ecclesiolae in ecclesia*),[14] *mixed* forms of 'type' can occur, representing dissent from within. Hence, quasi-sectarian movements can sometimes arise, manifesting disenchantment *within* the church type with the prevailing laxity or spiritual enervation of the church, but without actually leaving the confines of the ecclesiastical institution. And what Troeltsch would then call 'mystic' types are not uncommonly found within these ranks. This embellished notion of an *ecclesiola in ecclesia* is, as we shall see, especially illuminating for the fieldwork on the Trinity I conducted, and which I shall now move to describe.

To sum up this preliminary little methodological excursus: while many American sociologists over the years have dismissed Troeltsch's typology as being too cumbersome and fallible to be usefully extended to contexts other than the medieval and early modern Christian one he started with, others, especially more recently in Europe, would continue to support its *intra*-Christian usefulness, at least, as a significant hermeneutic device for analysis and descriptive insight, and as strangely prescient in some regards of fluctuating church–state relations and intra-church tensions in contemporary postmodern Europe. My own interest in it, as a theologian and proponent of *théologie totale*, lies largely in developing the fascinatingly brief (but merely programmatic) remarks Troeltsch makes right at the end of the *Social Teaching* about the patterning of different forms of *doctrine* in line with the different types of social organization he has outlined. Only three pregnant pages[15] are given to this task; but there, with a characteristically flamboyant wave of the hand, Troeltsch outlines what *christology* and *soteriology* might look like in 'church', 'sect', and 'mystic' types of Christianity

[14] Joachim Wach, *Sociology of Religion* (University of Chicago Press, 1944), 173–86.
[15] Troeltsch, *Social Teaching*, vol. II, 994–7.

respectively.[16] It represents a fascinating set of insights into the priorities of different sorts of theological approach and emphasis.

What I am doing, then, in this project of *théologie totale*, is extending this Troeltschian line of argument back to questions about the doctrine of God, and particularly about the place of the Spirit in the Trinity. That is why I wanted to investigate what was happening to the discourses of pneumatology in that wing of the contemporary (sectarian-tending) charismatic movement that had been contained within the 'church' type of Anglicanism, and thus represented a sort of *ecclesiola in ecclesia*, in Wach's sense. Were there any modern parallels here to the patternings, tensions, and theological divergencies I had found in my patristic study on the Trinity? As it happened, my membership of the Church of England Doctrine Commission provided me with precisely the opportunity to explore these questions, as I shall now explain.

FIELDWORK ON CHARISMATICS IN A UNIVERSITY TOWN IN THE NORTH OF ENGLAND

How can one investigate belief in the Trinity (or, more accurately, discourses about such belief) through fieldwork? That was my

---

[16] Thus, for instance, the 'Christ of the Church' is the universal redeemer who continues to work through the settled institutions, ministry, and sacraments of the established church order; the 'Church of the sect' is, in contrast, the stringent 'example and lawgiver' who allows his sectarian followers to pass through 'contempt' in this era, but promises full redemption and vindication at his return in the Kingdom; and the 'Christ of mysticism' is 'an inward spiritual principle, felt in every stirring of religious feeling' (ibid., vol. II, 994). Troeltsch goes on to aver, however, that in his own day only the 'mystic' type has 'produced a truly scientific theology, a real religious philosophy, based on universals, and with a hope of real development before it' (996); but its tragedy is that it 'finds it difficult to establish satisfactory relations with the churches, and with the conditions of a stable and permanent organization' (997). At this point it finally becomes clear where Troeltsch locates himself, somewhat uncomfortably, as a 'mystical' theologian who nonetheless realizes that the 'church' type must also be sustained if Christianity is to continue to have a profound influence on European culture.

question. Some work I had previously done on a British Council of Churches commission on 'Trinitarianism Today'[17] had provided some insight about what would happen if you came at that question directly, with the kind of survey that uses a questionnaire. The sociologist Geoffrey Ahern had been detailed by the British Council of Churches to find out about trinitarian commitment amongst London Christians of a number of backgrounds. In a short report endearingly entitled 'The Triune God in Hackney and Enfield',[18] he reported the unsurprising discovery that, while Christians of denominations officially committed to the doctrine of the Trinity tended to signal *notional* assent to it (they liked hymns that gave a verse to each person of the Trinity in turn, for instance), they were on the whole completely flummoxed if asked to give any cogent account of the doctrine in its developed, ontological form. This was arguably a quite unexceptionable finding, and also not very exciting in sociological terms – if a bit embarrassing for the denominations concerned.

Meanwhile, however, the Doctrine Commission of the Church of England, of which I was also a member, had been asked to write a book on the Holy Spirit. In part this was in response to what were seen in the Anglican hierarchy, I think, as the not totally welcome effects of the charismatic movement upon the Anglican parish system. It was said that Archbishop Robert Runcie had originally called for a series of what he called '*ice-blue* pamphlets on central doctrines of the faith', to be written by his new Doctrine Commission. No one in the commission was ever totally clear what the evocations of 'ice-blue' were in Runcie's own mind (was

---

[17] *The Forgotten Trinity*, ed. Alasdair Heron (3 vols.; London: British Council of Churches, 1989–91).

[18] Geoffrey Ahern, 'The Triune God in Hackney and Enfield: 30 Trinitarian Christians and Secularisation', *Religion Today* 2/3 (1985), 5–6.

he referring to the colour of the covers or the incisiveness of the contents?). But when applied to the doctrine of the Spirit, the message seemed (to me at any rate) depressingly clear: a bucket of cold theological water was to be thrown over the cavorting charismatics who were causing no little disturbance in the Anglican church at the time. Bridling a little at this evident lack of phenomenological objectivity, I offered to do some fieldwork at the highly popular and flourishing Anglican charismatic church in the northern university town in which I then worked (let me here call this parish 'St Matthew's').

This parish had undergone 'renewal' some ten years earlier, and thus could hardly be said to be in the first flush of frothy 'enthusiasm'. I myself had no particular axe to grind theologically, and little sense of what I was likely to find; I simply wanted to see and understand, since I had never visited this church before, but a number of my students were actively and enthusiatically engaged in it. Instead of quantitative questionnaires, I proposed to use 'qualitative' fieldwork methods: participant observation in services, and taped 'in-depth' interviews with a range of informants *representative* (in age, sex, and socioeconomic terms) of the congregation as a whole. As a sociological 'control' I also did a similar, smaller study of a more purely sectarian charismatic 'Fellowship' group in the same town.[19] This had split off from St Matthew's a few years

---

[19] I was assisted in developing this methodology by my then colleagues in the Sociology Department of Lancaster University. To term this study a full 'sampling' of the two congregations involved would perhaps mislead, despite the care taken to choose a range of different sorts of informants, since the number of interviews undertaken was limited: a dozen in-depth interviews were done with individual members of 'St Matthew's', and six with people from the Fellowship group. In some interviews more than one respondent was involved. In choosing my informants I was partly guided by suggestions from the leaders of the congregations, and partly took the initiative myself in inviting people to fulfil representative roles (half the informants were men; half women; about a third in the

earlier, ostensibly on the issue of infant baptism (which it opposed), and was in loose affiliation with the eschatologically oriented 'Restoration Movement', or more particularly the part of it based in Bradford.[20]

In the Anglican St Matthew's, morning worship had now reverted largely to the outlines of the official Anglican liturgy (at this time the Alternative Service Book), after an earlier phase in 'renewal' in previous years of more spontaneous (and sometimes rather uncontrolled) forms of service. All classes and ages were represented in the congregation, but there was now a noticeably dominant middle-class element, mainly from the university community. Clothes were informal, but conventionally neat and clean; indeed the younger men seemed to adopt a near uniform of white or brightly coloured well-pressed trousers, neatly clipped moustaches and strong whiffs of aftershave. This was a 'respectable' congregation. The sartorial dishevelment of the Fellowship group was marked in contrast, reminding me of Mary Douglas's suggestive

professions (clergy, academics, medical doctors); a third artisans or manual workers; and the remaining third students, housewives, or retired people). Likewise, about a third of the informants were under the age of 35, a third between 35 and 50, and a third over 50. All the informants were British and white (at the time, there were virtually no Afro-Caribbean families in the town, and none that I noticed in the two congregations; the town does however have a significant population of well-assimilated Pakistani Muslims). The participant observation in both groups took place over several months in this northern university town in the academic year 1988/9, and taped interviews (carefully reviewed later for analysis, but not transcribed) mostly took place the same year, while some remaining interviews from the Fellowship group were spread into the 1989/90 academic year. Each interview took 60–90 minutes, and was conducted either in the house of the informant or in my own house, depending on convenience for the person or family concerned. I took time at the start of each interview to explain my undertaking, my background, and to answer any questions the informants had about the use I would make of what was said. Formal permission to tape the interviews was received in each case. I also took brief notes while conducting the interviews, and more extensive notes after each one.

[20] A study of this movement as a whole was being researched at about the same time: see Andrew Walker, *Restoring the Kingdom: The Radical Christianity of the House Church Movement* (London: Hodder & Stoughton, 1988).

remarks about the connections between deliberately tatty bodily style and sectarian revolt against the dominant culture.[21]

The members of this latter group tended to be younger Christians (not necessarily younger in age); they also spanned an interesting range of class and educational backgrounds. There were some professional people here too, and a large gathering of students, but in general the ethos was definitely less middle class than in the Anglican congregation. Its leaders were artisans – a builder and a professional gardener. Manifesting a much purer 'sect'-like form than could be achieved within the episcopal structures of Anglicanism, and also a much more rigorous biblical fundamentalism, this group's maintenance of high levels of prophecy and public tongue-speaking in its worship distinguished it from what was now the norm in its Anglican counterpart. Here worship had already become somewhat formalized and sedate before the split-off; and indeed for those who left this was seen as a loss of contact with the Spirit's drive and purpose.

Was this a sign of decline and lack of direction in the Anglicans' case (as the Fellowship tended to read it), or rather a new phase of deepening maturity, a distinct pressure of the Spirit towards a new synthesis with tradition (as the Anglican minister read it)? To try to answer this, I needed to look at the witness of those concerned, and only from there begin to suggest a theological assessment based upon this. What was certain, however, was that we had here a fascinating correlation of sociological and theological factors, different attitudes to the Holy Spirit and prayer being aligned with different socially constituted groupings. To anticipate: the purer 'sect' form of the Fellowship, with its rejection of ordained ministry,

---

[21] For Douglas on 'smooth' versus 'shaggy' sartorial styles, and their social indications, see her *Natural Symbols: Explorations in Cosmology* (Harmondsworth: Penguin, 1973), 102.

commitment to egalitarian exercise of 'gifts' (and yet more strict refusal of teaching roles to women on fundamentalist biblical grounds), expected high feeling states as the norm in public prayer 'in the Spirit'; whereas the Anglican community, with its self-styled hybrid of 'sect'-type and 'church'-type organization (the episcopal structure being combined with lay 'elders' and much other lay leadership, including some cautious use of women in positions of authority), seemed to be moving towards a less sporadic and emotionally dramatic understanding of the Spirit, encouraged by its minister to believe that a new phase of the renewal had been entered, the original 'recovery of gifts' being succeeded by what he called the 'recovery of disciplines'.

Hence, as we shall see, issues about trinitarianism were encoded here, as were also questions about female power. But my formal questions in the interviews were focused primarily on practical matters about the Spirit and prayer. I asked three basic questions to each informant in both communities: about the initial encounter with renewal, about 'tongues', and about difficulties in prayer. (Questions or comments on gender or sexuality were allowed to arise more spontaneously in the discussion.)[22] I shall here report on the interviews tackling each theme in turn, and then comment theologically, ending with a few salient remarks on what also emerged from the interviews about concomitant attitudes to sex and gender.

---

[22] The interviews could thus be described as 'semi-structured'. The initial three questions to all informants were: 1. How did you first come into Christian renewal, and how would you describe prayer 'in the Spirit'? 2. Have you experienced the 'gift of tongues' yourself, and how do you assess the effect of tongues in your congregation? 3. What are the main difficulties you yourself confront in prayer? All informants answered these three main questions in their own ways, but I allowed other matters to emerge spontaneously, including comments on desire, gender roles and sexuality. It is noteworthy that in many interviews these latter issues did arise, despite not being part of the original brief of my Doctrine Commission undertaking.

1. The initial 'experience' of the Spirit

(a) Interviews

It was in questions concerning the initial 'experience' of the Spirit, and the continuing effects of regular prayer 'in the Spirit', that I found least divergence, indeed, negligible divergence, between the two groups. (In part this could of course be explained by the fact that most of the members of the Fellowship whom I interviewed had undergone initial renewal at St Matthew's before splitting from it.) The vexed question of the meaning of 'baptism in the Spirit' was not explicitly raised in the interviews, and, perhaps significantly, was not an issue for polemicizing by either group. But to the general question 'How has your prayer changed since you encountered renewal?', there were answers such as 'There was a sense of new excitement', or, 'It was so delightful to find that it was acceptable to be openly enthusiastic about God'. 'Affective' (positive emotional) states, then, were universally acknowledged, and the sense of a great release of feelings, especially positive feelings of praise and exaltation, that had previously been held back. But even more significant for my question about what in fact characterized the 'experience' of the Spirit, specifically, for these informants, was the reiterated remark that people had in a new way found prayer to be a 'two-way relationship', not just a talking at God, but God (the Holy Spirit) already cooperating in their prayer, energizing it from within, and no less also responding in it, alluring them again, inviting them into a continuing adventure. This was said to be 'the real thing', 'making yourself a channel for the Spirit's work', an intermingling of the human desire for God and the Spirit's interceding to the Father. So, most interestingly, the Romans 8 theme was clearly stated and acknowledged, even made central by these informants. With this then came the sense of prayer 'in the Spirit' becoming a uniting thread in life, 'an all-encompassing relationship', so that prayer became no longer one activity (or duty) amongst others, but the wellspring of all activities. Thus Paul's injunction 'Pray constantly' (1 Thessalonians 5. 17) was said to take on new meaning, as did Jesus's insistence on trust, faith, and confidence in prayer ('Ask, and it will be given you' (Matthew 7. 7)), even though it was admitted that one did not always get what one expected.

(b) Commentary

The actual prayer methods of the people interviewed were enormously varied, as varied as were the people themselves. It was taken for granted that there would be a commitment (indeed an intense commitment) to the usual range of verbal prayers, expressing penitence, praise, petition, and intercession; but beyond that most people also made regular and disciplined use of some sort of scriptural meditation. Moreover, it was striking how ingenious and resourceful people had been in working out structured patterns of praying suitable for their own psychological type or mode of life. One husband and wife had been particularly conscientious in their search for something that suited each of them personally, and afterwards I reflected that their preferred methods of prayer were almost indistinguishable from (respectively) Luther's 'Simple way to pray' (using each phrase of the Lord's Prayer meditatively in turn),[23] and Ignatius of Loyola's 'composition of place' in *The Spiritual Exercises* (thinking one's way imaginatively into a gospel scene).[24] Being of a fundamentalist bent, however, they had evidently preferred not to rely on anything out of 'tradition', but had

[23] 'A Simple Way to Pray', in Martin Luther, *Luther's Works*, ed. Jaroslav Pelikan, Helmut T. Lehman, and Gustav K. Weincke (St Louis, MO: Concordia, 1955–68), vol. XLIII, 193–211.

[24] Ignatius of Loyola, *Personal Writings: Reminiscences, Spiritual Diary, Select Letters including the Text of the Spiritual Exercises*, trans. and ed. Joseph A. Munitiz and Philip Endean (Harmondsworth: Penguin, 1996), 294–5.

painstakingly evolved their own ways in direct interaction with the Bible.

Likewise, it is worthy of comment that the already noted reference to Romans 8 (in relation to the crucial experience of the Spirit praying in one) did not in general lead to any clear and explicit reflection on the importance of this in *trinitarian* terms. The informants assumed without question that the Spirit was in some almost inexplicable way experientially distinct from the Son. But the possibility that this starting point might provide some sort of response to certain 'liberal' Anglican theologians then challenging the Spirit's distinct personal existence, or otherwise dismantling the doctrine of the Trinity, was far from their minds. Such matters did not in fact come up in the interviews. Clearly these theological controversies had not consciously impinged on them at all (as indeed would be true in most parish contexts).

2. The use of 'tongues'

(a) Interviews

My second question to the informants related more specifically to the question of 'tongues'. Here we can indeed chart a distinct difference of emphasis between the two groups studied. For whereas the Anglican charismatics at St Matthew's had now almost ceased to use tongues in public worship (the exception being the occasional, unplanned, and indeed eerily beautiful use of corporate 'singing in tongues'), the Fellowship group deliberately encouraged corporate praise in tongues, especially in the often jubilant and noisy introductions to their services, and claimed a much greater 'cutting edge' and 'specificity', too, to their public prophecies. The divergence may partly have resulted from the departure of some of the more 'activist' worshippers from the one group to the other. But there was also, implicitly, a different reading of 1 Corinthians 14 in play in the two groups. The Anglicans, curbed in public tongue-speaking to some extent by their minister, after some episodes which were thought to be excessive and unedifying, were now preferring in the main to keep their tongue-speaking as a private 'love language' *to* God (see 1 Corinthians 14. 2), having found a plethora of tongues and interpretation somewhat repetitive or trite (see v. 19). In contrast, the Fellowship was much more anxious to exhibit the 'gifts' in their full range (especially tongues and prophecy, understood as sent *from* God), and to witness to 'unbelievers' and potential converts (see vv. 21–5). Here, then, was a noticeable difference in opinion over whether the Spirit's presence always is, or should be, publicly or dramatically manifest.

But in fact it was in the private use of tongues that the most interesting material emerged in discussion with the Anglicans. For it was striking, again, how in certain ways their (very diverse) use of tongues converged spontaneously on certain themes from the contemplative traditions of Christianity, traditions with which most of them were not in any direct way familiar, and indeed against which the fundamentalist convictions of some of them would naturally prejudice them. Thus, whereas the dominical warning against 'vain repetitions' (Matthew 6. 7) made them wary of repetitive or mantric prayer, even of the 'Jesus prayer', they were ready to acknowledge that their 'tongues' often had a repetitive and formalized sound, and could be serving a similar function. Some, indeed, used 'tongues' as a regular discipline of private prayer. A memorable example was a charismatic plumber, who often prayed in tongues as he worked alone. ('There are some very prayerfully laid pipes in this area', he remarked with satisfaction.)

Similarly, whereas some saw silence in prayer as mainly an absence of thought, or a sign of perplexity, and wished to fill such silence with tongues, others could voice the thought that silence could actually be the 'point' or 'end' of tongues, that to which tongues naturally led. (Certainly this could sometimes be witnessed communally in the very sensitive and quiet use of 'singing in tongues' at the evening service at St Matthew's, ebbing away into intense stillness and corporate awareness.) Thus when faced with the charge of the Fellowship group that the Anglicans were losing their 'cutting edge' in playing down their public use of tongues and prophecy, the Anglican minister's response was, 'God is trying to speak to *us*: that should be the feeling.' Others said there had been a certain 'hardness' in some of the more strident public tongues, which had simply 'felt wrong'.

It was the diversity of the application and theological interpretations of private tongues that was most remarkable, however. It was said to be a 'short cut' to God, a direct release of joy or feeling, a way of 'getting out of the way' so that the Spirit could act directly, a prayer for when 'words failed', whether through loss, perplexity or grief, a means of becoming 'like a child' (see Matthew 18. 3), or, used authoritatively, a prayer for warding off danger. While only a few informants were familiar with, or happy with, the psychological language of 'releasing the unconscious' or 'exposing one's inner life' to God, all stressed what they perceived as the healing qualities of this prayer, its directness, and its short-circuiting of normal checks and defences. Above all the theme of 'ceding to the Spirit' was stressed, the way in which tongues averted one's normal and natural tendency to 'set the agenda', especially in the areas of counselling and illness. Tongues were found to reach directly to the root of a problem, so that 'if one did not know what to pray for before, one does afterwards' (see again Romans 8. 26). In sum, it was found in the Anglican community that tongues were continuing to be used in diverse ways, in private prayer, in small house groups, and in the semi-private counselling or healing sessions which attended evening communion. But more overt or spectacular usages of tongues in public contexts had become the prerogative of the Fellowship group.

(b) Commentary

The Anglicans, with almost no exception, were emphatic that tongues were 'not the be all and end all', although they admitted they might not have said that a decade ago (at the beginning of the renewal at St Matthew's). They felt that this gift had 'fallen into place', and it was not necessarily for everyone; whereas in the Fellowship it was expected as 'normal' for all 'real Christians', and seemed to be being used in a much more overt and self-conscious way as an (effective) instrument of conversion alongside the other 'gifts'. Only a few informants, however, knew anything of the instances of 'tongue-speaking' found in spiritual writers dotted through the Christian tradition. Interestingly here, in writers as contextually diverse as the desert fathers and Teresa of Ávila (as the minister at St Matthew's had discovered through his own research), what is noteworthy is how little is made of the phenomenon of tongues: it is simply a natural outflowing of expressiveness in one already deeply committed to prayer. It is recorded of abba Ephraim, for instance, that his prayer was sometimes like 'a well bubbling out of his mouth' (*Apophthegmata Patrum*, Ephraim 2). Over a thousand years later, Teresa's autobiography quite passingly refers to a type of prayer in which 'The soul longs to pour out words of praise ... Many words are then spoken ... But they are disorderly' (*Life*, ch. 16). And there are many other such scattered examples from the tradition, giving the lie to the suspicion that this gift has been totally dormant since the apostolic age. 'Singing in jubilation', likewise, is seen by Augustine and others as a wholly natural way of letting the Spirit pray in one: for 'this kind of singing (*jubilum*) is a sound which means that the heart is giving birth to something it cannot speak of' (*Sermons on the Psalms*, 32.8). What these examples perhaps show, then, is that charismatic gifts within the 'church' type have traditionally not been made much of, but more often assimilated to the contemplative (or 'mystic') mode.

But again, as we have already intimated, only a few of my informants were beginning to take note of the parallelism in charismatic and contemplative traditions, or to explore the burgeoning popular literature on this theme of the 'recovery of disciplines' from such traditions, although this was clearly being encouraged by the Anglican minister (who has since gone on to write a book on renewal peppered with such ecumenical quotations). Once again, then, one felt that St Matthew's was at a point of decision: whether to modify its exclusive biblicism, accept a quieter form of worship, and turn to a broader and more intellectual assimilation of tradition; or whether to reassert the more overtly 'enthusiastic' worship of some years previously, and engage consciously in 'power evangelism' along the lines of the American evangelist John Wimber (who was much discussed in the interviews).[25] A small minority wanted much more public tongue-speaking to re-emerge (and it is significant that a few of these people left the church during the period of this research); others saw its dangers as 'an excuse not to think'. Exactly, however, at the axis of this decision also lie the issues encoded in our third question.

[25] See, e.g., John Wimber, *Signs and Wonders and Church Growth* (Placentia, CA: Vineyard Ministries, 1984).

3. Prayer and failure, prayer and aridity, prayer and depression

(a) Interviews

It was in this area that the greatest ambivalence was found in the interviews, and the ambivalence cut across the two groups. Does 'failure' in prayer, or the common states of dryness ('aridity') and depression when afflicting those who pray, indicate that the Spirit is necessarily inactive or impeded here? Is the Spirit's active work in any sense compatible with human failure and weakness? These were the questions I posited under this last heading.

'Failure' in prayer was confronted movingly in one interview with an Anglican 'elder', an Oxford-educated scientist in late middle age, a man who for long years had wanted to 'come into tongues'. Repeatedly his friends had prayed for this, but to no avail. The same man's wife was also virtually crippled by back pain; again, repeated prayer had brought little relief. It was poignant for me, as the interviewer, to have to ask how he could explain this. His response was that he could only finally 'bow to God's sovereignty'; and in relation to tongues, after great disappointment, he had come to accept 'I've just got to be me, and that's the Lord's job.' When I tentatively enquired whether such evident humility could not itself be a work of the Spirit, he assented, though there was a sense that this was a new idea. (One might juxtapose the thoughts recorded by John Cassian here: 'Wonders and powers are not always necessary, for some are harmful and are not granted to everyone . . . Humility is the queen of all the virtues' (*Conferences*, 15.7).)

Attitudes to aridity in prayer were mixed, too. Many of those interviewed felt that joyousness should be the norm (and in the case of one member of the Fellowship group, this was particularly emphatically expressed); but all when pressed admitted to phases of dryness themselves, most explaining them as correlated to stress or other passing human factors, such as the menstrual cycle. Only one person, interestingly, surmised that dryness might actually be in some circumstances a sign of progress, of the Spirit 'driving one into the desert' to 'sharpen one's thirst' (see Mark 1. 12–13 and parallels). But no sustained explanation of this was made; there was no reference by the informants, for instance, to John of the Cross's detailed explication of this phenomenon as the prayer of 'the night of sense', moving one on into 'contemplation', a form of prayer emotionally less satisfying than before, even felt as a 'failure' to pray, and yet characterized by a continuing and restless desire for God (*Dark Night of the Soul*, 1.8–10).

On depression, however, there was the widest range of response. A minority of people (in both the Fellowship and the Anglican church) felt that depression was largely self-absorption and should be dealt with rapidly and effectively by prayer and exhortation. People in both groups believed in the devil and the demonic but on the whole were not happy with the idea that individual demons caused illness or depression (this was a view powerfully influential in the area, however, as a result of the 'demonic deliverance' liturgies of a 'healing centre' recently established locally: both groups I interviewed were suspicious of this centre and its activities). This sort of localized personification of evil had been deliberately averted by the minister within the Anglican group through his teaching and preaching. In a particularly interesting interview with a psychiatrist, who was also a member of the Anglican congregation, it was admitted that being a Christian was sometimes a distinct 'risk factor' in depression, because of the possible mood swings from a high affective state into the reverse – the rigorous standards imposed upon the self, and the feelings of further guilt if prayer was not effective in relieving the condition. Often she found the best way through was to set aside theological language altogether, and insist 'This isn't a sin problem; you have a health problem that can be effectively treated with drugs.' It was important, then, that religiously committed people should feel no guilt or shame about accepting medication when needed. The same doctor was, however, wary of saying the Spirit could in any way be working actively in and through a depression, especially not through severe psychotic states, although she conceded that 'less severe episodes' could sometimes lead to a 'greater dependence on God'.

In general, then, there was an agreement amongst those interviewed, and especially amongst the Fellowship members, that Christians should not normally be depressed, and that their mood should primarily be characterized by joy. Once again there was only one commentator, the Anglican minister himself, who strongly urged that to demand the continuous maintenance of a high feeling state was actually 'unbiblical'. 'What of Gethsemane, not to speak of the prophets and the psalms?', he parried. The same person distinguished importantly between clinical 'depression' and spiritual 'desolation'. The former he saw as a recognized 'illness', and, just as Jesus had in the gospel stories invariably responded to those who requested healing from sickness, so in this case, too, he believed, the sufferer should rightfully pray to be relieved. In the case of spiritual 'desolation', however (and he admitted depression and desolation might be difficult to disentangle without the discernment of an experienced spiritual guide), one could be confronting the particular activity of the Spirit itself, moving one on into a painful new phase of growth, a sharing in some sense in Christ's own passion.

(b) Commentary

It was clear that here I had reached a theological crux (and I use that word advisedly) in my investigations. If the Spirit's activity was deemed in some sense incompatible with 'low' feeling states, then either a necessarily sporadic understanding of the Spirit's activity was in play, or else there was a lurking dualism (as in the questionably orthodox early fifth-century Macarian homilies, where Satan and the Spirit wage war with equal force for the overlordship of the 'heart', the Spirit being associated particularly with the 'feeling of assurance'). But what then of the possibility of genuinely Christlike dereliction? Could it be that the Spirit would sometimes lead one to this? Such thoughts about the Spirit are of course already foreshadowed occasionally in the New Testament (not least in the Pauline purple passage, Romans 8. 11, 17). But they have been spelled out since then with the profoundest practical and psychological insight by spiritual writers as diverse as Diadochus of Photicē in the East (in the fifth century) and John of the Cross in the West (in the sixteenth century). Diadochus, for whom 'regeneration' in the Spirit is central, speaks of God deliberately 'receding' at times 'in order to educate us', to humble the soul's tendency to 'vanity and self-glory'; through 'feeling ourselves abandoned ... we become more humble and submit to the glory of God' (*One Hundred Texts*, 89, 69). This is somewhat akin to John of the Cross's first 'night of sense', where prayer seems to lose all its former sweetness. Much more terrible, however, is what John describes of the trials and disorientations of the second 'night of spirit', in which God draws so painfully and purgatively close that the experience is akin to that of a log being thrown into a devouring fire (*Dark Night*, II.x). If such as this, then, might truly be an implication of Paul's invitation to be compelled by the Spirit into the sharing of Christ's passion, then it has to be said that such an idea was one which only a few of those interviewed in our survey had begun to reflect upon, if at all.

Here too, then, it may be that the charismatic movement within Anglicanism was facing a dilemma, and one, though earthed in the most practical pastoral issues, that has fundamentally *trinitarian* implications: is the Spirit only to be a 'triumphalist' Spirit, bearer of joy and positive 'feeling'? Or, if this is Christ's Spirit, breathed out of his scarred body, 'one in being' (*homoousion*) with Father and Son, must one not allow as much for the fire of purgation (T. S. Eliot's 'flame of incandescent terror',[26] if you will) as for the refreshment of the comforting dove? Could it be that the acceptance of Christo-morphic *pain* is part and parcel of the full acceptance of trinitarianism in the 'church' type of Christianity?

On this, the Anglican charismatics interviewed in my research seemed poised for an *implicitly* trinitarian decision, increasingly nudged in that direction by the teaching – and newly adopted scholarly reading – of their minister; whereas the Fellowship group, in contrast, strongly resisted the idea of a possible connection between 'low' feeling states in prayer and deepened spiritual and doctrinal maturity. This is, however, an issue that needs more careful reflection, not least because such a move (as those with a well-developed 'hermeneutic of suspicion' will immediately see) could lead to some rather chilling implications for women and underlings in the 'church' type, if they were then exhorted to accept *all* pain and sufferings without demur. This was, however, far from being yet the case in the two communities I studied.

These, then, were the preliminary results of my investigations amongst charismatics of two sorts in a northern university town, and I think they reveal some important new strands in our trinitarian *théologie totale*. Let me now briefly draw together my conclusions on this chapter's investigation.

---

[26] T. S. Eliot, 'Little Gidding', 4, in *Four Quartets* (London: Faber, 1979), 41.

CONCLUSIONS: RICHES AND EMBARRASSMENTS

What my investigations seemed to confirm, first, was the thesis I have already formulated on a historical and textual basis, that 'sectarian' forms of social organization normally go along with a non-trinitarian pneumatology. The sense of the Spirit may be a vibrant one, of a dramatic and powerful visitant, but this visitation is sporadic, and the bearer of *particular* ecstatic manifestations and 'high' feeling states. The complexification of the thesis, however, comes with the Anglican charismatics, because, as we might expect in a Wachian *ecclesiola in ecclesia*, we found the Anglicans *initially* attracted to a sectlike pneumatology, as was still clearly evidenced in the Fellowship; but, over time, and under pastoral pressures of various Christo-morphic kinds (as well as under guidance from a minister increasingly mixing with the ecclesiastical hierarchy and senior members of the university), a nudging towards reflective trinitarianism was evidenced. Quieter worship, a greater respect for 'tradition', and some dawning recognition of the convergence between charismatic and contemplative spiritualities, were significant accompaniments here. Instead of a merely cynical reining back into the rationality of the Logos (suggested in my last chapter as a nervous way of tempering the Spirit's independence), the perception of the Spirit *over time* amongst these Anglican charismatics was more truly affected by implicitly christological issues of prayer and pain, prayer and desolation, prayer and apparent failure. In this way their discourses about the Spirit were subtly changing. If life in Christ, and thus in intimate relation to the Father, necessarily involved such stages of human testing, then it must be consistent with life in the Spirit too, otherwise the 'persons' would be divided. In this way the Anglicans' emergence into conscious trinitarianism was *earthed* in profoundly pastoral eventualities and spiritual testing.

Thus, to return to the social and theological 'patterning' of trinitarianism that I already suggested in my last chapter, perhaps we must now restate its workings in the form of a somewhat paradoxical thesis. Whereas trinitarianism does indeed seem the prerogative of the structured 'church' type, the precarious balancing of the 'mystic' form of this trinitarianism (that which, at the opening of this chapter, I called the pressure to a radical and personally 'assimilated' orthodoxy') is given new life, oftentimes, by slightly *outré* elements within the church type. Reinvigorated trinitarianism – trinitarianism earthed in prayer and pastoral practice, not simply imposed creedally by authority from above – is likely to arise from reforming minorities with at least sectlike *tendencies*, but often also under the influence of leaders with an intellectualist and 'mystic' *attrait*, ones capable of reframing the technicalities of trinitarian thought in line with these pressing personal issues. Whereas, in contrast, merely notional trinitarianism, subscribed to with the lips but not with the heart, is likely to be the result of *loss* of 'enthusiasm', loss of prayer discipline, loss of a vibrant pneumatology: we recall again the evidences of the 'Triune God in Hackney and Enfield'.

Finally, as for women's and gender issues, and attitudes to 'sexuality', these have by no means been forgotten here; but the evidence on these topics in my fieldwork was circumstantial, as I have explained, and also somewhat paradoxical (indeed, rather depressing overall to a contemporary feminist). For the biblical fundamentalism of many of the charismatics (in both groups) led to an effective subordination of women in these congregations, at least where leadership and teaching roles were concerned: the biblical (or rather Pauline and deutero-Pauline) clamp on their potential in these areas was deemed normative.[27] Not that women

---

[27] See, e.g., 1 Cor. 11. 2–16; 14. 33b–35; Eph. 5. 21–33; Col. 3. 18; 1 Tim. 2. 11–15; 5. 3–16.

did not exercise independent, vigorous, and visible ministries of various sorts in both groups, just as Troeltsch would have expected in the 'sect' realm in general; but the problem of 'headship' precluded explicit teaching roles in public in the Fellowship completely, and made it a complicated matter of negotiation at St Matthew's. Ironically, it was the 'church' type of authority in the Anglican group that had led to directives *from above* that women should move towards some minor leadership roles. (There was now one woman elder, for instance, and occasional women preachers: this development had been explicitly promoted by the local suffragan bishop.) This was a cautious, and fairly new, development, and had no counterpart in the Fellowship group. But by now, in the late 1980s, it had become a matter of Anglican order, rather than of sectarian revolt!

As for matters of eroticism and sexuality, although there was some reluctance in both the groups to speak of these things too overtly, it was interesting that the issues came up spontaneously, and quite frequently, in interviews not explicitly devoted to these topics. At least amongst the more mature and articulate Christians in the Anglican group, there was a rather shy admission that regular invocation of the Spirit and a deepening of prayer was likely to lead to an initial intensification of sexual temptation rather than the opposite: the spectre of 1 Corinthians 11, and its attendant problems, still hung visibly in the background. One potential scandal at St Matthew's, I discovered *en passant*, had only been narrowly averted; and it was acknowledged in this regard that the need for spiritual direction and personal accountability in leadership roles, especially, was a strong *desideratum*. In the Fellowship group, too, one of the two leaders was certainly aware of the need for care in this area of such a strong connection of spiritual expansion and *eros*, but acknowledged that this was far from being a conscious arena of teaching in his group, except insofar as standard biblical mores were of course emphasized. On the surface, the erotic realm was heavily policed by traditional biblical values in the Fellowship; the other side of this commitment was the regular occurrence of joyous intra-Fellowship weddings, especially between student members of the group. The breakdown of marriage was, by contrast, almost impossible to discuss.

In sum: my fieldwork investigation had, indeed, discovered both spiritual riches and some theological embarrassments, but not necessarily of the sort I might have expected when I set out on the task. My initial aim, when working for the Church of England Doctrine Commission, had been to educate myself, as far as possible without prejudice, about the impact of charismatics on the Anglican church, and to investigate their theological differences from independent charismatic groups outside episcopal jurisdiction. More theoretically, my attempt was to illuminate implicit doctrinal choices by correlating them to divergent social and ecclesiastical forms. In the case of the former aim, I must record here emphatically in closing the impact that both communities made on me as a theologian: not only was I enormously impressed personally by the spiritual seriousness of the people in both these groups; I was fascinated both by their explicit, and also by their more implicit, *theological* commitments and divergences, as recorded here. If their lack of precise knowledge of technical trinitarian niceties was in some sense theologically 'embarrassing', their fresh spiritual insights and their inadvertent recovery of rich strands in classic tradition were 'treasures' indeed. Yet they were indeed *different* from one another: different in theological priorities, different in social and economic status, different in their attitudes to women and their roles, and – above all – different in the precise content of their learned and taught discourses on the Spirit.

If we return finally to Troeltsch, then: have his sociological insights, and especially his disputed suppositions about a 'mystic' type alongside the 'church' type and the 'sect' type, been newly vindicated in this investigation? In my view, they have. For I did indeed – if this narrative has been effective in its interpretation and its message – encounter patternings of correlated social and theological difference between the two groups strikingly in accord with Troeltsch's insights. And – more subtly – I also hinted at the significance of personal leadership within such groupings which evidenced what Troeltsch came to call the 'mystic' type: the intense personal passion to spiritual depth, the drive to intellectual comprehension, the willingness to offer somewhat uncomfortable leadership beyond what an existing group already entertained. I have also traced more lightly, but afresh, the curious entanglement of such issues of sociological and theological 'types' with pressing questions of gender, sexuality, and female roles of authority.

In Chapter 6 I shall return to the uncomfortable paradoxes we have once more unearthed here – to the tension between biblical directives about the subordination of women, on the one hand, and a 'mystic' trinitarian model earthed in prayer that might somehow transcend and destabilize such subordinationism, on the other. But first there is another piece of the jigsaw method of *théologie totale* that urgently needs to be put in place; for it brings to bear, on the problematic entanglement of desire, gender, and trinitarian thought that has been revisited here, the fresh insights of the world of imagination and of visual symbol. Accordingly, in the next chapter we shall move to a visual and imaginative sphere of theology, and turn an iconographic page in the *théologie totale* by asking: how can one appropriately represent the Trinity as an art form (if at all)?; and what implications does the history of trinitarian *iconography* have for the question of sexual and gender 'subtext' in our theological understanding of divine persons-in-relation? How do power and gender figure in the cultural artifacts of Christian worship of the Trinity, and how do their messages relate to the lessons of deepened spiritual engagement such as I have charted in this chapter? To these issues I now turn.

* * *

BIBLIOGRAPHIC NOTE

RETURN TO SOCIOLOGY OF RELIGION: TROELTSCH AND HIS THEOLOGICAL SIGNIFICANCE

My own work on Troeltsch started with a study of his Christology (*Christ without Absolutes: A Study of the Christology of Ernst Troeltsch* (Oxford University Press, 1988)); and it was there that I first came to understand the under-appreciated *theological* acuity of his great sociological study, *The Social Teaching of the Christian Churches* (2 vols.; London: George Allen & Unwin, 1931). Troeltsch wrote this work in constant conversation with his friend Max Weber, although Weber's views on 'sect' and 'charisma' are significantly different from Troeltsch's: compare Max Weber, *Economy and Society* (Berkeley: University of California Press, 1978); and Max Weber, 'Charismatic Authority' and 'The Routinization of Charisma', in *Theory of Social and Economic Organization* (Glencoe, IL: Free Press, 1947), 358–63 and 363–86. For critically sympathetic recent studies of Troeltsch's work on the *Social Teaching*, see Friedrich Wilhelm Graf and Trutz Rendtorff, eds., *Ernst Troeltschs Soziallehren: Studien zu ihrer Interpretation* (Troeltsch-Studien 6; Gütersloh: Gütersloher Verlagshaus, 1993); Arie L. Molendijk, *Zwischen Theologie und Soziologie: Ernst Troeltschs Typen der christliche Gemeinschaftsbildung: Kirche, Sekte, Mystik* (Gütersloh: Gütersloher Verlagshaus, 1996); and Lori Pearson, *Beyond Essence: Ernst Troeltsch as Historian and Theorist of Christianity* (Cambridge, MA: Harvard University Press for Harvard Theological Studies, 2008).

For critical discussions of Troeltsch's typology of 'church, sect, and mystic', see Theodore M. Steeman, 'Church, Sect, Mysticism, Denomination: Periodological Aspects of Troeltsch's Types', *Sociological*

Analysis 36 (1975), 181–204; W. R. Garrett, 'Maligned Mysticism: The Maledicted Career of Troeltsch's Third Type', *Sociological Analysis* 36 (1975), 205–23; William H. Swatos, 'Weber or Troeltsch: Methodology, Syndrome, and the Development of Church–Sect Theory', *Journal for the Scientific Study of Religion* 15 (1976), 129–44; and K.-F. Daiber, 'Mysticism: Troeltsch's Third Type of Religion Collectivities', *Social Compass* 49 (2002), 329–41. Matthew P. Lawson, 'Sects and Churches, Conservatives and Liberals: Shades of Max Weber in the Sociology of Religion in America, 1904–1993', *Research in the Social Scientific Study of Religion* 6 (1994), 1–33, illuminatingly applies church–sect typology to more recent developments in North America and indicates how Weber's and Troeltsch's insights have been taken up afresh by contemporary sociologists of religion, albeit critically and in a changed key. Crucial in these shifts in North America has been the work of Robert Wuthnow at Princeton: see especially his *The Restructuring of American Religion: Society and Faith since World War II* (Princeton University Press, 1988).

In England, an important programmatic essay by Ian Hamnett published as long ago as 1973 ('Sociology of Religion and Sociology of Error', *Religion* 3 (1973), 1–12) signalled a turn against the presumption that sociology of religion is necessarily anti-theological; and David Martin, *Reflections on Sociology and Theology* (Oxford: Blackwell, 1997) extends this exploration with his characteristic insight.

Two recent compendia on contemporary sociology of religion contain essays on the state of the field in sociology of religion, both methodological and philosophical, and are useful foils for my current retrieval of Troeltsch (as a sociologically *non*-reductive theologian): Bryan S. Turner, ed., *The New Blackwell Companion to the Sociology of Religion* (Oxford: Wiley–Blackwell, 2010); and Peter B. Clarke, ed., *The Oxford Handbook of the Sociology of Religion* (Oxford University Press, 2009).

FIELDWORK TECHNIQUES

I have been guided by a number of studies in qualitative fieldwork technique, both sociological and anthropological. While carrying out my initial investigation of Anglican charismatics my primary guides were: Janet Finch, *Research and Policy: The Uses of Qualitative Methods in Social and Educational Research* (London: Falmer Press, 1986); Alan Bryman, *Quantity and Quality in Social Research* (London: Routledge, 1988); and Kvale Steinar, ed., *Issues of Validity in Qualitative Research* (Lund: Studentlittertur, 1989). More recent works of relevance include: James D. Faubion and George E. Marcus, eds., *Fieldwork is not what it used to be: Learning Anthropology's Method in a Time of Transition* (Ithaca, NY: Cornell University Press, 2009); Michael Herzfield, *Anthropology: Theoretical Practice in Culture and Society* (Malden, MA: Blackwell, 2001); John H. Goldthorpe, *On Sociology: Numbers, Narratives, and the Integration of Research and Theory* (Oxford University Press, 2000); David Silverman, *Interpreting Qualitative Data: Methods for Analysing Talk, Text, and Interaction* (2nd edn; London: Sage, 2001); and Amir B. Marvasti, *Qualitative Research in Sociology: An Introduction* (London: Sage, 2004).

Timothy Jenkins, *Religion in English Everyday Life: An Ethnographic Approach* (Oxford: Berghahn, 1999) has inspired my attempts to combine religious sensitivity and methodological honesty; Mary McClintock Fulkerson, *Places of Redemption: Theology for a Worldly Church* (Oxford University Press, 2007) is another scholar who finds this kind of ethnography creative theologically from a feminist perspective.

I would like to record my gratitude to three younger-generation American sociologists of religion who have helped me develop and refine the methodology of this chapter: Matthew P. Lawson, Paul Johnson, and Michael Lindsay.

THE CHARISMATIC MOVEMENT AND ITS ANGLICAN PENUMBRA

There is a plethora of popular books, both Protestant and Catholic, on charismatic renewal. Amongst the best are Simon Tugwell, OP, *Did You Receive the Spirit?* (London: DLT, 1972); Ian Petitt, OSB, *The God Who Speaks* (London: DLT, 1989); and (from Anglican charismatic circles) Cyril Ashton (with Jack Nicholls), *Church on the Threshold: Renewing the Local Church* (London: DLT, 1991), and Cyril Ashton, *Threshold God: Discovering Christ in the Margins of Life* (London: DLT, 1992). For the British (and especially Anglican) scenario, also see Edward England, *The Spirit of Renewal* (Eastbourne: Kingsway Publications, 1982); *The Charismatic Movement in the Church of England: Report of a Working Group* (London: CIO Publishing, 1981); David Martin and Peter Mullen, eds., *Strange Gifts? A Guide to Charismatic Renewal* (Oxford: Blackwell, 1984); Peter Hocken,

Streams of Renewal: The Origins and Early Development of the Charismatic Movement in Great Britain (Exeter: Paternoster Press, 1986); Colin Craston, ed., *Open to the Spirit? Anglicans and the Experience of Renewal* (London: Anglican Consultative Council, 1987); and Tom Smail, Andrew Walker, and Neil Wright, *Charismatic Renewal: The Search for a Theology* (London: SPCK, 1993).

Recommended studies by historians and social scientists include: Thomas J. Csordas, *The Sacred Self: A Cultural Phenomenology of Charismatic Healing* (Berkeley: University of California Press, 1994); Stephen Hunt, Malcolm Hamilton, and Tony Walters, eds., *Charismatic Christianity: Sociological Perspectives* (New York: St Martin's Press, 1997); Simon Coleman, *The Globalisation of Charismatic Christianity: Spreading the Gospel of Prosperity* (Cambridge University Press, 2000); and Stephen Hunt, *A History of the Charismatic Movement in Britain and the United States of America: The Pentecostal Transformation of Christianity* (Lewiston, NY: Edwin Mellen, 2009).

CHAPTER 5

Seeing God: trinitarian thought through iconography

This chapter is devoted to exploring my supposition that Christian art, and indeed the realm of the imagination in general, must hold an indispensable place in a feminist *théologie totale*. The testing ground for this thesis in this volume will be an examination of significant examples from the history of the iconography of the Trinity. My previous two 'foraging raids' into the tradition (via patristic theories of prayer, and contemporary fieldwork on charismatics) have established revealing social patternings in the history and contemporary practice of trinitarian belief, and have brought to consciousness the 'messy entanglements' of political, sexual, and doctrinal agendas in any such trinitarian thinking and expression. We have by now seen the heady mingling of themes of desire and pain, politics and authority, gender and empowerment, with this normative trinitarian doctrine of the faith in any of its particular manifestations. Both in neglected texts, and in neglected personal narratives from the field, the doctrine of the Trinity has been cast into new light, and it has begun to become clear how many 'levels' of reflection on a central doctrine are relevant to a *théologie totale*. It is now time to investigate the aesthetic realm, the powerful arena of fantasy and of the imagination, and see what this adds further and creatively to our theological reflection.

In moving to examine iconographic expressions of the Trinity, part of what I shall be looking for, first, is some sort of substantiation or supplementation of my thesis of thematic 'entanglement' – in this case between art, gender, politics, and theology. What will become manifest in this chapter is that the visual representation of a doctrine in cultural artifacts (especially one that seeks to portray, as in the Trinity itself, *ideal* divine 'relations') is often hugely revealing of coded and subliminal messages about normative human relations in society, church, and family. 'The medium is the message' indeed; and representations of power and gender that are given as doctrinally 'orthodox', but simultaneously carry all kinds of extra social and political ballast, demand close and critical attention.

But there is also another side to this iconographic endeavour, another basic intention in my project, which is more positive theologically than the 'hermeneutics of suspicion' which must necessarily inform this first, critical approach. And that rests on the assumption that there is a revelatory *irreducibility* about visual symbolism that will not simply translate without remainder into the verbal. 'The symbol gives rise to thought', as Paul Ricoeur's memorable slogan reminds us.[1] That is: art does not simply illustrate doctrine as a kind of anodyne teaching aid for something already settled theologically elsewhere. No, theological art at its best can enable – in a way that on this supposition *only* the arts can – doctrine's creative new expression, animus, and efficacy. And if this supposition is correct, then the artist may be the one on whom one could best and first rely for the creative new redirection of symbolizations of the divine that is still so evidently needed in the contemporary Christian feminist quest. One may well ask, too, in line with the investigations of the last two chapters, whether there is any evidence in the iconographic tradition to connect the 'mystic' type, or contemplative, with such creative symbolic redirections.

---

[1] Paul Ricoeur, *The Symbolism of Evil* (Boston, MA: Beacon, 1967), 347–57.

These, then, are my two main intentions in this chapter: to provide a discerning 'hermeneutics of suspicion' about historic visual depictions of the Trinity, on the one hand, and a quest for creative symbolic trinitarian redirections, on the other.

But it is also important to be clear what I am *not* attempting in this chapter. I am not attempting (and could not in any case attempt in this brief compass) a scholarly survey of all the main available types of visual trinitarian representation in the history of Christian art, with suitable art-historical analyses of them. When I first started collecting slides and pictures of the Trinity, many years ago now, there was a very meagre set of scholarly treatments available on this topic; and it was indeed part of my interest to utilize these materials systematically in the teaching of early Christian doctrine. Some of my discoveries on that score are hinted at in what follows. But since that time, not only have a number of excellent scholarly studies of this topic been published, especially in relation to early Christian art, but also I myself have become clearer about what sort of job this material is intended to do in the particular context of my *théologie totale*. And this I must express carefully. It is important that the reader understands that this chapter should be perused more as a visual and imaginative 'magical mystery tour', with suggestive guiding notes, than as an exhaustive scholarly-historical analysis, with representative illustrations. In other words, if 'the medium' is indeed to be 'the message', let the medium speak here in all its creative messiness and multivalence. The business of detailed scholarly analysis of the art forms will be mentioned briefly when it throws particular theological light; but such scholarly analysis is not the main ambition of my undertaking in this particular chapter. As with the other aesthetic explorations planned for later volumes of this systematics (on poetry, music, and liturgy, respectively), here is the moment in the systematic project when one explicitly invites a certain seepage from the unconscious in one's response to the art form.[2] To allow oneself to be caught off guard, disturbed, intrigued, irritated, freshly inspired or even reduced to mirth by such an experiment is precisely part of the searching of dark corners that my method bespeaks.[3]

But this is why, before we examine the visual itself, a further word about methodology is needed, if only to ward off possible misunderstanding or negative criticism. It is easy for a feminist critic using visual materials to be accused of *eisegesis*, or the 'affective fallacy', so-called. The danger is that she will be dismissed as having merely read anything she wants into the artwork. However, there is a ready answer to this charge. As with the interpretation of texts, so with the interpretation of art (as Hans-Georg Gadamer argued magisterially in his great study of hermeneutics): all interpretation involves a 'fusion of horizons' which is never *merely* the recapitulation of the original meaning of a text or work of art. But it is worth recalling that Gadamer himself is careful, too, to distinguish such an 'horizon' from a mere ideological prejudice,[4] and this is a vital point for providing a nuanced defence of feminist art-historical assessments. As Gadamer writes: 'A person who has no horizon is [one] who does not see far enough and hence *overvalues* what is

---

[2] That is why, at the end of Chapter 2, I described the endeavour in this chapter as a kind of 'semiotic' interlude – an opening up of the unconscious realm.

[3] My first public use of this material was in 1988 at the Lambeth Conference, during a session organized by Mary Tanner on feminism and the Anglican communion. Visual images of the Trinity were projected on to the big screen while I supplied theological comment and the assembled bishops watched in darkness. The effect for some bishops on their assessment of feminist critiques of 'patriarchy' was forceful and positive; others were shocked and irritated and a few left the assembly in protest. Overall, however, the experiment was judged a success: approaching feminist theological questions via visual images of the divine cut through standard defences in a remarkably powerful and creative way.

[4] In fact Gadamer himself uses the German word *Vorurteil* ('pre-judice' or 'pre-judgement') in a positive sense; but the contrast I am myself after here will be clear.

nearest.'[5] So one must be careful, on Gadamer's understanding, never simply to *impose* a hasty contemporary agenda on artistic interpretation without at least initial sensitivity about a number of factors that may illuminate the origins and history of an artifact's meaning. Such a sensitivity (to social, political, or liturgical contexts) is of course also entirely in line with the goals and methods of a *théologie totale*.

Thus, certain contextualizing questions will always play in the background as one considers a striking representation of the Trinity. Do we, for instance, possess accompanying texts or rituals that throw light on the original placing and meaning of the artwork? What iconographical conventions were in play in its original creation? What were the intentions of the donors of the artwork (if known)? What light does the original social or political context throw? But just as importantly: how was the work then received and used? And in its contemporary reception, how is it now responded to artistically and theologically? Rather differently, and in terms of aesthetic response, how is the eye directed as one examines the artwork – upwards, downwards, round and round – and what might this convey theologically? More contentiously, certainly, but not I think to be ruled out a priori: how might one adjudicate on psychoanalytic interpretations, such as Carl Jung's on the Trinity (which I shall explore briefly but critically below); or on the central theme of post-Lacanian French thought (already discussed in Chapter 1) that artistic expression, when not wholly dominated by the history of male 'masters', allows space for a (so-called) 'feminine' form of creativity to cut *through* the normal conventions of verbal discourse?

[5] Hans-Georg Gadamer, *Truth and Method* (London: Sheed & Ward, 1975), 269, my emphasis.

In what follows, then, I shall attempt to avoid any eisegesis of the crass sort (such as would count as a 'prejudice' in common English parlance); and occasionally I shall allude to as much of the background or social context of a painting, icon, drawing, or sculpture as scant space allows here, providing further leads for investigation in the bibliographic note that follows. But I certainly shall not feel obliged to rest solely with the so-called 'original' meanings of these artworks, even supposing we could establish those with any degree of certainty. And that, as we shall see, is in any case often a moot point. For art by definition often escapes such controlled analysis: that, ultimately, is the point of this 'semiotic' interlude.

THE TRINITY IN CHRISTIAN ART: AN INVITATION TO THEOLOGICAL RESPONSE

It is however possible by way of introduction to the visual materials presented in this chapter to say something about a few main themes that confront anyone who explores the doctrine of the Trinity through the lens of art. Being pre-advised of these points of interest can genuinely contribute to one's appreciation without dictating particular responses.

The first, and fascinating, point is that the iconographical evidence concerning early representations of God as Trinity by no means obviously coheres, historically speaking, with the development of the doctrine of the Trinity as it is characteristically presented in the history of ideas, or in the textbook accounts of early church theology. The dominant early iconographical motifs (first, the baptism scene of Christ of Mark 1. 9–11 and parallels, in which the Father's voice, the Son, and the Spirit all feature; and secondly the so-called 'Old Testament Trinity' of Genesis 18. 1–10, in which three mysterious angels appear to Abraham and Sarah) are both *tritheistic*-tending visually, as well as having an anthropomorphic emphasis on the male figures involved. And there is no obvious or clear shift of gear in the fourth century, as we might expect, in the face of the debates of the later Arian controversy, into a new interest in stressing the *homoousian* unity of the three 'persons' visually. (In fact, one of the great fascinations about the iconography of the Trinity *in toto* is how one can hope to express the divine *ousia* appropriately at all in visual terms.) Some long time after the normative propagation of trinitarian orthodoxy in the late fourth century, then, we still find free-wheelingly scattered symbolic representations of the trinitarian 'persons' simply plastered together: there is a complete lack of embarrassment about this seeming freedom and 'unorthodoxy' in visual terms. This is surely in itself highly significant and worthy of theological comment: it bespeaks a kind of symbolic excess in aesthetic responses to the Trinity which the church not only tolerated but actively condoned. When we remember that many of the Christian church's adherents at this time were illiterate, or at least too poor to possess expensive scrolls to read at home, this feature of aesthetic and liturgical life – which for many would have dominated over private reading of theological texts – is all the more marked in its significance.

Secondly, when more studied attempts at greater doctrinal correctness in representations of the Trinity do appear, especially in the medieval period in the West, the results are now usually somewhat ridiculous, if not actually grotesque, to our modern consciousnesses. Moreover, when they become over-didactic and quasi-geometrical in their attempts at theological precision, the unintended effect is seemingly often a collapse back, for the popular mind, into an effective unitarianism of the (male) Father figure: the theological effort of understanding trinitiarian 'relations' and 'processions' is seemingly too abstruse to root itself successfully into the symbolic imagination.

All this serves as a fitting reminder of what can, and cannot, be attempted in the business of visual divine representation – what *can* be stated and painted, and what cannot. What we find, however, is that the richest and most suggestive symbolism for God as Trinity often goes along with what might be called an appropriately 'apophatic' corrective reminder. The most 'successful' visual representations of the Trinity, that is, do not attempt to *describe* what it is like *chez God*,[6] but rather to stir the imagination, or direct the will, beyond the known towards the unknown, prompting symbolic 'hints half guessed'.

Thirdly, the gender and political themes in these representations will doubtless speak for themselves, although they may remain contentious hermeneutically, and thus open to further debate. Such associative themes become most obvious in the later Middle Ages, when Greek East and Latin West start to diverge fascinatingly in iconographical theory and convention, not least over the vexed issue of the Trinity's 'processions',[7] and over the place and significance of their iconic representation. In the West, a new location of the Trinity, visually, in the events of the cross, now puts *pain and death*, and the relations of the (anthropomorphically male) Father and Son, to the fore; there is then, as even from the start in the early baptism theme, a danger of the Spirit's near redundancy, a loss of the 'third'. The simultaneous 'feminization' of the Spirit in some paintings, and the regular replacement of the Spirit by the Virgin Mary, represent important implicit relocations of female power and presence, but arguably serve more to shore up cultural stereotypes of 'femininity'

---

[6] To use a memorable phrase of my colleague Janet Martin Soskice.

[7] That is, the modes of relationship and mutual implication between the divine 'persons'. For considered reflection on this matter for the purposes of this systematic project, see Chapter 7. The visual materials in this chapter are however remarkably revealing of various symbolic alternatives, both 'successful' and theologically misleading.

rather than dissolve them. There are, however, exceptions to this rule in which the dominance and forceful beauty of the place of the Virgin presents a different visual impact.

In Eastern iconography of a similar period, in some contrast, what I termed in Chapter 3 the 'mystical' rendition of an 'incorporative' vision of the Trinity, finds *some* unofficial mode of instantiation iconographically, on my rendition, in the 'Three Ages of Man' icon, with its trinitarian overtones, as well as in its feminized counterpart in the 'Anna Trinity' (in which St Anne, the Virgin, and the Christ child are portrayed in the same spatial relations). The Spirit is in much less danger of neglect here than in most Western counterparts; but the visual 'hierarchalizing' of the 'persons' (to 'match', if you like, the layered order of the Byzantine state and church), is deeply redolent of those ecclesiastical arrangements, and thus reminds us at least as much of the 'linear' model of the Trinity as of the 'mystical'. Indeed, in all these themes, which present themselves evocatively via the artwork, we shall find recapitulations of theological issues discussed in earlier chapters, but often with fascinating new twists, elisions, and emphases inviting further thought.

THE ARTWORK

One further introductory reflection must guide us throughout our tour of the trinitarian artwork. For the whole story of Christian art, of course, *starts* with an apophatic silence or visual erasure in the first two centuries of the Common Era; and this beginning may in itself prove abidingly significant for our reflections on art and the Trinity. Before the third century there is no 'Christian art' as such at all,[8] whether on

---

[8] Unless one counts, for example, a possible crucifix at the site of Pompeii, or a *graffito* at Rome ridiculing the crucified 'God' of the Christians, both dating from the first century CE.

account of a Jewish fear of idolatry, a political fear of persecution, or a Hellenistic squeamishness about materiality. The mystery of this early aniconism remains disputed, as is often the case in 'arguments from silence'.[9] But in the world of the third-century Roman catacombs, Christian art suddenly bursts forth for the first time; and we enter a magical new realm of visual symbolic allusion: Old Testament typology for Christian salvation dominates, haunted always by the themes of death and new life in Christ. And immediately, visual suggestions of the emerging Christian trinitarian belief start to appear. But they are only such – intimations and allusions – at first. Let us start our tour of visual trinitarianism, then, in third-century Rome.

In third-century catacomb art (see Figure 1) we already meet nascently the two basic and original loci of visual trinitarianism in the Christian tradition: this so-called 'Old Testament Trinity' of Genesis 18. 1–10 (Abraham welcoming the three mysterious angels, which have more anonymous variations later which I shall call the 'identical triplets' representation); and the scene of Christ's baptism, which takes us back to the 'economic' history of the Trinity as it unfolds in Christ's ministry.[10] In both these types of catacomb representation, anthropomorphic visualization dominates – although in this rough catacomb wall painting the angels are decidedly ungendered.[11] But it is also important to acknowledge that in neither of these early types of representation in the catacombs is there any obvious or fully developed *trinitarian* assumption in play. It has been shown, for instance (through an analysis of

[9] I prefer the anti-idolatry argument: see the discussion (admittedly controversial) in Paul Corby Finney, *The Invisible God: The Earliest Christians on Art* (Oxford University Press, 1994), esp. 15–98.

[10] One may find the earliest examples of the baptism scene already in catacomb art: see, e.g., Robin M. Jensen, *Living Water: Images, Symbols and Settings of Early Christian Baptism* (Leiden: Brill, 2011), figure 1.1 on 12.

[11] Unlike the later Western medieval representations of three identical men or boys: see below, e.g., figs. 17, 28, 29.

1. The catacomb of the Via Latina, Rome: Abraham's vision at Mamre
(Genesis 18), third century

relevant patristic *texts* on Genesis 18 at the time), that the trinitarian
gloss was by no means dominant in the early period: a reading of
Genesis 18 in terms of angelology or christology was just as usual.[12]
The sense conveyed however is that, for these painters, 'God' still
primarily connotes the *Father*, and suitable care is being taken not to
attempt to represent him directly at all.

Some three centuries later, in the sixth-century Rabbula gospels
of Syriac-speaking provenance (with its emphatically high doctrine

[12] On this point, see Lars Thunberg, 'Early Christian Interpretations of the Three Angels in
Gen. 18', *Studia Patristica* 7 (1966), 560–70.

of the Spirit; see Figure 2),[13] the fiery association of the Spirit is interestingly maintained alongside the dove at the baptism of Christ. But it is important to underscore that, by this time, this fiery trait was the exception rather than the rule. In general, after Nicaea in the empire (except in direct representations of Pentecost), that association of power and fire with the Holy Spirit was lost iconographically. Looking ahead, we may see that loss as significant: the more 'cooing' and self-effacing the dove as Spirit, the more danger of its quasi-'feminization', or (perhaps the same thing) its near redundancy. But such is not the danger in this Syriac-speaking context. Note here too, in the Rabbula gospels, the convention of the hand from the heavens, which, as in the multiple hands painted in the Jewish synagogue at Dura Europos,[14] represents the Father's active intervention but without any direct visualization of him.

In the Ravenna baptistery of the Arians (Figure 3), in contrast (also from the sixth century), a youthful Christ is flanked (seemingly to achieve visual balance) by John the Baptist and a male personification of the River Jordan, based on pagan prototypes. This is not the last time, as we shall see, that extraneous anthropomorphic figures enter the 'trinitarian' magic circle (here understood only in a derived, Arian sense). The effect, of course, is of a more demonstrably *male*

---

[13] The fiery rendition of the Spirit's work is especially evident in the poetic theology of the third-century Syriac authors Ephrem and Aphrahat, and that same emphasis also finds memorable expression in the early fifth-century Macarian homilies. In the early Syriac tradition the baptism of Jesus is also interpreted as his simultaneous 'ordination', as may be also suggested in this artistic representation. For relevant discussion, see Robert Murray, SJ, *Symbols of Church and Kingdom: A Study in Early Syriac Christianity* (2nd edn; London: T&T Clark, 2006), esp. 80–1, and S. P. Brock, *Holy Spirit in the Syrian Baptismal Tradition*, Syrian Churches 9, ed. J. Vellian (Poona: Anita Printers, 1979), esp. 11–14.

[14] See Kurt Weitzmann and Herbert L. Kessler, *The Frescoes of the Dura Synagogues and Christian Art* (Washington, DC: Dumbarton Oaks Research Library and Collection, 1990), plates 4, 7, 49, 152, 177–9.

2. Christ's baptism in the Rabbula gospels, sixth century

3. Baptism of Christ, Baptistery of the Arians, Ravenna, *c.* 500

configuration, but also of a perplexing but powerful syncretism of
Hellenic river gods and biblical figures. Perhaps particularly in imperially supported Arian circles, art could allow what – elsewhere –
'orthodoxy' would not.

4. A 'Trinity' of British divinities (mother goddesses?): *Genii Cucullati* (hooded deities), Housesteads Fort, Northumberland, third century

The trouble is, of course, that these two earliest types of 'trinitarian' representation that we have now looked at (the 'Old Testament Trinity' and Christ's baptism) show no obvious means of achieving any idea of *homoousian* unity at all. The religious imagination could easily be accused (and this well after fourth-century 'orthodoxy' had been achieved, but then fought over in successive waves of Arianism) of veering towards *tritheism* – as in the delightful British divinities from the Roman wall at Housesteads, suitably dressed up for the Northumbrian weather (Figure 4). Long-existent pagan alternatives of such a tritheistic kind were not hard to find, especially in the Middle East,[15] and could easily seem to be echoed in any representation of the Trinity that

---

[15] Representations of the Egyptian gods Isis and Osiris with a bird are especially suggestive parallels: see Sylvie Cauville, Jochen Hallof, Hans van den Berg, OSA, Alain Lecler, Mohamed Abou el-Amayem, and Yousreya Hamed, *Le Temple de Dendara: la porte d'Isis* (Cairo: Institut Français d'Archéologie Orientale, 1999), plates 18, 70.

merely painted three identical figures, or two such figures with a third attendant of some sort.

Occasionally, in the early Christian period, however, a flash of *sui generis* artistic genius and originality breaks through the mould of convention and of dominating male anthropomorphism. One striking example is a mosaic of 'Christ's monogram in a circle of doves', from the mid-fifth-century baptistery at Albenga (Figure 5). The *Chi-Rho* symbolism representing Christ and his cross cuts across and through three (trinitarian) concentric circles with Alphas and Omegas, also representing Christ but in his eternal relation to the Father. Twelve apostolic doves indicate the spiritual overflow into the world of Christlike life in baptism. Hence the Spirit, far from being neglected here, is alluded to, summoned, and *replicated* in the apostolic effects of baptism. The particular visual impact of this circular vision of God, as well as its simultaneous 'mandala'-type symbolism of the self (if one is favourably disposed to psychoanalytic readings),[16] is something we shall have reason to reflect on further shortly, for it seems to have particularly powerful resonances for the evocation of transformed Christian life.

Rather different, but no less unique and effective, is the 'throne of God as a trinitarian image', in Saint Prisca, Santa Maria Capua Vetere (in Campania) (Figure 6). As André Grabar notes in his own commentary on this representation, it too has the quasi-tritheistic 'defect of . . . using symbols that do not take into account the idea of the identity of the three persons';[17] but a modern feminist might add, by way of compensatory riposte, that at least it does not fall

---

[16] For an introduction to Carl Jung's theories on the mandala as symbol of the self, see *The Portable Jung*, ed. Joseph Campbell (Harmondsworth: Penguin, 1976), 323–455, esp. 324–9 (on the mandala) and 434–6 (on the functions of the self).

[17] André Grabar, *Christian Iconography: A Study of the Origins* (London: Routledge & Kegan Paul, 1969), 115.

5. Christ's monogram in a circle of doves, mosaic from the baptistery,
Albenga, 450–500

into any crass male anthropomorphism for God.[18] Indeed, its
approach to visual trinitarianism is one of some subtlety and

---

[18] In the classic words of Mary Daly, 'If God is male, the male is God', in *Beyond God the Father: Towards a Philosophy of Women's Liberation* (revised edn; Boston, MA: Beacon, 1993), 19.

6. The throne of God as a trinitarian image, Saint Prisca,
Santa Maria Capua Vetere, early fifth century

imaginative power. By indicating the mysteriousness of the 'Father' – this time by an empty throne (empty, that is, except for the Word's equally mysterious presence in the form of a scroll whose reading must be *heard*) – it again signals an apophatic dimension, a space which cannot be filled by idolatrous imagery but only by attending to the gospel. Further, the dove-Spirit is by no means here neglected, but loomingly guards, and seemingly protects, the space of the Father–Son mystery, thereby perhaps indicating a brooding presence which sustains the divine unity.

Possibly more fascinating still is the reconstruction, by Robert Murray (from iconographic bits and pieces that will be familiar to those who know the sixth-century mosaics of Rome and Ravenna),[19] of the destroyed basilica of Nola, contrived and described in considerable detail in a poem by St Paulinus (353–431) in his Letter number 32 to Sulpicius Severus (Figure 7). What is so intriguing here is the

---

[19] Especially the allusions to the mosaics of Sant'Apollinare in Classe, Ravenna: see Antonio Paolucci, *Ravenna* (London: Constable, 1971), 57–66.

7. St Paulinus' mosaic of the Trinity at Nola, fourth to fifth century:
a reconstruction by Robert Murray, SJ

quite unashamed, but arguably mutually corrective, uses of a number
of *different* symbolizations for each divine 'person'. 'Christ is represented by a lamb', writes Paulinus, 'the Father's voice thunders forth
from the sky, and the Holy Spirit flows down in the form of a dove. A
wreath's gleaming circle surrounds the cross [representing *another*
dimension of Christ in his earthly life, note], and around this circle
the apostles form a ring, represented by a chorus of doves'. 'The holy
unity of the Trinity *merges in Christ*', goes on Paulinus – perhaps
somewhat unconvincingly in terms of doctrinal exactitude: 'but the
Trinity has its three-fold symbolism'.[20] This, indeed, is symbolization
of the Trinity by a form of mutual bombardment of images, a strategy
to which we shall have reason to return in due course for further, more
sustained, theological reflection. But whether it really succeeds in

[20] Paulinus of Nola, Letter 32.10 (my emphasis), in *Letters of Paulinus of Nola* (ACW 35–6; 2
vols.; Westminster, MD: Newman, 1966–7), vol. II, 145.

conveying any obvious sense of divine *unity* is highly questionable, despite Paulinus' poetic attempts to stress such. What is once more so noteworthy, then, is the apparent official acceptability of such a public artistic visualization when it was ostensibly, at any rate, so far from obvious *homoousian* orthodoxy. Yet under this apse at Nola the holy sacramental mysteries were celebrated, and the faithful adored a vision of God that doubtless impinged on their consciousnesses at least as powerfully as the biblical words and theological commentary they heard declaimed from altar and pulpit.

One is thus left musing, in this early period of Christian art, on the relationship of written or spoken creedal precision in matters of trinitarianism (which had, after all, cost the church dear theologically and politically), and a notable range of mandated artistic licence in expressing the same truths. The relative lack of ecclesiastical control, and the free play of imagination and symbolic bombardment manifest in the most creative and thought-provoking examples of visual trinitarianism we have already surveyed, stood in contrast to the more stylized representations of the 'Old Testament Trinity' and the baptism scene, which themselves made no obvious attempt to conjoin the three 'persons', despite the various attempted allusions to divine (Fatherly) intervention and mystery.

When we turn, in contrast, to specifically Western developments in the later Middle Ages, new types of visual trinitarianism appear and rapidly become dominant. They are on the one hand more daring in their implication of the divine Trinity in the sufferings of Christ, and on the other hand evidence a greater concern (sometimes an almost laughably pedantic concern) about doctrinal orthodoxy and precision.

It is in the new so-called 'Throne of Grace' (*Gnadenstuhl*) representation of the Trinity, emerging in the thirteenth century, that the events of the cross start to dominate trinitarian visualization and conceptuality in the West. Figure 8 shows one of the earliest of

8. Throne of Grace, Wiesenkirche Altar, Soest, *c.* 1250–70

this type from the mid thirteenth century; but examples are manifold from about 1400 CE onwards. Daring at the time, as Gertrud Schiller underlines, this type of trinitarian representation was at first developed in relation to a new theological emphasis on the outworkings of the eternal Trinity in the life and death of Jesus (the so-called *opera sanctae trinitatis ad extra*).[21] But in visual effect, and well before Luther's celebrated theology of the cross, this visual type of the Trinity seemingly welcomed the wounded human Christ into the inner life of the eternal Godhead, at a period of intense European suffering through famine, plague, and political strife. Thus Christ here simultaneously becomes the elevated *corpus Christi* of the eucharistic sacrifice.[22] The emphasis, note, is not – at least initially – on an empathetic Father, but on a stern and merciful acceptance by him of the 'satisfaction' for sin effected in Christ's death. And all the drama in this early example of the *Gnadenstuhl* resides in the relationship of the (all-male) Father and Son; the Spirit, we might say, is virtually redundant to the theme, and indeed is unmentioned in the biblical narratives of the cross (except perhaps by indirect allusion in the gospel of John to the outflowing of water, as well as blood, from the body of the dead Christ).[23]

Hence it is not surprising to find the Spirit actually missing form this *Gnadenstuhl* visual type on occasion. As my former colleague in medieval studies at Lancaster University, Meg Twycross, used to

[21] See Gertrud Schilller, *Iconography of Christian Art* (2 vols.; London: Lund Humphries, 1971), vol. II, 219–20.
[22] On this important medieval transition to a profound emphasis on the sufferings of Christ in both theology and art, see R. W. Southern's famous essay, 'From Epic to Romance', in his *The Making of the Middle Ages* (London: Pimlico, 1993), 209–44.
[23] See John 19. 34, in which Christ's body is pierced to prove that he is already dead. But perhaps even John himself already intends a double entendre: the blood and water that flow out may also indicate the sacraments of eucharist and baptism (with a special allusion to the Spirit in the latter).

say of this form of trinitarian representation: 'Hunt the pigeon!'; for the dove is often small, shadowy, and hard to see. In the case of Figure 9 the Spirit has disappeared altogether, being seemingly unnecessary to the immediate text and context. This may be an unintended consequence of the popularity of the *Gnadenstuhl* visual representation of Trinity. But one might hypothesize that it also witnesses to a less than vibrant pneumatology in the theological thinking that attends the type. There was, however, to be a striking pneumatological corrective in a slightly later variation on this popular theme, which also more daringly stressed the 'impassible' Father's affective compassion for the Son.

This significant variation on the *Gnadenstuhl* representation of the Trinity, termed by the iconographers the *Not Gottes* (The Pain of God), emerged originally in Burgundy at the very end of the four-teenth century, and acted as a certain corrective and theological extension to the earlier form. Figure 10, by an anonymous 'Master of Danzig', is somewhat later, dated 1440. Here the Father supports the *dead* Christ, note, and the Spirit is accorded a somewhat more prominent position. According to Gertrud Schiller (although I am somewhat doubtful about both the theological orthodoxy and the historical veracity of this interpretation), the dove here 'was added to mark the divinity of Christ who was to all appearances dead'.[24] Certainly the dove visually represents a linking force between an ostensibly separated Father and Son at this moment of death and deposition; but since the Spirit itself is not incarnate, only the Son can actually undergo death. Nonetheless, the new configuration of the 'persons' in this type of trinitarian representation possibly begins to *suggest* full divine implication in human passibility, even though that was, and remains, technically 'unorthodox' if it is applied directly to

---

[24] Schiller, *Iconography*, vol. II, 220.

9. Initial D and God the Father enthroned, English psalter, mid fourteenth century

10. *Not Gottes* (The Pain of God), anonymous master, St Mary, Danzig, 1440

the Father. It is another example of art seemingly outstripping technical orthodoxy to make a striking spiritual point. This trend is only intensified in later manifestations of this same visual type, as painterly conventions further bend towards new humanistic realism.

Thus, in the quite differently expressed conventions of later Renaissance art, El Greco's variation on this *Not Gottes* theme (Figure 11) achieves, it must be said, a profoundly affecting

11. *The Holy Trinity*, El Greco, 1577

compassionate vision of the Father, causing Elisabeth Moltmann-Wendell and Jürgen Moltmann (in their jointly authored feminist volume, *Humanity in God*) to eulogize what they see as his 'motherly' features.[25] But this is a case where I think we do have a rather clear instance of contemporary eisegesis, and one with gender associations which may well not achieve the intended goals, even of the Moltmanns themselves. For one may well question whether a 'motherly Father', as supposedly in this representation, is a *desideratum*, if what this means is that such a Father is *good* at empathetic suffering. For then the result is actually a reassertion of a particular societal stereotype about 'femininity' or motherhood, and one surely not intended by the artist himself.[26] El Greco's 'Father' is indeed of remarkably compassionate and affective visage; but there seems to be no good iconographical, historical, or theological reason to insist that this compassion is specifically '*motherly*'. The gender themes we may choose to find encoded in such representations must at least bear the test of critical, self-reflexive scrutiny.

And that is why we also have to be careful when we come to reflect on the encoded messages about intense or bloody pain and suffering which emanate from the trinitarian (or non-trinitarian) representations of the cross in the late medieval West – a matter on which the East already had misgivings at the time, preferring its own more measured iconographic conventions. Figure 12 shows an earlier variation on the *Gnadenstuhl*, the theme of 'Christ in the Winepress', which was highly popular on the eve of the Reformation, and does indeed emphasize with almost shocking force the sacrificial pain at the heart of Christ's eucharistic self-offering.

---

[25] See Elisabeth Moltmann-Wendell and Jürgen Moltmann, *Humanity in God* (London: SCM, 1984), esp. 40–50.

[26] This is to repeat a concern already mentioned in Chapter 1: see especially the second subsection in the bibliographic note.

12. *Christ in the Winepress*, anonymous master, Bavaria, *c.* 1500

The Spirit, note, is absent, and therefore – in comparison with the softened visage and pneumatological presence of the later *Not Gottes* – the visual impact of the Father–Son relation is quite differently conveyed. But *is* this a twisted exaltation of pain which might be termed sadomasochistic – 'S and M theology', as the radical feminist Mary Daly famously insisted? Is it the regrettable replacement of the pagan mythological 'tree of life' with a masculinist 'torture cross', as she put it?[27] Such was clearly far from the minds of the original viewers, for whom the eucharistic wine – and thus the life-giving divine locus of salvation – would have been central at a time of great European turmoil and sickness. But it is certainly appropriate today to ask more probing questions about the apparent legitimation here of pain and physical punishment *in the very life of God*; for unlike the theological texts of the time which discoursed on 'satisfaction' for sin, visual representations added to that the *particular* evocations of painterly expression in the Father's and Son's faces. And these could be very various and suggestible.

So perhaps even more strikingly in this regard, in Hans Holbein the Elder's memorial for Augsburg (Figure 13), painted right on the eve of the Reformation, are these themes of pain and punishment writ large, and now attended by an extra layer of explicit gender associ-ation. The vengeful Father here sheathes his sword, but only in the face of the pleadings of the Son's wounds and the Virgin's baring of her breast. (Note how the Virgin has here *replaced* the near redundant Spirit.) Above the Man of Sorrows are the words: 'Father, see my red wounds, help men in their need, through my bitter death'. Above the Virgin we read: 'Lord, sheathe thy sword that thou hast drawn and see my breast where the Son has sucked'. The pleadings thus establish a hierarchy of significance: the Virgin's significance resides in her pointing away from herself to the Son, and thence to the Father. Underneath, the faithful line up in what Paul Tillich once called the medieval 'mystic' view of the crowd. As Tillich put it: 'The crowd is completely dominated by the over-arching idea that it represents'.[28] For there is no personalized individuation in the crowd here. Note

[27] See Mary Daly, *Gyn-Ecology: The Metaethics of Radical Feminism* (Boston, MA: Beacon, 1990), 73–105.
[28] Paul Tillich, *On Art and Architecture* (New York: Crossroad, 1987), 9.

13. Hans Holbein the Elder, memorial, Augsburg,
the Man of Sorrows and Mary intercede, 1508

that all the women are arranged under the Virgin, the men under the Son. From a modern feminist perspective we might well want to ask: what sort of vision of ideal male or female existence is here presented to the viewer? Does the male viewer identify primarily with the Father, or the Son (or both)? What messages for women are encoded in the Virgin's pleading posture?

Again, in Figure 14, a slightly earlier painting of the Man of Sorrows and Mary, the Virgin effectively replaces the Holy Spirit in this quasi-trinitarian image, in which the Father is represented as an episcopal or papal figure. Yves Congar OP is amongst those modern theologians who have commented perceptively on the regularity of this type of visual replacement of the Spirit by the Virgin in the medieval West;[29] but by the end of the third volume of his own magisterial study of the historical forms of pneumatology he is ready to propose – as a systematic alternative – that it would be a good idea to 'feminize' the Holy Spirit in a slightly different way as a concession to modern women's interests, and in witness to the sporadic, and especially early Syriac, such gendering of the Spirit.[30] What he unfortunately fails to engage with from his twentieth-century perspective, however, is the far from liberating effect of a 'feminine' principle in the Godhead if she is, as here, still ranged in what is obviously the lowliest place in a descending hierarchy, where the ultimate point of authority is visually male and quasi-papal. To be sure, Mary is the highly significant point of *entry* to the divine in this picture (look at the donors at the bottom of the picture, to whom Mary is their nearest source of comfort and salvation); and Mary is, thus, too, the mediator here of resurrection faith (for the rest of the painting, not shown here, is about doubting Thomas, to whom Christ presents his wounds). But we are left in no doubt, visually, about Mary's appropriate 'place' in relation to Father and Son: she is the blessed 'feminine' *conduit* to their saving interaction.

---

[29] Yves Congar, OP, *I Believe in the Holy Spirit* (3 vols.; London: Chapman, 1983), vol. I, 163–4.

[30] Ibid., vol. III, 155–64. I present a critique of Congar's well-intended 'complementary' move here in '"Femininity" and the Holy Spirit?', in Monica Furlong, ed., *Mirror to the Church: Reflections on Sexism* (London: SPCK, 1988), 124–35.

14. Man of Sorrows and Mary, part of an altarpiece,
Konrad Witz and workshop, Basle, 1450

It would be an interesting and compensatory Protestant tale if we could show that the Lutheran reform effected an immediate purgation of inner-trinitarian visual themes of punishment and cruelty, hierarchy and dependence, at the same time as it attempted to sideline Mariology. In fact, however, the evidence of the early period of Lutheran reform suggests a strong *unwillingness* to change iconographically in this regard. Luther explicitly forbade over-disgusting gashings and drippings of blood on the body of Christ; but in a 1560–70 painting by Lukas Grunenberger from a Lutheran context (Figure 15), the familiar sword-waving by the Father remains as a central visual feature, even despite Luther's well-known resistance to any suggestion of a manipulative intra-divine sacrifice, and his preference for a reworked atonement theology of penal substitution that would properly accommodate his central insistence on 'justification by faith alone'.[31] It would, of course, doubtless be too much to expect a *direct* artistic representation of all these fundamental theological shifts in atonement theology, subtle and complex as they are; at best what we get here in Grunenberger, as signal of this seismic theological change, is the central placing of the Father–Son 'substitution' negotiation in the context of a complete narrative history (from Fall to Cross), and a certain softening of the threatened Fatherly violence by the presence of the comforting dove and the lack of any overt wounds on the Son. Yet in other respects the painterly conventions of divine threat and sacrificial submission have not changed from their pre-Reformation visual

---

[31] See for instance Martin Luther, *Lecture on Galatians 1535*, commenting on Galatians 3. 13: 'He has and bears all the sins of all men in His body — not in the sense that He has committed them but in the sense that He took these sins, committed by us, upon His own body, in order to make satisfaction for them with His own blood', in *Luther's Works* (55 vols.; St Louis, MO: Concordia, 1955–86), vol. XXVI, 277. For Luther's views about visual representations of Christ's wounds, see Schiller, *Iconography*, vol. II, 226.

15. 'The Trinity as Allegory of Fall and Redemption',
Lukas Grunenberger, 1560–70

counterparts. Here one might say, then, that artistic convention somewhat lagged behind Protestant theological reform, rather than anticipating it.

However, in a slightly earlier, indeed very early, Lutheran woodcut by Peter Dell (Figure 16), a nice inner-trinitarian relocation is significant for another reason. At the centre is the *Gnadenstuhl* – with, again conservatively, an episcopal or even papal Father figure still in evidence. When we search for the dove, however ('Hunt the pigeon!' again), we find it has flown

16. Throne of Grace, wood relief, Peter Dell the Elder, 1548

now to the left-hand side of the woodcut to hover over, and ostensibly provide legitimation for, the new powers of the reforming preacher in the pulpit. Hence the Lutheran balance of Christ as Word and Sacrament is here visually represented by a new twist on the traditional iconographical trinitarian theme of the 'throne of grace': on the left of centre, the dove 'baptizes' and authorizes the Lutheran preacher who conveys Christ's Word; on the right, the altar remains as place of encounter with Christ's sacramental and ubiquitous 'real presence'.

If we turn away now from the specifically pain-centred and eucharistic orientation of the *Gnadenstuhl* and *Not Gottes* types of rendition of the Trinity, we should bear in mind that the medieval

West also, and concomitantly, continued pedagogically with a version of the 'identical triplets' form of representation of the Trinity with slightly individualized touches to distinguish the three 'persons'. This type was, it seems, essentially didactic, but – as with the much earlier 'Old Testament Trinity' forms – did little to express divine unity, except by the near 'identicality' of the figures and their garb. Figure 17 presents a characteristic French manuscript example in which one has to look closely to find the hints which indicate which 'person' is which.

So the problem here, as ever, was of an apparently unguarded and unmodified tritheism; hence we find well-meaning 'modalist' correctives, such as the three-nosed (and three-bearded) manuscript illustration of the Trinity, illustrating the *Speculum Humanae Salvationis* (Figure 18), which was to have great and widespread influence theologically via the impact of its text and exegesis.[32]

Even more grotesque, one might argue, if not plainly ridiculous, is this *homoousian* version of the events of Genesis 18 in an English manuscript of the thirteenth century (Figure 19). One can well surmise how such an ingenious representation must have been motivated by the fear and danger of visual tritheism. In compensation, this well-meaning commitment to trinitarian orthodoxy has produced a three-headed monster, to somewhat ludicrous effect. Yet the convention of such three-headed representations of the Trinity was not unusual at this time; and one might argue that they lead the viewer back, by a sort of shock tactic, from the story of the three mysterious angelic visitors to Abraham and Sarah in

[32] See Adrian Wilson and Joyce Lancaster Wilson, *A Medieval Mirror: Speculum Humanae Salvationis 1324–1500* (Berkeley: University of California Press, 1984) for the history and influence of the *Speculum* tradition of illustrated works of popular theology, which were designed to instill in the reader, through vivid use of typological analysis, the urgent need for salvation and the threat of eternal damnation.

17. The Trinity, fifteenth-century French manuscript

18. Trifaced Trinity, *Speculum Humanae Salvationis*, from *Ein Spiegel menschlicher Behaltnuss*, Augsburg, c. 1476

Genesis 18, to an insistence on the correct understanding of divine unity prefigured there.

An intriguing and unusual alternative on the *homoousian* insistence is presented by Figure 20, which shows an illustration in the thirteenth-century Lothian Bible and is a remodelling of Father and Son, with interposed Holy Spirit (evidently expressing the Western commitment to the *filioque* clause), in terms of *one* pair of shared knees! My point raised in the introduction to this chapter is now, I hope, well taken: ingenious Western medieval attempts to paint 'three persons in one substance' in some *literal* way tend only to veer towards the risible. Yet there is a certain charm and originality here as well, the oddity of the arrangement itself 'giving rise to (theological) thought'.

19. Abraham adoring a three-headed Trinity, English Psalter, *c.* 1260

20. Six days' work of creation, Lothian Bible, thirteenth century

21. Arms of the Trinity, stained-glass window, St Andrew's Church,
Greystoke, Cumbria, fifteenth century

Yet when such attempts at visual orthodoxy are conjoined, as
they regularly were in the later medieval period (Figure 21), with
didactic and quasi-geometric demonstrations of how Father, Son,
and Spirit can all be God ('Deus') while *not* being identical with
each other ('Pater non est Filius', etc.), doctrinal error is seemingly
averted; but the danger, as is often remarked in modern trinitarianism's reaction to the divide between 'economic' and 'immanent'
Trinities, is of turning the eternal, ontological life of the Trinity into
a celestial puzzle, seemingly well removed from any impinging on
the life of the believer. The diagram tells the viewer what can, and
cannot, be believed if orthodoxy is to be maintained; but whether
this evokes any imaginative and internalized commitment to God
the Trinity is less easy to surmise.

Such a dilemma is indeed touchingly expressed in a little piece of
medieval stained glass to be found near the sacristy in Bristol
Cathedral (Figure 22). The Trinity, here represented by the clover

22. The Trinity in Paradise, Bristol Cathedral, late medieval

leaf which St Patrick used to expound its truth, appears to be shut away inside a little sheep-pen or garden. The enclosed space could represent the life of Paradise, or possibly the virginal motherhood of Mary, as the 'enclosed garden' of Song of Songs 4. 12, one of the variations in Marian iconography which became popular in this period. Thus the Trinity is safe no doubt from harm; but also safely removed, perhaps, from having any known or direct effect on the ordinary life of the simple believer, except as expounded sermonically once a year on Trinity Sunday. The mysterious God as Trinity is seemingly kept far away in a celestial sanctuary.

From a modern feminist perspective, moreover, the loss of a vibrant and effective visual trinitarianism of the 'economy' of salvation is worrisome mainly because of what often replaces it in the popular imagination. By this I mean that the alternative can be a collapse into an effective unitarianism, where God *is* Father (and so, by implication, as Daly quipped, 'the male is [indeed] God'). Figure 23, which presents a telling manuscript detail from the late fifteenth century, is an example of such a 'God' as judge, attacking simultaneously the world, the flesh, and the devil with a three-pronged weapon.

This dual Western visual trinitarian tendency, then, with a certain fatal *combination* of a sense of difficult and remote celestial geometry qua Trinity, on the one hand, and, simultaneously, the reduction of the Trinity to the Father, on the other, becomes arguably more marked as we approach the modern period (as in a drawing of *Æternitas* of 1610; Figure 24). Here the new modernistic interest in medicine and human physiology is combined with the period's equal rigour in mathematics, making 'eternity' a matter of triune geometry with a male, fatherly, human face. Gone are the charming and ingenious medieval attempts at visual orthodoxy which, to the modern eye, can give rise to mirth; instead, there is

23. God the Judge, manuscript, Brussels, *c.* 1488

24. *Æternitas*, Matthäus Greuter, 1610

perhaps an intimation here of modernity's coming assault on the very coherence of the notion of Trinity, in the light of critical and scientific thinking.

All our recent illustrations have traced a Western trajectory, in which a concentration on Christ's death is one marked feature, and a problematically abstruse didacticism, another. But what of the Byzantine East, with its quite different and well-codified conventions of iconography, its perception of the icon as a *non*-propositional 'door to the sacred', and its tendency to emphasize an Athanasian salvation through Christ's reconstitution of humanity (rather than through 'satisfaction' for sin)?

I shall return shortly to the further flowering of the 'Old Testament Trinity' type in Orthodoxy, for which Eastern iconography is justly renowned. But for the moment it is a more unofficial (indeed, officially debarred) representation of the 'Trinity' that interests me more in the first instance. Figure 25 shows a hierarchical visualization of the 'persons' of the Trinity (officially named 'The Three Ages of Man'), which emerges only in the late fourteenth and fifteenth centuries, and is I think a most telling indirect symbolization of the Cappadocian doctrine of the Trinity, as already preliminarily discussed in Chapter 3. 'The Holy Spirit proceeds from the Father *through* the Son', as Gregory of Nyssa has it and as this icon portrays visually. Note that there is no danger in this Eastern approach of the Spirit's *redundancy*: indeed the eye rests centrally here, for the Spirit is the crucial point of entry into the life of God. And yet the ascent that is then required, via the Son to the Father (who himself is 'source' and 'cause' of the other two 'persons'), is also a vivid visual reminder of the structured organization of the Orthodox church, and indeed perhaps even of the ordered relations of emperor and patriarch.

There is, however, another (and more subversive) way to read this icon, an insight which I owe to Graham Ward. In a private communication with me (written after a showing of my trinitarian slides), he wrote:

Is the hierarchical reading [of this icon] the only [possible] one, the dominant one? Could we not suggest that the emphasis in the picture is in fact not on the overshadowing [Father], but *centre* of the picture, the Spirit, the indefinable, ineffable and mysterious heart of God? The Spirit

25. Divine fatherhood, School of Novgorod, fourteenth century

image is the focusing and organizing one [here], if we take an alternative paradigm for the symbolic organization of space. The focusing Spirit then 'deconstructs' the hierarchical. The hierarchical and concentric become two moments of paradoxical tension within the picture ... the Spirit image challenges and acts as a critique upon the far too literal [male] presentation of God as Father and Son ...

Now if this alternative interpretation also convinces us, then what might be achieved here is of course precisely that subtle balance of the contemplative *prioritizing* of the Spirit (and yet without collapse into tritheism) that I was gesturing towards in my third chapter, and which seems creatively to dissolve again any rigid hierarchical ordering of the 'persons'. This particular iconic representation therefore leaves us with a paradox: is the sense of downward linear *order* too strong to allow any such fruitful destabilization in the Spirit? Or is the gaze so magnetized towards the centrally placed Spirit that it there becomes transfixed and *transformed*? These are paradoxes to which we shall find ourselves returning in Chapter 6, as we consider further the contribution of the Cappadocian fathers, and especially of Gregory of Nyssa, to the history of trinitarian thought.

Be that as it may, we certainly do have a wonderfully humorous gendered *reversal* of this same type in the Eastern 'Anna Trinity', so called, in which (as in Figure 26, which shows a Greek fifteenth-century example of the type) a kind of visual reversed pastiche of the icon we have just seen is achieved, and the female powers of grandmother (St Anne) and mother (the Virgin) over the Christ-child are strongly asserted.

The 'Anna Trinity' had an even more considerable vogue in the late medieval West, too.[33] Figure 27 shows an example from *circa*

---

[33] See Pamela Sheingorn, 'Appropriating the Holy Kinship: Gender and Family History', in Kathleen Ashley and Pamela Sheingorn, eds., *Interpreting Cultural Symbols: Saint Anne in Late Medieval Society* (Athens: University of Georgia Press, 1990), 169–98.

26. St Anne enthroned with the Virgin and Christ, Greek, fifteenth century

27. 'Anna Trinity' from an *Horae*, Simon Vostre, Paris, *c.* 1500

1500, and, significantly, the women are here visually supplanted at the top by the male divine figure. The devotion to St Anne at this time had an important societal setting in the West in connection with debates about inheritance laws; and the enclosing power of the grandparental figure here has a certain recurring psychological impact. And it puts, you might say, the male Christ-child *in his place*, albeit still importantly centre stage as the object of grand-maternal and maternal adoration.

Was the Virgin's power in the late medieval West, however, such as effectively even to make her in some circumstances a fourth member of the Trinity in unofficial piety and practice? The icon-ography of the coronation of the Virgin, such as in the representa-tion by Jean Fouquet in the *Book of Hours of Étienne Chevalier* (Figure 28), might have seemed to suggest it; and this indeed was a well-established visual trope long before the official papal prom-ulgation of the doctrine of the Assumption in the mid twentieth century. For a psychoanalytic commentator such as Carl Jung, this notable ecclesiastical development was a sign that the Church had at last recognized the need to invite the suppressed 'feminine' into the magic divine mandala.[34] As Jung himself admitted, however, the solution is only ecclesiastically acceptable if the Virgin is kept at a suitably lower level of subordination, as indeed is evident in Fouquet's other representation of this same theme (which precedes the enthronement in his illustrations): the coronation of the Virgin.

Jung himself, however, had apparently no conscious inkling of the way in which his view of the so-called male 'anima' (the

[34] For Jung, selfhood (represented by the mandala) must always be constituted by four parts or functions: C. G. Jung, *Psychological Types* (London: Routledge & Kegan Paul, 1971). For Jung's comments on the promulgation of the doctrine of the Assumption of Mary, see his letter to Victor White, OP: Ann Conrad Lammers, Adrian Cunningham, and Murray Stein, eds., *The Jung–White Letters* (London: Routledge, 2007), 157–60.

28. Enthronement of the Virgin, Jean Fouquet, *c.* 1455

proposed contra-sexual dimension of the male psyche) was infused with a *stereotypical* understanding of 'femininity', which he simply took for granted.[35] Yet his romantic view of 'femininity' is, as we have already indicated in relation to the Moltmanns' work, one that contemporary feminism is likely to find suspect, for it appears to reinscribe the very gender presumptions that Jung himself sought to overcome in his theory of contra-sexual 'integration'. In following Jung here, Leonardo Boff's more recent theological solution of 'hypostatizing' the Marian 'feminine' in specific relation to the *Spirit* is less obviously quarternian than Jung's approach (and thus more conscious of the problems of heterodoxy that Jung's proposed adjustment to the Trinity involves); but it is just as obviously problematic, I have argued, where its vision of stereotypical 'femininity' is concerned.[36] For what is changed in such a stereotype, if it is merely projected into the Godhead? It is in this way remainingly chastening to return to the visual symbolism of a Fouquet (see Figure 29): that the 'feminine' should be enthroned may not, therefore, be to ensure that the crowd's male gaze is in any way transformed in its own existing gender presumptions.

When, however, as Figure 30's depiction of the fifteenth-century statue of Mary now in the Musée de Cluny, Paris, the Virgin actually contains *within* herself the whole mystery of the Trinity, the visual assertion of devotion to the female is made the more complete, though at the cost, of course, of total 'orthodoxy'. For here even the Father is subjected to Mary's enclosing and superior power; and the statue, when closed, has the Virgin ruling over the whole earth as the primary point of fecundity and authority. Once

---

[35] C. G. Jung, 'Anima and Animus', in *Two Essays on Analytical Psychology* (London: Routledge & Kegan Paul, 1966), 188–211.

[36] See Leonardo Boff, *The Maternal Face of God: The Feminine and its Religious Expressions* (London: Collins, 1989), reviewed by this author in *Heythrop Journal* 42 (2001), 102–4.

29. Coronation of the Virgin, Jean Fouquet, *c.* 1455

again, the visual imagination outstrips what is doctrinally 'correct', becoming the exception that proves the doctrinal rule: the 'feminine' divine is manifestly adulated; but what this means for ordinary (sinful) women in the church is perhaps less obvious.

30. Statue of Mary, opened to reveal Father and Son, fifteenth century

When, in contrast, the *Spirit* is 'feminized' (as it seemingly is in a unique fourteenth-century example from the village church in Urschalling, Bavaria; Figure 31), it is again unclear that such idealized 'femininity' (and it is still disputed amongst the iconographers whether this figure *is* a female) is doing more than mediating between Father and Son, as the visual Augustinian *vinculum amoris* – the 'bond of love'. Despite earlier feminist excitement about this find,[37] I myself do not regard this striking one-off artistic example as a daring 'proto-feminist' move, either: such a presumption is surely entirely anachronistic. Rather, if the Spirit here *is* intended to be female (which seems to me likely), what we seem to have is the artful projection of a compliant and mediating 'femininity', by a male artist, into the life of God. The mysterious vulva shape painted below the Spirit, moreover, is perhaps evidence of a longing for the incorporation of something 'female' that is yet more earthy and physiological, rather than merely psychological, into the realm of the Godhead. But whatever we make of it, this particular medieval Bavarian wall painting is indeed a *sui generis* representation of the Trinity, and again one that presses well beyond what is strictly orthodox doctrinally. The contemporary imagination is thus both challenged and disturbed by it, precisely because its gender compensation is so unashamed and so overt.

Yet, in a different and marked way, the subterranean pathology of Western ideas of inner-trinitarian relations when visually gendered is most profoundly summed up, for me, by an earlier miniature from an eleventh-century Winchester manuscript, often wittily nicknamed the 'Winchester Quinity' (Figure 32). A *homoousian* eternal Father and Son on the right together rehearse the

---

[37] See Moltmann-Wendell and Moltmann, *Humanity in God*, 101–3 on the Motherhood of the Holy Spirit in relation to this wall painting.

31. The Trinity with a 'feminine' Holy Spirit, Urschalling, Bavaria, *c.* 1390

32. The Trinity, English manuscript miniature, 1012–20, the 'Winchester Quinity'

events of salvation – treading down the devil, Arius, and Judas. Significantly excluded, however, from their inner (and all-male) magic circle is everything associated with the 'feminine': with inspiration (in the form of a rather dejected-looking Holy Spirit); with the Virgin; and with the fragile baby human nature of the Christ-child (the Son being represented here for a second time) on the left. Again, the critical gendered assessment which I hazard here (and which seems to escape the standard art historical analyses),[38] is I think legitimately called out by the intense sense of exclusion signalled in the left-hand portion of the picture. For it is clear where the real power, the real locus of salvific activity, resides in this remarkable manuscript miniature: the left-hand figures, in contrast, strain to gain entry into that salvific realm of eternal male spiritual authority. Has the sense of 'feminine' exclusion from the realm of male divinity ever been more masterfully expressed?

'THE SYMBOL GIVES RISE TO THOUGHT'

Let me now repeat what I stated at the outset of this chapter: if one wishes to demonstrate unambiguously the historic capacity of the church to gender inner-trinitarian relations, while yet emphatically denying that it is doing so, it is to the history of Christian art that one must make first appeal. By now there can be little doubt in the reader's mind of this prevailing paradox in classic Christianity: the persistent orthodox refrain that God, qua God, is beyond gender; and the equally persistent appearance of gendered visual representations of that God, often in forms which vividly display cultural assumptions about 'normative' gender roles. Yet this unofficial gendered trinitarian visual story I have been tracing so far in this

[38] Compare Schiller, *Iconography*, vol. I, 8.

chapter, in all its intriguing and sometimes disturbing variety, is not yet the whole picture.

If existing family, political, and societal patternings and expectations such as the ones we have now surveyed were often writ revealingly large on the history of trinitarian iconography, especially in the medieval West, then there were other occasional *sui generis* and creative moments too, in both East and West, which seemed to question and destabilize such expectations; and it is with a few of these unusual instances that I wish to finish this chapter. For it may be that here we can begin to signal a creative way forward in symbolizing the Trinity, both visually and theologically. As I insisted at the outset, traditional trinitiarian iconography may incur in the first instance a contemporary hermeneutics of suspicion, and a keen urge to purge manifest idolatry; but it may also release the imagination precisely towards the means of such purgation, and so towards new and creative symbolizations. We turn now to some such intriguing possibilities at the close of this chapter.

One such release may occur through the strategy of simultaneous visual bombardments by different trinitarian images. In the late fifteenth-century east window in Holy Trinity Church, Goodramgate, York (Figure 33), for instance, a certain mutual correction is created by juxtaposing several of the possible visual 'trinities' of 'persons' in the Western tradition in a unique way. There is the *Not Gottes*, or exposition of the Corpus Christi, at top centre (in honour of the donor, the Revd John Walker, who was a member of the York Guilds of Corpus Christi); but also, directly underneath the *Not Gottes*, there is a form of the 'identical triplets' Trinity pictured at the Coronation of the Virgin. Finally, to the left of that image is another alternative family grouping – a quarternal variation on the 'Anna Trinity': the child Jesus, the Virgin, and her parents Joachim and Anna. Along with the additional presence of

33. Holy Trinity Church, Goodramgate, York, the Trinity Window, 1470/1

many other saints in the east window, the result – both trinitarian and quarternian – is at least a restless *shifting* of the trinitarian terms, which disallows the eye or mind from coming to a halt with one representation only, or with one gender only. The tactics are indeed reminiscent of that much earlier symbolic approach of Paulinus of Nola, with his willingness to allow many different visual allusions to exist side by side and so both complement and destabilize each other.

Another *sui generis* novelty may be found, earlier, in the work of Joachim of Fiore (1135–1202), whose attempt to map the 'persons' of the Trinity along the course of cosmic history brought him under fire for his heterodox thinking. Here, in his hotly disputed *Figurae* (preserved in a manuscript of Joachim in Corpus Christi College, Oxford; Figure 34), we have an arcane exposition of three over-lapping circles, across all three of which is written the secret name of God. Probably falsely accused of tritheism by the Fourth Lateran Council in 1215 (or so his modern defender Marjorie Reeves argues), Joachim succeeded at least in strengthening pneumatolog-ical significance by granting a distinct third circle to the 'age of the Spirit' (which is not however *separated* from the other two circles, but was intended to supersede the 'age of the church'). The circular diagram form also evidently withdraws from gendered anthropo-morphic dangers, and Reeves believes and argues that these inter-laced circles explicitly anticipate Dante's vision, in the *Paradiso*, of concentric circles enclosing a human face.[39] But whether or not this direct influence on Dante is right, we shall begin to understand, as we move to the end of this series of images, the vital importance of the visual circular movement as an undermining, or corrective, to

[39] Dante was indeed an admirer of Joachim's work: see Marjorie Reeves, *Joachim of Fiore and the Prophetic Future: A Medieval Study in Historical Thinking* (rev. edn; Stroud: Alan Sutton, 1999), 64–6 (on Dante) and 26 (on the condemnation of 1215).

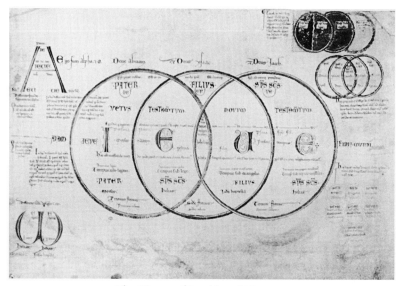

34. The *Figurae* of Joachim of Fiore, *c.* 1200

the straightforwardly linear or hierarchical ascent and descent of divine order more commonly found in visualizations of the Trinity.

Thus in a memorable trio of mad March hares from Paderborn Cathedral (Figure 35), I take it that the cavorting of the hares, their confused *circular* flurry, is an important gesture towards *perichoretic* coinherence – the uniting of three via their ecstatic dance of interaction and delight. Thus the ears of the hares form a perfect divine triangle, even as their movement constantly keeps the figures turning and bringing new perspectives to the fore. By using a figure of nature, rather than the more common gendered anthropomorphisms of the Trinity, this sculpture injects the idea of divine intra-trinitarian delight, careless frolicking, and even erotic excess, all the while holding the movement within its circular frame.

All three of these last images are already imaginatively suggestive, labile, in the same way as some of the earliest, experimental symbolisms discussed above were. But I shall now conclude with a

35. Hare Window, Paderborn Cathedral, early sixteenth century

further four representations in which (in the case of the two male artists, first) such a movement or change of traditional direction marks also a profound and conscious reworking of the trinitarian visual 'types' they have inherited; and in the case of the two women mystics' depictions with which I shall end, there is for both, significantly, an altogether *sui generis* novelty about their visions, and, with that, a profound sense of circular movement too.

Rublev's reworking of the traditional 'Old Testament Trinity', first, is now so well known and overused as to have lost some of its initial impact; yet even on a cursory viewing it is an extraordinary achievement of balance and harmony (see Figure 36). Much has been written on this icon, both art-historically and devotionally;[40] but several particular points are important for our theological

[40] Especially to be commended is Gabriel Bunge, *The Rublev Trinity: The Icon of the Trinity by the Monk-Painter Andrei Rublev* (Crestwood, NY: St Vladimir's Seminary Press, 2007).

36. The Trinity, Andrei Rublev, 1411

purposes here. To begin with, rather as in the early catacomb renditions of Genesis 18, the angel figures are not clearly male or female, but elusive presences who beckon us into their communion; and the eye moves naturally around, in circular motion, among the three, as one is invited to wonder which 'person' is which (itself a gesture towards *homoousian* unity). The highest figure in the circle, then, interestingly, is not allocated to the Father, but to the Son – who gestures towards the eucharistic dish as his own particular point of reference; but the inclination of the heads to the figure on the left still gently resummons the Eastern sense of the Father's position as 'source' and 'cause' of the other two 'persons', even as the circular movement to a large extent modifies this sense of hierarchy. Most striking of all, however, is the sense of *inclusion* into the divine circle: the viewer gradually grasps that the eucharistic elements are intended as the means of such incorporation into this divine circle of gentle movement and mutual submission.

Just as remarkable as Rublev's reworking of the Eastern 'Old Testament Trinity' theme, though much less well known, is William Blake's sketched reworking of the Western 'Throne of Grace' type (Figure 37). For he turns it *literally* inside out. The Father, again not noticeably male, bends to embrace the Son *face to face* on the (absent, but allusively suggested) cross. The Spirit is huge, encompassing, and bodily; its outstretched wings mirroring the cruciform shape of the Son's arms. It is as if, on the one hand, the dispassionate Father's gaze of the original medieval *Gnadenstuhl* (see again Figure 8 above) has been transmogrified into the anguished parent of a dying child; yet, on the other hand, and in contrast, the turned-around Christ is veritably leaping into the Father's arms, in an ecstasy of simultaneous joy and costly gift. And because the vibrant presence of the Spirit (no 'Hunt the pigeon!' obscurity here) so exactly emulates the shape of the Son's

37. The Trinity, sketch by William Blake, *c.* 1793

outstretched arms, the viewer experiences the movement of death precisely as a leap into life. Here is the circle of divine desire perfectly enacted, under the aegis of the Spirit's own longing love.

It is worth comparing these last two works of male artistic genius with one of the unique trinitarian visions of the twelfth-century Benedictine mystical theologian Hildegard of Bingen. The one shown in Figure 38, to my mind, anticipates the concentric circles of Dante's *Paradiso* at least as significantly, if not more so, than Joachim of Fiore's *Figurae*. As is so often the case, Hildegard's own written *interpretation* of her vision in the *Scivias* is rather less exciting (or less subversive) than the picture itself might suggest.[41] At the

---

[41] See Hildegard of Bingen, *Scivias*, 2.2.2., *trans.* Mother Columba Hart and Jane Bishop (CWS; New York: Paulist Press, 1990), 161–2.

38. The Trinity, *Scivias Codex*, Hildegard of Bingen, 1150–1200

heart of the Trinity here stands the mysterious figure of the Word, hands raised in a humble posture of blessing. As Hildegard had this figure illuminated, it is not *obviously* male (although in her commentary Hildegard takes that as read). But the seeming anonymity of the Christ figure here recalls, to my mind, the 'stretched' vision of the 'Son' in what I called the 'incorporative', contemplative model of the Trinity (in Chapter 3); for the Son appears here as the archetypal human, greeting us with humility, gentleness, and welcome. The silver outer circle represents the Father, significantly not anthropomorphized at all; and the inner burnished-gold circle is the Spirit, significantly rediscovering its fiery individuality here, albeit by symbolic allusion. Although Hildegard herself does not quote Paul in her own commentary on this vision, the sense of moving into the mysterious human heart of the Trinity via the Spirit evoked here recalls the Pauline stricture 'No one can say "Jesus is Lord" *except* by the Holy Spirit' (1 Corinthians 12. 3). There is, of course, no danger at all of the Spirit's prophetic redundancy in the mystical work of Hildegard, for whom the fire of the Spirit is a constant and central theme. But we are struck here in this particular vision, above all, by the condensation of trinitarian insight into the face of *Christ*, a Christ who welcomes the viewer into the divine movement of the cosmic circle precisely by his posture of human vulnerability and defencelessness. Yet it is a defencelessness which is supremely powerful: both demanding submission, and representing it in perfect form.

Finally, I end with a modern pastel by another woman, Marlene Scholz (at the time of composition a Dominican nun studying modern trinitarian theology in London) (Figure 39). This is, it seems to me, a near perfect visual representation of the type of contemplative trinitarianism towards which my argument has been moving in this volume, and it deftly releases the imagination towards such a vision. The 'Christ' figure here is an anonymous pray-er. The Spirit, significantly both dove *and* fire, is received at the point of the heart's vulnerability. The 'Father', not anthropo-morphized in any direct way as male, is represented *both* as the

39. 'Blessed Trinity', Marlene Scholz, late twentieth century

everlasting arms reaching *down*, *and* as the circular unknown vortex into which the pray-er is being caught *up*. The downward move-ment is thus returned – balanced – by an upward one; and both are taken up into the 'apophatic' whirl of a circular tunnel reaching out and up to the unknown. As with the Blake drawing, the modern sketchiness of the pastels allows a sense of indeterminacy and ubiquitous anonymity for the central Christ figure; and the sense of unlimited, participatory ascent into the divine life is gloriously conveyed by the movement of the upper, beckoning circle.

CONCLUSIONS AND FORECAST

Let me now attempt some final conclusions from this chapter's lengthy exploration, especially with this last, modern pastel still in mind. In some ways, of course, I do not want to essay 'conclusions' that would stifle or shut off further imaginative reflection that may arise from these art forms; so my remarks here are brief and recapitulatory, even as they also point us forward. It will be recalled, however, that we set out in this chapter with two conflicting and paradoxically related goals: to find in these art forms a means and goad towards the *purgation* of (often unconscious) idolatry; and then to *redirect* our minds, hearts, and imaginations towards a new participation in the trinitarian God. As we have discovered, these paradoxically related undertakings can sometimes coalesce remarkably, even in the form of one single artwork.

So these selections from the history of Christian trinitarian iconography have underlined afresh for us the importance, first, of symbolic ingenuity and novelty in trinitarian theology, ingenuity that often comes, in both East and West, from the prophetic or 'mystical' wing of the church. It is these factors which disturb as well as reassure; and thus they have the power not only to *reinvigorate* old symbolism (as, say, Rublev and Blake do), but actually to *redirect* it (as Hildegard and Scholz do) with wholly new ideas, movements, and configurations. And we have seen enough, I trust, to recognize the difference between visual trinitarianism on the one hand getting bogged down in literalism or ideology, and on the other (in its most creative and original moments) pointing out *beyond* literalism and ideology to something both richly symbolic and at the same time apophatic in its imaginative dimensions.

Moreover, a visual approach to the Trinity gives us some more *particular* points of warning. There is the danger, first, of *losing* the Spirit figure – the significant, destabilizing, 'third' – especially also through loss of the vivid power of fire symbolism. There is the importance, too, of the avoidance of crassly literal male anthropomorphisms, or an over-dominance of the Father–Son relationship to the exclusion of the Spirit. There are also the positive ways in which sketchiness or indeterminacy of gender can, rather than clinically androgynizing the members of the Trinity, sometimes signal the incorporation of both men and women into participation in the life of God. And there are the means by which the symbolic uses of movement in the artwork (especially circular movement, or movement up and down), can overcome the rigidity of any hierarchical 'linear' model of the Trinity. These seem to me to be the most important particular points of principle we have learned from our survey. Yet these abstract lessons pale, frankly, in comparison with the irreducibility of their visual instantiation.

Let us remember these visual themes, however, as we move on next to a further unfolding of the patristic material left off in Chapter 3; for with the various lessons of the intervening chapters, and the garnering thereby of theological resources from a number of unexpected sources, we are now in a position to attempt a more explicit unravelling of the gender overtones and implications of the normative patristic trinitarian theologies of the Greek and Latin churches (as represented here by Gregory of Nyssa and Augustine, respectively). We shall also move to a more profound reflection on what might be the significance of what I have called the 'apophatic turn' in a trinitarianism focused on the activity of contemplation; and on how such a turn might affect, in some unexpected ways, the status, well-being, and empowerment of women.

To those tasks my next chapter turns.

* * *

BIBLIOGRAPHIC NOTE

ICONOGRAPHY OF THE TRINITY

My own collection of visual trinitarianisms has been built up over the years from a number of diverse sources. For some of the main ones I drew on originally, see André Grabar, *Christian Iconography: A Study of its Origins* (Princeton University Press, 1968); Engelbert Kirschbaum, Günter Bandmann, and Wolfgang Braunfels, eds., *Lexikon der christlichen Ikonographie* (8 vols.; Freiburg: Herder, 1968–76), especially the articles 'Trinität' and 'Heilige Geist'; Frederik van der Meer and Christine Mohrmann, *Atlas of the Early Christian World* (London: Nelson, 1958); Michael Gough, *The Origins of Christian Art* (London: Thames & Hudson, 1973); Gertrud Schiller, *Iconography of Christian Art* (2 vols; London: Lund Humphries, 1971–2); Heinrich Schipperges, *The Holy Trinity* (Freiburg: Herder, 1955); David Talbot Rice, *Art of the Byzantine Era* (London: Thames & Hudson, 1963); Antonio Paolucci, *Ravenna* (London: Constable, 1971); Gabriel Bunge, *The Rublev Trinity: The Icon of the Trinity by the Monk-painter Andrei Rublev* (Crestwood, NY: St Vladimir's Seminary Press, 2007); Leonid Ouspensky, *Theology of the Icon* (2 vols.; Crestwood, NY: St Vladimir's Seminary Press, 1992); David Bindman with Deirdre Toomey, eds., *The Complete Graphic Works of William Blake* (London: Thames & Hudson, 1978). I would also like to acknowledge my indebtedness to Fr Robert Murray, SJ, who greatly assisted me in my original development of a slide series on the Trinity in Christian art. More recently there has been an unusally creative outpouring of work on visual trinitarianism, which has much enriched my own understanding: see especially François Bœspflug, 'The Trinity in Christian Visual Arts', in Gilles Emery and Matthew Levering, eds., *The Oxford Handbook of the Trinity* (Oxford University Press, 2011), 472–86; François Bœspflug, *La Trinité dans l'Art d'Occident* (Strasbourg: Presses Universitaires de Strasbourg, 2000); David Brown, 'The Trinity in Art', in Stephen T. Davis, Daniel Kendall, SJ, and Gerald O'Collins, SJ, eds., *The Trinity: An Interdisciplinary Symposium on the Trinity* (Oxford University Press, 1999), 329–56; Robin M. Jensen, 'Theophany and the Invisible God in Early Christian Theology and Art', in Andrew B. McGowan, Brian E. Daley, and Timothy J. Gaden, eds., *God in Early Christian Thought: Essays in Memory of Lloyd G. Patterson* (Leiden: Brill,

2009), 271–96; Robin M. Jensen, 'The Trinity and the Economy of Salvation on Two Early Christian Sarcophagi', *Journal of Early Christian Studies* 7 (1999), 527–46; Gesa Thiessen, 'Images of the Trinity in Visual Art', in Declan Marmion and Gesa Thiessen, eds., *Trinity and Salvation: Theological, Spiritual, and Aesthetic Perspectives* (Oxford: Peter Lang, 2009), 119–40; Gesa Thiessen, 'Imaging the Dogma of the Trinity', *Communio Viatorum* 51/1 (2009), 4–21; N. Silanes and J. Gonzalez, eds., *La Trinidad en el Arte: Lenguajes Simbólicos del Misterio* (Salamanca: Ediciones Secretariado Trinitario, 2004); Severino Dianich and Timothy Verdon, eds., *La Trinità di Masaccio: Arte e Teologia* (Bologna: Edizioni Dehoniane, 2004); Katharina Herrmann, *De Deo Uno et Trino: Bildprogramme barocker Dreifaltigkeitskirchen in Bayern und Österreich* (Regensburg: Schnell & Steiner, 2010); Barbara C. Raw, *Trinity and Incarnation in Anglo-Saxon Art and Thought* (Cambridge University Press, 1997); Roseline Grimaldi-Hierholz, *Images de la Trinité dans l'art* (Fontainebleau: R. Hierholz, 1995); Susie Paulik Babka, 'The Trinity in the *Gnadenstuhl* Motif: Illustrating the Cross as an Event of the Triune God', in David C. Robinson, ed., *God's Grandeur: The Arts and Imagination in Theology* (Maryknoll, NY: Orbis Books, 2007), 17–37; Jeffrey F. Hamburger, *Rothschild Canticles: Art and Mysticism in Flanders and the Rhineland circa 1300* (New Haven, CT: Yale University Press, 1990).

EARLY CHRISTIAN ART AND THE PROBLEM OF DIVINE

REPRESENTATION

The question of the original Christian restriction on visual representations of the divine remains a matter for intense discussion: see especially Paul Corby Finney, *The Invisible God: The Earliest Christians on Art* (Oxford University Press, 1994); Thomas F. Mathews, *The Clash of Gods: A Reinterpretation of Early Christian Art* (rev. edn; Princeton University Press, 1999); Sr Mary Charles Murray, 'Art and the Early Church', *Journal of Theological Studies* 28 (1977), 303–45; Sr Mary Charles Murray, *Rebirth and Afterlife: A Study of the Transmutation of some Pagan Imagery in Early Christian Funerary Art* (Oxford: BAR, 1981); Sr Mary Charles Murray, 'Artistic Idiom and Doctrinal Development', in Rowan Williams, ed., *The Making of Orthodoxy: Essays in Honour of Henry Chadwick* (Cambridge University Press, 1989), 288–307; Robin M. Jensen, *The Invisible God: The Earliest Christians on Art* (Oxford

University Press, 1994); Robin M. Jensen, *The Substance of Things Seen: Art, Faith, and the Christian Community* (Grand Rapids, MI: Eerdmans, 2004); Robin M. Jensen, *Face to Face: The Portrait of the Divine in Early Christianity* (Philadelphia: Fortress Press, 2005); Robin M. Jensen, *Living Water: Images, Symbols and Settings of Early Christian Baptism* (Leiden: Brill, 2011); James A. Francis, 'Verbal and Visual Representation: Art and Text, Culture and Power in Late Antiquity', in Philip Rousseau, ed., *A Companion to Late Antiquity* (Oxford: Blackwell, 2009), 285–305; James A. Francis, 'Late Antique Visuality: Blurring the Boundaries between Word and Image, Pagan and Christian', in David Brakke, Deborah Deliyannis, and Edward Watts, eds., *Shifting Cultural Frontiers in Late Antiquity* (Aldershot: Ashgate, 2012), 139–49; Hans Belting, *Likeness and Presence: A History of the Image before the Era of Art* (Chicago University Press, 1994).

ART, INTERPRETATION, AND THE PROBLEM OF 'EISEGESIS'

In this chapter I have only been able to discuss this far-reaching art-historical conundrum briefly: namely, how does the 'eye of the beholder' legitimately contribute to the 'meaning' of an artwork? But, as discussed in the chapter, I have primarily been guided by the hermeneutical principles of Hans-Georg Gadamer, *Truth and Method* (London: Sheed & Ward, 1975), and Paul Ricoeur, *The Conflict of Interpretations: Essays in Hermeneutics* (Evanston, IL: Northwestern University Press, 1974), which can, I argue, be appropriately extended to the visual realm. From rather different facets of theological commitment, Aidan Nichols, *The Art of God Incarnate: Theology and Image in Christian Tradition* (London: DLT, 1980), and George Pattison, *Art, Modernity and Faith: Towards a Theology of Art* (Houndsmills: Macmillan, 1991) also repay study, and both address this issue with acute theological questions in mind. Margaret Miles's feminist theological interpretation of classic visual materials, *Image as Insight: Visual Understanding in Western Christianity and Secular Culture* (Boston, MA: Beacon, 1985), has been savaged in the past by art historians insistent on her so-called 'affective fallacy': see especially J. W. Dixon, 'Image as Insight: Review Essay', *Journal of the American Academy of Religion* 58 (1990), 267–76; Whitney Chadwick, *Women, Art and Society* (London: Thames & Hudson, 1990) is appealed to by Miles in riposte: deep questions are at stake here about the fundamental way cultures 'signal', however subliminally, their various commitments through the aesthetic realm.

ART AND PYSCHOANALYTIC INTERPRETATION: THE
TRINITY / QUARTERNITY

Carl Jung's account of the symbolic import of the Trinity (and its incompleteness, in his view, without a fourth element representing 'integration' in the self) is discussed in 'A Psychological Approach to the Dogma of the Trinity', in *Psychology and Religion: West and East* (Princeton University Press, 1969), 107–200. Underlying this is Jung's theory of gender and the 'contra-sexual' in each of us: see his 'Animus and Anima', in *Two Essays on Analytical Psychology* (Princeton University Press, 1966), 188–211, and 'The Syzygy: Anima and Animus', in *Aion: Researches into the Phenomenology of the Self* (Princeton University Press, 1968), 11–22.

Intriguing as these theories remain for interpreting certain classic representations of the Trinity, they ultimately have to be assessed on theoretical and philosophical grounds.

CHAPTER 6

'Batter My Heart': reorientations of classic trinitarian thought

In the last three chapters I have taken the reader on diverse 'foraging raids' into the history and contemporary practice of trinitarianism, with the aid of the interdisciplinary techniques of a *théologie totale*, and with the special impetus thereby to search for doctrine's lost coins in dark and neglected corners. I have tried above all to demonstrate how deeply trinitarian conceptuality 'bites' in unexpected places, how strangely it permeates even the most basic human preoccupations with sex, power, pain, death, and primary parental relationships; and, at the very least, what I hope will have emerged from these explorations of text, fieldwork, and art is some substantiation of my claim that no doctrine of the Trinity, as charter and paradigm of perfect *relationship*, can be completely innocent of political, familial, and sexual associations. Whatever the abstract form of trinitiarian ontological speculation in its purest conceptual and theological expression, its implications reach all the way down, personally and culturally, and spiral out-wards in ways often beyond the control of ecclesiastical authorities.

But that is not all; for other, doubtless more contentious, sub-theses have been at work in what I have said so far. There has been a sociological hypothesis about 'church'-type Christianity's need for a subversive element within its bounds if trinitarianism is to be perennially reinvigorated by response to the Spirit; and a concomitant hypothesis about the (relative) suppression of a 'prayer-based', or 'incorporative', doctrine of the Trinity within the 'church' type, for fear of its liberating or potentially disordering implications.

Then there was the thesis that became all the clearer through iconographic evidence, of the tendency towards the symbolic subordination of women as part and parcel (even if unconsciously) of the cultural 'packaging' of trinitarian faith at the imaginative and cultural level. And so we have learnt that the rhetoric of an appealing 'equality' and mutual 'in-dwelling' (*perichorēsis*) in classical trinitarianism is often, in practice, not quite what it seems. That is one of the first and obvious lessons, if we are to take seriously our method's acknowledgement that doctrine, in its widest sense, is purveyed in multiple forms and at multiple levels of cultural and imaginative engagement (Chapter 2, above). What follows, of course, is that the self-reflexive task of the 'hermeneutic of suspicion' in a *théologie totale* can never come to an end; but as we emphasized with equal insistence at the start of this volume, such suspicion can never have the last word either: the Spirit always blows afresh to purge, enlighten, and inflame, and *it blows where it wills*. While the seductive tug of idolatry is an ever-present danger, there is always also the deep propulsion to find in God, through the Spirit, the way to the true goal of human longing.

How, then, as the obvious question continues to press, are we to know the *difference* between false trinitiarian consciousness, on the one hand, and conformity, through the Spirit and in the Son, to the very life of God, on the other? How, in particular (after the revealing lessons of Chapter 5), are we to avoid both the Scylla of a trinitarianism that declares sexuality and gender irrelevant to the question of God, and also the Charybdis of a trinitarianism that appears to mandate, albeit covertly, a subordinating or denigrating assessment of women's roles?

In returning now in this chapter to two of the great founding fathers of classic patristic trinitarianism, Gregory of Nyssa in the East and Augustine of Hippo in the West, we confront this dilemma with new seriousness. For at the start of this book I promised that the theological lessons to be drawn from their pioneering trinitarian work could be thrown into revealing new light if we trace how their themes of desire for God, on the one hand, and human desire for each other as sexed and gendered beings, on the other, are in different ways correlated and aligned. Of course they are both also deeply aware (although they express this truth via different tropes) of the *infinite* difference between the divine, trinitarian life, and the human life of sexual temptation and struggle; yet there is also something in both their contributions that draws these realms tightly and analogically together in the uniting theme of desire, and so illuminates with special force the dilemma still set before us: what *are* the signs that engagement with the trinitarian God in prayer is authentically salvific and transforming, and what are the signs of the presence of a distorting and sinful false consciousness that tragically drives us in a contrary, and idolatrous, direction, and renders 'sexuality', especially, a realm of division, pain, and strife?

In writing in this comparative way about Gregory of Nyssa and Augustine, however, there are several serious interpretative pitfalls to be avoided. Three such problems in particular need to be named at the outset, if only to exorcise the possible dangers they may create in the realm of contemporary theology.

INTERPRETATIVE DANGERS

So there is ground-clearing to be done here before we can read and hear the texts of Nyssen and Augustine afresh. First, as we hinted in the Prelude, there has been a long-standing trend in twentieth-century theology to drive wedges between so-called 'Eastern' and 'Western' trinitarianism, and to utilize the Cappodocian fathers (Basil the Great, Gregory of Nazianzus, and Basil's brother Gregory of Nyssa) as pedagogical opposites, or contrasts, to the 'Western' work of Augustine.[1] The oft-repeated, but quite misleading, pedagogical slogan that 'The East starts from the three and moves to the One', and that the 'West', in contrast, 'starts from the One and moves to the three', had become by the 1970s so prevalent and so widely assumed in systematic theology,[2] that any attempt to compare Gregory of Nyssa and Augustine was simply taken to conform to some such pattern. The detailed story of how this fixation got its hold is a complex and fascinating one, and need not detain us here.[3] Suffice it to say that it arose at least in part from the need of an exiled Russian Orthodox school of theology, fleeing the Russian revolution, to re-establish a confident identity over against a prevailing Western neo-Thomism, which itself – ironically – was in the process of an increasing self-reform via new appeals not only to Augustine's thought but also to the insights of the early Greek patristic corpus. Nonetheless the 'East'–'West' disjunction

[1] It should be said that only quite recently has patristic scholarship come to give Gregory of Nyssa pride of place as the representative 'Eastern' patristic trinitarian exponent of the fourth century, even over Basil and Nazianzen; the revival of interest in Nyssen's distinctive and original thought is a twentieth-century phenomenon in the West, strongly influenced by the so-called *nouvelle théologie* movement within French Catholicism, and by the work of Jean Daniélou in particular.

[2] The rhetorical contrast is rightly attributed to the late nineteenth-century Jesuit Théodore de Régnon, *Études de théologie positive sur la Sainte Trinité* (4 vols.; Paris: Victor Retaux, 1892–8), vol. I, 428–35, amongst many other locations, but usually wrongly understood. He himself intended the contrast to apply not to the Cappadocians and Augustine – whom he rightly saw as sharing most trinitarian assumptions – but to the continuing Eastern tradition in comparison with later Western scholasticism.

[3] I have supplied a brief orientation to these complex exegetical issues in my 'Afterword: "Relational Ontology", Trinity, and Science', in John Polkinghorne, ed., *The Trinity and an Entangled World: Relationality in Physical Science and Theology* (Grand Rapids, MI: Eerdmans, 2011), 184–99.

rhetoric attained a certain dominance; and it was to continue to mesmerize exponents of systematic theology for some decades to come. Only in the last couple of decades, and then only slowly, have some of the more egregious misreadings arising from this disjunctive pedagogy been seriously challenged by detailed patristic study; and now systematic theology (which tends to lag behind technical advances in patristic scholarship) needs to take heed. This is my first caveat.

Secondly, one of the later manifestations of this same 'East'–'West' contrast school of trinitarian theology was a certain self-flagellating tendency amongst its 'Western' exponents to adulate the 'Eastern' trinitarian alternative, as they saw it, and especially to hold it up as an *imitable* prototype for ecclesial and social relations. And thence was born what came to be called 'social trinitarianism'. It was argued, for instance, that since the 'Eastern' model of the Trinity 'started from the three and moved to the One', it presented a vision of 'persons' in mutual 'communion' which could prove the ideal prototype for a political or church programme set on resisting the destructive individualism of the Enlightenment; whereas the 'Western', 'Augustinian' model of the Trinity was blamed for being nastily 'proto-Cartesian' in its implications in comparison. The 'West', it was argued, had already been seduced in Augustine well towards the modern solipsistic sense of selfhood which was later associated with Descartes' philosophy, and had read it instead on to God in Godself, making God in the image of the modern, *individual* mind.

But this interpretative line of approach was as flawed as the first trend which had spawned it; it sought to project certain anti-'Enlightenment' agendas directly into the life of God, thereby unconsciously creating a new idolatrous project of social utopianism while also seriously misreading the Enlightenment figures who had become the new 'whipping boys' of this 'Eastern' trinitarian project.

Ironically, the reading of the Cappadocian fathers which supposedly sustained this vision was itself strangely misleading exegetically.

A further, and third, wrinkle within this latter school of thinking was that it also attracted to itself some theologians notably sympathetic to the feminist cause (although not as critical of the classical tradition as the more radical feminist theologians of the time). On this 'softer' feminist and social trinitarian option, then, Augustine could be blamed for much of the evils of 'Western' individualistic and masculinist thinking, including his supposedly 'anti-body' theology and his 'male' mentalist trinitarianism; whereas the 'East' seemed in contrast to favour a high vision of 'relationship' and 'mutuality' implicitly supportive of women's projects. More radical feminists were, in contrast, critical of Christian trinitarianism *tout court*, and not just the 'Western' form of it: for them, the spectre of God as Trinity was simply the 'Men's Association' writ large, or even an incitement to battery and rape (in the tradition seemingly mandated by John Donne's famous sonnet, 'Batter My Heart, Three-Person'd God', to which we shall return at the end of this chapter). And somewhere in between these two positions (which already lay at opposite ends of the feminist theoretical spectrum) were feminist patristic scholars who were simply suspicious of all attempts from the period of early Christian theology to purvey a vision of divine perfection that appeared to demand, as an anthropological correlate, either asexuality or subordinate sexuality for women subjects.

Since the immediate backcloth of much recent 'systematic' work in the theology of the Trinity has been marked by one or more of these three sets of presumptions, it requires a certain tour de force to struggle into a new hermeneutical setting, and especially if one seeks to nudge the discussion of the Trinity, feminism, and gender forward towards a more creative – but also more spiritually demanding – theological moment. Quite apart from the fact that some of these influential twentieth-century readings of the patristic texts were intrinsically problematic, we can now see that it was entirely naïve to argue that as long as one conceptualized God as Trinity in *relationship* (and perhaps threw in a touch of Eastern Orthodox promise for good measure), all would be well and feminist critiques would dissolve into *perichorētic* harmony and mutuality. There was something awfully wrong with this falsely optimistic closure; just as there was something equally wrong with the opposite, and wholly pessimistic, conclusion that God as Trinity could never be anything but an abusive, masculinist God bent on punishment and destruction.

In the course of this chapter I shall do my best to lay aside any further polemics against these three sorts of 'pre-understanding' that so notably captured the imagination of twentieth-century systematic and feminist theology. To be sure, I am still in inevitable mental conversation with some of the important earlier feminist literature in this vein, as will be evident in what follows. But since my own approach to gender and feminism is so different (see Chapters 1 and 2), I often find myself unable to 'mesh' with these earlier feminist goals and presumptions. Instead I propose to return, to some degree newly uncluttered, to some of the texts of these two great founding fathers of Greek and Latin trinitarianism respectively, Gregory of Nyssa and Augustine. For it is not, I shall argue, that the 'West' was, already in Augustine, nastily proto-individualistic or 'Cartesian' or abstract in its trinitarian thinking, whereas the 'East' was ever rich with relational insight. Rather, *both* authors' trinitarian thinking was undeniably rife with a 'gender subtext' that we have yet to detect and unravel; and *both* were engaging profoundly, albeit in different contexts and with different points of difficulty, with what I have called the 'messy entanglement' of sexual desire and desire for God. If I am right, then to display how Gregory and Augustine struggle in these different, and perhaps mutually corrective, ways with this problem will be to point our way towards some sort of constructive trinitarian and anthropological solution. This will not, however, be one that simply rests with them unchanged, or adulates one over the other, but one which learns from them both and confronts this 'messy entanglement' more directly. As we shall see, the issue of divine trinitarian 'apophatic' mystery will here intersect significantly, and creatively, with incorrigible questions of gender, desire, passion, and asceticism. Gregory and Augustine, for all their obvious differences on these questions of gender, do in important ways also converge most remarkably in their final ontological vision of the trinitarian Godhead, and in their perceptions of its radically transformative potential for human life.[4]

GREGORY OF NYSSA (335–C. 395) AND AUGUSTINE OF HIPPO (354–430): A FIRST COMPARISON IN SYMBOLIC CONSTELLATIONS

The comparison of Gregory and Augustine will also take us back, with new and opened eyes, to one of the central paradoxes that bedevils contemporary feminist and gender theories and which was at stake above in Chapters 1 and 2. We might call this the paradox of 'equality and difference'. For modern and postmodern feminists and gender theorists in their different schools (liberal, radical, socialist, psychoanalytic, pragmatist) are still torn, and must I think remain torn given their secular assumptions, between the assertion of women's

---

[4] In what follows, I want to express my particular gratitude to Lewis Ayres for critical conversations over the years, which have helped me refine my thesis in this chapter.

equality with men in the public workplace (which concern tends to abstract from physical difference) and the assertion of women's physiological and psychological *difference* from men (which concern endangers the reimposition of gendered subordination). Even the attempt in pragmatist postmodern gender theory to undermine altogether the cultural fixation on the 'gender binary' (see Chapter 1) finds itself constantly pressed back to this dilemma in one way or another.

Illuminatingly, Gregory and Augustine also seem to anticipate this contemporary dilemma, but with very different modes of resolution given their theistic assumptions. Gregory points, as we shall see (and he does this with the crucial aid of a strongly apophatic dimension to his vision of spiritual growth), to the possibility not merely of women's spiritual 'equality' with men, but even of their potential ascetic superiority. His theory involves a fascinatingly labile perception of the role of 'gender' and its own subordination to a more fundamental propulsion to godly *desire*. Augustine, at least by the time of his later work, remains insistent on women's lasting – indeed eternal – bodily 'difference' from men, and struggles mightily with how to square this commitment with his equally strong intuition that women are spiritually and mentally equal to men before God (here he too appeals to Gal. 3. 28), yet constantly in need of physical protection from the violation that sinful men may wreak upon them. Both writers, we should note, are as dedicated as each other to probing the scriptural witness on gender,[5] though with somewhat different emphases, and are equally aware of its intriguing ambiguity and openness; both are profoundly

---

[5] Amongst the most important scriptural passages on gender with which Gregory and Augustine engage are: Gen. 1, Gen. 2, Mark 10. 1–12 (and parallels), Mark 12. 18–27 (and parallels), Gal. 3. 28, 1 Cor. 7. 1–16, 1 Cor. 11. 2–16, Eph. 5. 21–33, 1 Tim. 2. 8–15, and – for Gregory – the *Song of Songs*. As we shall see, some of these passages are given greater significance over others by both exegetes, since much depends from the outset on whether Genesis 1 is read through Genesis 2, or vice versa.

affected by Platonic and neo-Platonic insights on 'desire', although neither of them succumbs to an unquestioning assimilation of that philosophical tradition (as has often been held against them both); and certain important changes occur in both of their renditions of it through their careers. Finally, both are staunchly committed to a 'Nicene' trinitarianism, in which the espousal of perfect divine 'hypostatic' relations in the Trinity is conjoined with a deep sense of divine mystery and the ultimate incapacity of the human to 'tape', or mentally control, the inner workings of the life of the triune God.

Where, then, does their trinitarian thought diverge, and where is that divergence importantly connected – symbolically and analogically – with their difference of understanding about the nature of the sexes?

We cannot, first, ignore the crucial autobiographical differences on matters of sex which must, to one degree or another, have affected the two men's reflections on these topics, even if the precise nature of this influence remains speculative and difficult to assess. Gregory was married in his earlier life, and only later (after his wife's presumed death: the historical details here are obscure) embraced the celibate commitment of an ascetic and bishop. This makes his witness and insights on gender and sex peculiarly interesting: it is strung along a diachronic development which parallels his own move from married life to celibacy. In his work we rarely find any revulsion against sexual activity as such – on the contrary, it forms the increasingly vital metaphor for the relationship of the soul to God in Godself; and even in his public address to Christian neophytes (the *Catechetical Oration*) Gregory extols human genitalia as a matter for honour rather than for shame.[6] In Augustine's *oeuvre*,

---

[6] Gregory of Nyssa, 'An Address on Religious Instruction', 28, in Edward R. Hardy, ed., *Christology of the Later Fathers* (Philadelphia: Westminster Press, 1954), 306–7.

in contrast, the problematic and guilt-ridden extra-marital sexual relations of his early life (unforgettably charted in the *Confessions*) form an indelible backcloth to his later, theologically mature, reflections on women, sex, marriage, and the ascetic life. We should not, however, fall prey to an earlier feminist presumption that Augustine is thereby rendered body- or woman-*hating*. Still, the texture of his affirmation of the body and of sexual relations before God is undeniably different in tone from Gregory's; and it is not a coincidence that for the most part Augustine eschews theological and spiritual reflection on the erotic metaphors of the *Song of Songs*. It is rare in Augustine for the pleasures of sex to be spoken of positively as such, as opposed to his granting of a high theological importance to reproduction in Christian marriage.

My concern in what follows is to ask probing questions (suitable to a *théologie totale*), about how different aspects of these two writers' thinking, not usually put together, might mutually illuminate one another.[7] To get to the heart of the 'messy entanglement' of sexual desire and the desire for God, I shall ask about the *constitutive* connection between what these authors say on 'sexuality' and women on the one hand, and on God as Trinity and the quest for God in prayer and spiritual practice, on the other. How do their texts on these subjects – not usually so put together, but all vitally concerned with the issue of *relationship* – combine to throw light on the possible 'sexual subtext' in their trinitarian theologies?

---

[7] A justly famous essay by Rosemary Radford Ruether, 'Misogynism and Virginal Feminism in the Fathers of the Church', in *Religion and Sexism: Images of Women in the Jewish and Christian Traditions* (New York: Simon & Schuster, 1974), 184–211, long ago highlighted the different views held by Gregory and Augustine on the doctrines of creation and the nature of the sexes. What follows is both a strong implicit critique of Ruether's reading of the two authors, and yet also remains indebted to her primary insights about the importance of the comparison. I have however extended the range of comparisons to include the matters of prayer and the Trinity, which are central to this book's concerns.

Let me anticipate my comparative thesis in its broad outlines first, before turning back to supply some more revealing details about each author's work individually.

In the case of Gregory of Nyssa, first, we find in his great last commentary works, especially, a spirituality of *erōs* stretching up into darkness and into loss of mental control. And in this yielding to the unknown which the *nous* (intellect) here undergoes, we are presented with a striking primary subtext of male sexual desire and release (though one that also tips over into metaphors of womb-like receptivity). So it is not I think insignificant to discover that Gregory (who, bemusingly enough to the exegetes, was married when he wrote his first asceticial treatise, *De virginitate*) lauds 'virginity' *not* on the grounds that sexual activity is in itself intrinsically dangerous or polluting; instead, he argues, the call that some have to celibacy should be on the grounds of desiring, by way of ascetic witness, to suspend the normal social order, to stop reproducing in order to avoid the endless cycle of birth and death – to echo in that way, in fact, the eternal nature of the trinitarian Godhead. And so here we come to how the nature of God as Trinity 'fits' anologically into this picture as Gregory presents it, even from the time of his earliest writings. As we have seen in Chapter 3, the Spirit in Gregory's later apologetic works is the divine outreach – the lure, the attraction, if you wish – into the Godhead. And Christ, in the terms of the *Song of Songs* on which Gregory wrote a strikingly beautiful commentary late in life, is the 'bridegroom' of the soul. But all three 'persons' are ultimately equally unknowable or 'incomprehensible' in the darkness of superseded reason to which the soul *yields* in submission to the bridegroom.

Perhaps, then, we can now begin to see the 'constitutive connections' between these different areas that are being explicated. At the symbolic heart of Gregory's system is a very particular kind of *loss* of control, a yielding to the unknown in God in a desire without end. This is no less true of the 'spirituality' of his exegetical works than of his later trinitarian theology as expressed in them, in which – as an ontological correlate – a glorious confusion of metaphors is applied to a trinitarian God who slays his lovers in the Spirit and loves them without reserve in Christ.[8] In neither arena is sexual metaphor worrisome for Gregory; indeed, it turns out to be indispensable: for it is deeply redolent of that never achieved union with the divine nature towards which Gregory constantly and restlessly strives.

But what about Augustine? Here, if I am right, the correlations line up somewhat differently, and with a set of emphases and interests which have profoundly affected Western Christendom ever since. The Platonic and neo-Platonic theme of 'desire' for God is of course as central in Augustine as it is in Nyssen (in the famous words of the *Confessions*: 'You have made us for yourself, and our hearts are restless till they rest in you');[9] and desire for God also remains to the fore in Augustine's theory of prayer in his later career. But his attitude to women and sex, which, as we shall see, is mixed and complex, is crucially different from Gregory's in at least this respect: even normal marital sexual activity is *intrinsically* worrisome to Augustine because of the revolt of the male body –

---

[8] A more detailed account of these points is given in Sarah Coakley, 'Re-Thinking Gregory of Nyssa: Introduction – Gender, Trinitarian Analogies, and the Pedagogy of *The Song*', in *Re-Thinking Gregory of Nyssa* (Oxford: Blackwell, 2003), 1–13 (for an examination of the zany proliferation of metaphors used for the Trinity in Nyssen's *Song* commentary, including 'male' and 'female' namings); and also in my '"Persons" in the "Social" Doctrine of the Trinity: Current Analytic Discussion and "Cappadocian" Theology', in *Powers and Submissions: Spirituality, Philosphy and Gender* (Oxford: Blackwell, 2002), 209–29 (for a critical rereading of the standard twentieth-century account of Gregory's apologetic trinitarianism).

[9] *Confessions* I.1, trans. Henry Chadwick (Oxford University Press, 1998), 3.

the phallus – against the man's rational will to have complete control over himself.[10] The rightful *harmony* between the rational activities of the mind – memory, understanding, and will – in their normal operations, and in mutual relation to the body, is thus disordered, disturbed in sex. Physical sex, for Augustine, undermines the ideal of control or 'mastery', of one's self (as he puts it in the famous passage on continence in *Confessions*, x.29).[11] It is, however, only *God* who can finally supply the (graced) control that human, ascetic effort constantly fails to achieve.

Yet the contrast with Gregory's spiritual emphasis on the indispensability of *loss* of mental control in the allegory of Moses and Mount Sinai is striking. It is hardly surprising, then, that Augustine's mature trinitarian theology (expressed in his *De trinitate*) is – at least at one important level of analysis – a theology of cooperative, harmonious, *ordered* mental activities in God. Just as memory, understanding, and will operate, or should operate, harmoniously and cooperatively in the human subject, and the body be subject to the will, so too – at a higher and perfected analogical level – the divine persons are mutually and harmoniously cooperative, one with another. That is what God is *like* for Augustine – to the extent, that is, that the human mind can comprehend the nature of God at all. It is of course true that Augustine will come to contrast what *normal* human reasoning, even at its best, can achieve by way of order and insight, and what a final and more direct 'contemplative' response to the beatific vision will be like; and – as with Gregory – he is ever aware of the mysteriousness and infinite

---

[10] *Concerning the City of God against the Pagans*, XIV.16, trans. Henry Bettenson (Harmondsworth: Penguin, 1984), 577.

[11] 'By continence we are collected together and brought to the unity from which we disintegrated into multiplicity', *Confessions* 10.29, trans. Henry Chadwick (Oxford University Press, 1998), 202. It is only God, for Augustine, who can effect continence, as a gift of grace; the Stoic vision of *human* self-mastery is finally a chimera for him.

difference of the divine life from the created order: by the end of the *De trinitate* he has even declared *all* his previously rehearsed analogies for the Trinity inadequate (*De trinitate*, XV.7, 11–14). Nonetheless, the goal he has in mind is one of final blessedness in clarity and certainty – not perfection in darkness and loss of mental control.[12]

Perhaps in this first, broad brush-stroke attempt at comparison of our authors, the drift of my analysis may be becoming clear. I seek to probe the symbolic themes and substantive preoccupations which unite their *particular* views on relationship at all levels; and I seek to display how, for them, these various levels of relationship intersect analogically. As we turn now to examine Gregory's and Augustine's positions in a little more detail, some further surprises will, however, await us. In the case of each author I shall look briefly, first, at his view of the nature of the human and the sexes; second, at his theory of prayer and spiritual development; and third, at his understanding of God as Trinity. I shall then attempt to give further evidence of how these themes mesh – or, at occasional and revealing moments, significantly fail to mesh. What will emerge is a conclusion that is admittedly paradoxical but nonetheless profoundly suggestive for the systematic proposal to be finally essayed in the last chapter. For what disjoins Gregory and Augustine in their theory of gender in all its evocations, nonetheless simultaneously and surprisingly conjoins them in their epistemology of desire and their ontology of divine trinitarian mystery. What starts as a new

---

[12] Only consider *De trinitate* XV.25, 45: 'We shall see the truth there without any difficulty, and shall enjoy it to the full because it is most clear and most certain. Nor [*sc.* at that point, in the beatific vision] shall we seek anything by the reasoning of the mind, but by contemplating we shall perceive' (Augustine, *The Trinity*, trans. Stephen McKenna (Washington, DC, Catholic University of America Press, 2002), 513). We may contrast this with the dark perfection of 'never arriving', which is characteristic of Nyssen's vision for life after death.

attempt to illuminate the difference of their central controlling metaphors ends, most surprisingly, in a certain ironic metaphysical convergence. Let me now explain.

GREGORY OF NYSSA ON GENDER, PRAYER, AND THE TRINITY [13]

Gregory's view of the nature of the human and the sexes, first, is best illuminated by looking at his thoughts on creation and eschatology, and then back again at his early treatise *On virginity*. Both originally and ultimately, for Gregory, the human person is what one might call 'humanoid' (or perhaps 'angeloid') – neither male nor female in any commonly accepted sense. This intriguing idea is expounded in Gregory's famous reflections about a 'double creation' in his treatise on *The making of humanity* (chs. 16–17), which has occasioned much recent exegetical comment. It is all a matter here of how Gregory interprets Genesis 1. 27: 'God created man in His own image; in the image of God he created him, male and female he created them'. Taking Galatians 3. 28 as a text to play off *against* this ('in Christ there is neither ... male [and] female'), Gregory argues that Genesis 1. 27 should be taken in two parts, as the Hebrew text itself suggests: first a non-physical, non-sexed, angelic creation; and only then, with the Fall becoming imminent, sexual differentiation. (Thus on this view, note, gender differentiation into two is implicitly connected with moving towards the fallen state.) So too, in reverse, at the general resurrection, says Gregory

---

[13] I am here condensing into a short overview what I have discussed in more detail in several other writings: again, in Coakley, *Powers and Submissions*, ch. 9; in Paul Gavrilyuk and Sarah Coakley, eds., *The Spiritual Senses: Perceiving God in Western Christianity* (Cambridge University Press, 2011), ch. 2; and in Sarah Coakley, *The New Asceticism: Sexuality, Gender and the Quest for God* (London: Continuum, 2013), ch. 1.

(in his oration *On those who have fallen asleep*), our bodies will lose their sexual differentiation, but – interestingly – all become quasi-'female' in relation to God, being, as Verna Harrison glosses him, 'impregnated with life from God and giving birth to various forms of goodness'.[14]

Women, then, paradisally and eschatologically, might be seen as honorary *sexless* 'men' (and the contrast with Augustine here will be highly important). But in some sense men are also, eschatologically, honorary sexless 'women'. Of course, even to put it thus is arguably to miss the subtlety and elusiveness of what Gregory is after; for in prioritizing Genesis 1 over Genesis 2 in this way, Gregory seems to be implying that the binary gender difference does not play the *defining* role in our true spiritual – or even bodily[15] – identity at all; so earlier feminist critics who have dismissed Gregory's ploy as a mere erasure of women's distinctiveness and stature surely miss the point. Yet postmodern theorists also err in thinking that Gregory can thereby be constrained into a contemporary *secular* agenda of 'gender fluidity': his understanding of what constitutes authentic human existence before God eludes even these 'transgressive' categories.

The most interesting (and perhaps test-) case of gender reversal or transformation in Gregory's work is found in his adulation of his elder sister Macrina, and especially in his treatise *The Life of Macrina*. Macrina, qua virgin, and in virtue of her outstanding

---

[14] See Verna Harrison, 'Male and Female in Cappadocian Theology', *Journal of Theological Studies* 41 (1990), 441–71. Note the background importance here both of Jesus's words (Mark 12. 25) 'when they rise from the dead, they neither marry nor are given in marriage', and of the Platonic idea of 'spiritual procreation' as a replacement for physical reproduction in the higher realm of philosophy.

[15] Even angels, of course, have a special sort of visible 'body': when Gregory speaks of transformed bodiliness he invariably has the mysterious 'spiritual body' of 1 Corinthians 15 in mind.

ascetical prowess, is set up as an awesome model in her quality of 'male' *erōs* – desire for God. (Here Gregory is using 'male' to indicate a particular cultural and philosophical value.) Thus can Gregory remark admiringly at one point that Macrina could even be seen as a 'man' in this regard.[16] But she is also, most interestingly, the cause in Gregory of the production of a strong, 'womanish', *affective* response – which in turn brings about a lively philosophical debate between them about how intellect and affect should properly relate. Thus, in his treatise *On the soul and the resurrection*, Gregory dialogues with Macrina on the problem of the relation of affectivity (or passion) with reason, interestingly projecting on to her an initially rigorist rejection of the emotions (which today we might normally take to be 'masculinist'), while he takes the part of defending passion. Gradually they together work out in dialogue a more integrated and transformative vision of the passions in relation to the soul; for both body and soul are in due course to be brought to final perfection in the resurrection body (it is in fact 1 Corinthians 15 which frames the narrative of this philosophical dialogue, at both beginning and end).

In short, there are already all kinds of interesting 'sexual/textual' play in Gregory's work, designed to reverse, complexify, and confound what modern feminists have dubbed the body-hating stereotype of the 'Platonist' 'Man of Reason'. Whatever Gregory has in mind for the resurrection life, it will certainly not conform to anything we can catch and hold in gender stereotypes *in this world*. But ultimately, and originally, we are, according to him, all 'humanoid/angeloid', rather than physically 'sexed' into male and female at all. Yet even after death we shall still remain, on his vision of

---

[16] *Life of Macrina*, in Anne M. Silvas, *Macrina the Younger, Philosopher of God* (Turnhout: Brepols, 2008), 109–48, here 110; GNO VIII/1, 370–414, here 370–1.

ongoing ascetical transformation, questing, longing, desiring, and – in the elusive sense discussed in Chapter 1 – thus still 'gendered' in relation to *God*, even despite the loss therein of 'sexed' differentiation.

What, then, is the particular virtue of virginity, according to Gregory? (Both Gregory and Augustine of course share the view – not to them contentious – that virginity is a better state than marriage, although Gregory insists that well-ordered marriage is infinitely better than badly ordered celibacy.) Perhaps the most important point here, well brought out by Peter Brown in his magisterial study *The Body and Society*,[17] and already intimated above, is that Gregory nowhere suggests, in his early tract *De virginitate*, that sexual activity is intrinsically lustful, worrisome, or a matter of guilt. Rather, if virginity is finally *better* than marriage, it is because it puts desire for God above all else; and so it stops procreation, and thus the whirlygig of birth and death, and the jostling for social standing, in a world of class and civic competition with which the high-born Cappadocians were well familiar. The undergirding motif here, at least as Brown avers, was one of renewed eschatological expectation:

For Basil and Gregory, neither the universe nor the city was secure. All creation was poised in tense expectation of the return of Christ ... Both sensed acutely the power of the ancient, civic urge to pile up wealth, to gather kinsmen, and to beget descendants ... it was to tame [this urge], and only incidentally to tame the sexual urge, that Basil had written with passionate exactitude on the model of life to be practised in his 'brotherhoods'.[18]

Thus, in his own early treatise *De virginitate*, Gregory argues – and note again the constitutive connection with the doctrine of God –

---

[17] Peter Brown, *The Body and Society* (London: Faber, 1988), 285–304.   [18] Ibid., 303.

that virginity is moulded on the chaste relations of Father, Son, and Holy Spirit. Why? Because by avoiding *death* – that is, procreation – we may emulate eternity: 'it was never possible for death to be idle while human generation was active by means of marriage', he says; whereas virginity 'is a fellow citizen of the entire celestial nature because its impassibility accompanies the superior powers and is inseparable from divine realities'. The 'constitutive connection' between virginity and the divine nature is thus explicitly made by Gregory himself. However, for him this does not mean that married asceticism does not have its own value and glory; it is all a matter, as he puts it, of the 'right aiming' of desire (at God) and of its appropriate 'moderation' in all matters of good physical pleasure.[19]

But what about Gregory's view of spiritual development, next? How does this connect with our undergirding (and multi-levelled) theme of 'relationship'? It is in his late work the *Life of Moses*, most memorably, that Gregory tells the allegorical story of the soul's ascent to intimate relationship with the divine. As with Philo and Clement before him, Moses's ascent up Mount Sinai is for Gregory the 'type' of the contemplative's quest for God. In this treatise, Moses moves in three stages from the light of the Burning Bush (interpreted as the light of the incarnation), through cloudy

---

[19] *De virginitate*, 2; GNO VIII/1, 253. It should be acknowledged that, on occasion in his writings, especially in his mid career (e.g., in Oratio VII of his *Homilies on Ecclesiastes: An English Version with Supporting Studies*, trans. Stuart George Hall and Rachel Moriarty (Berlin: De Gruyter, 1993), 123 (GNO V, 409), citing 1 Cor. 14. 35 with approval), Gregory does refer without demur to biblical injunctions about the subordination of wives to husbands in marriage, something that he nowhere draws attention to in his early *De virginitate*. It might seem, then, that he largely reserves the capacity for the more radical forms of gender transformation to the realm of women ascetics. However, asceticism is a calling that he regards as appropriate to all Christians, whether married or celibate: he regards a good marriage climaxing, after children are grown up, in duteous service to the poor. In this sense the boundary between marriage and the ascetic life is a porous one for Gregory.

darkness in the wilderness, to the thick darkness of the peak of Mount Sinai, the climax of the ascent. The language, even in the Greek, may strike the reader as sexually symbolic:

> as the soul makes progress [says Gregory], and by a greater and more perfect concentration comes to appreciate what the knowledge of truth is, so much the more does it see that the divine nature is invisible. It thus leaves all surface appearances, not only those that can be grasped by the senses, but also those which the mind itself seems to see, and it keeps on going deeper until by the operation of the spirit it *penetrates* the invisible and incomprehensible, and it is there that it sees God. The true vision and true knowledge of what we seek consists precisely in not seeing, in an awareness that our goal transcends all knowledge and is everywhere cut off from us by the darkness of incomprehensibility.[20]

Thus, the classic Platonic goals of light and clarity and achieved perfection are extraordinarily reversed by Gregory into darkness and obscurity and a perfection that 'never arrives' (as he puts it in his treatise *On perfection*):[21] now we see that the goal of the Christian life is a very particular kind of *loss* of control. At this point, as Gregory explains in his *Commentary on the Song of Songs*, the soul has to wait for the spouse (Christ) in darkness, relying only on the 'spiritual senses' of smell, taste, touch, and feeling.[22] The ascent of ('male') *erōs* thus tips over into what we might call a dark womblike receptivity. Verna Harrison draws attention to Gregory's concept of 'spiritual procreation' as the goal for both sexes here, qua ascetics: the human person becomes a 'receptacle created to be filled with the

---

[20] *The Life of Moses* 376d–377a; GNO VII/1, 86–7, in *From Glory to Glory: Texts from Gregory of Nyssa's Mystical Writings*, ed. Jean Daniélou, trans. Herbert Musurillo (Crestwood, NY: St Vladimir's Seminary Press, 1961), 118, my emphasis.

[21] *On Perfection* 285d, in *Ascetical Works*, trans. Virginia Woods Callahan (Washington, DC: Catholic University of America Press, 1987), 122; GNO VII/1, 86–7.

[22] *Commentary on the Song of Songs*, VI, in *Homilies on the Song of Songs*, ed. Richard A. Norris (Atlanta, GA: Society of Biblical Literature, 2012), 191–201; GNO VI, 180–8.

life of God and in response to pour forth that life both to God and neighbor'.[23]

But what, finally, of Gregory's trinitarianism? How does it 'fit' (in some analogical sense) with the above – or does it? Earlier, in Chapter 3, it was noted that Gregory's late exegetical writings have many of the aspects of the prayer-based 'incorporative' model of the Trinity we discussed there (as well they might, granted the priority Gregory grants to the Spirit's lure into the life of the Godhead). But although the Spirit is there prioritized experientially, Gregory's understanding of inner trinitarian relationships in some of his more doctrinally polemical writings is – as was seen in Chapter 3 – more infected by a safe 'linear' and hierarchical ordering of the persons than is suggested by Paul's vision in Romans 8 of the 'reflexive' answering of Spirit to Father in and through the prayer. As emerges from Gregory's famous treatise *Ad Ablabium, on 'Not three Gods'* (and despite his insistence there on the strict *homoousian* equality of the persons), it is clear that Gregory sees messages from the divine side running *downwards*, in an ordered flow from the Father (who is 'source' and 'cause' of the other two), through the Son, to the Holy Spirit; and then the 'ascent' from our side reverses the order *upwards* (*Ad Ablab.*, 125c, 128a). As Gregory puts it in one of his letters (previously attributed to Basil; *Ep.*, 38, 4): 'One must

---

[23] Harrison, 'Male and Female', 470. In Luce Irigaray's extraordinary post-Freudian reading of Plato's allegory of the cave (in 'Plato's *Hystera*', in *Speculum of the other Woman* (Ithaca, NY: Cornell University Press, 1985), 243–364), she sees the allegory of the cave as a masculinist rejection by Plato of the maternal womb (the cave) in his quest for the hegemony of reason (the light). If we can grant something to Irigaray's Lacanian psychoanalytic method of analysis here (see again Chapter 1 above for an assessment), then by the same token one might detect, in terms of *Gregory's* reversal of gender metaphors in *The Life of Moses*, a striking *return* to the womblike themes of darkness and receptivity when reason (*nous*) is finally superseded at the height of the ascent. On this reading there is an ultimate dethronement of the *nous*, a return to darkness and receptivity: Plato's 'cave', one might say, is re-entered, but at a higher level of spiritual consciousness.

first be enlightened by the Spirit, in order to ascend to the Son and thence to the Father'. In other words, the radical epistemic slippage at the height of Moses's ascent in the *Life of Moses*, which seems to dissolve all structured order and hierarchy, even in the God who is encountered, does not find any consistent or clear counterpart in Gregory's understanding of the Trinity in his mid-career defences of trinitarianism, which remain (as in his brother Basil's *De sancto Spiritu*) clearly structured and ordered – as Moses's earlier stages of the ascent are structured and ordered. There are apparently no sudden reversals here (despite all the rhetoric of the 'incomprehensibility' of the divine persons), which might ostensibly signal another and more profound 'apophatic turn'. If we want to find a resolution to this difficulty – this apparent lack of 'fit' between apologetic-trinitarian and later exegetical treatises – we have to ferret out the wilder trinitarian analogies of those later writings: less philosophically precise, to be sure, than those in the apologetic discourses, but freed up into a remarkable poetic and erotic licence. Here, archers and arrows, winds and billowing sails, and human erotic lovers become the new analogues of the freedom of inner-trinitarian relations, and of their transfiguring relation to us.[24]

AUGUSTINE ON GENDER, PRAYER, AND TRINITARIANISM

But now let us compare all that we have found here in Gregory with the case of Augustine. Again, I shall look for correlations between Augustine's view of the person (man and woman), of the life of prayer, and of God as Trinity. Whereas the final interest in Gregory is in *loss* of control, in yielding to noetic darkness, a much more

---

[24] Again, see my treatment of the Trinity in the *Song* commentary in *Re-Thinking Gregory of Nyssa*, 1–13.

dominant emphasis in Augustine, I suggest (at least until a certain modification in his last anti-Pelagian writings), is the quest for corporate and controlled *order* – at the level of life in the Trinity, of the city (*polis*), and of relations between the sexes. This is not of course to imply that Augustine is lacking a sense of the utter mysteriousness and transcendence of God (a God who, according to him, is no less mysterious qua incarnate): again and again in his sermons he will stress that we cannot 'understand' the Word, but merely 'hunger for it'.[25] Yet running through the *Confessions* and the agony of his own failed attempts at sexual continence is the ongoing struggle for 'order' over chaos – an order that he finally realizes can *only* be supplied by God and divine grace; and we should not therefore be surprised to find this trope exercising itself in other dimensions of Augustine's theology.[26] Let us now examine these central themes in Augustine of order, control, and place.

The contrast with Gregory on the nature of the person, first, is well brought out by looking at Augustine's view of paradisal sex in the *City of God*, book XIV. For Augustine, in contrast to Gregory, Genesis 1. 27 is understood as a one-stage event: right from the start God created man and woman, and this grants to woman a validated *Ur*-status as physically different. It is as if Genesis 1 already

---

[25] See, e.g., Sermon 117.3 in *Sermons*, trans. Edmund Hill, ed. John E. Rotelle (New York: New City Press, 1992), vol. III/4, 210: 'We are not now discussing . . . possible ways of understanding the text . . . it can only be understood in ways beyond words . . . it wasn't read in order to be understood, but in order to make us try to discover what prevents our understanding, and so move it out of the way, and hunger to grasp the unchangeable Word, ourselves thereby being changed from worse to better.'

[26] Margaret Miles's feminist reading of *The Confessions* also comes to the conclusion that 'order' is Augustine's chief obsession in that work, such that, she claims, books X–XIII of *The Confessions* lack the attractive restlessness of the earlier sections; for 'hierarchical order – everything in its place – has overcome the chaos in which the objects of lust relentlessly butt against and displace each other . . . Order . . . can [only] be . . . incarnated in the continent body': *Desire and Delight: A New Reading of Augustine's Confessions* (New York: Crossroad, 1992), 133.

anticipates Genesis 2 and the creation of Eve out of Adam's rib: difference and dependence (of woman on man) are of foundational significance right from the start. All this is to be contrasted with Gregory, with his ingenious rendition of Genesis 1. 27 and his relative lack of interest in the story of Adam's rib. 'There is no denying', Augustine emphasizes in contrast, 'the obvious evidence of bodies of *different* sex, which shows that it would be a manifest absurdity to deny the fact that male and female were created for the purpose of begetting children' (*City of God*, XIV.22). Sex and pro-creation are good, then, for that purpose alone; and according to the later Augustine, we shall still be physically (and recognizably) men and women at the end times, eschatologically.[27] What is really worrying to Augustine in the post-Fall condition, however, is male loss of control in sex: the revolt of the body against the cooperative mental work of memory, understanding, and will – especially against the will. Thus what is nasty and 'shameful' about sex (and our private parts are rightly called *pudenda*, he says, again in contrast to Gregory) is the independent revolt of the male phallus. Augustine expatiates on this at some length in the *City of God*, book XIV.22–6: men would like to be able to move the phallus at will, that is, 'like our hands and feet'; but there is 'this resistance, this tussle between lust and will'. If there had been no Fall, then children could have been conceived dispassionately – and, interest-ingly, with the woman remaining *intacta*. For Augustine, this would seemingly have been a preferable (if somewhat unimaginable) arrangement. But rather than snigger at this suggestion, we might well consider whether Augustine's concern here is not at least as

---

[27] See Margaret Miles, *Augustine on the Body* (Missoula, MT: Scholars Press, 1979), 52–77, 117–25, for the differences between the earlier and later Augustine on this point.

much for women's physical safety from assault and abuse, as for the desired male sense of ordered physical control.[28]

Where then does this leave physically differentiated women? Answer: in a very ambiguous position – nowhere better expressed, perhaps, than in the fascinating and disputed book XII of the *De trinitate*. The argument here has, I fear, been misrepresented by some earlier feminist exegetes.[29] There are, it seems, two sides to Augustine's view of women which remain somewhat unresolved, and are paradoxically expressed in this section of the *De trinitate*. On the one hand, there is a strong conviction in him that woman are *mentally* equal to men. On the other, scriptural authority (especially the vexed 1 Corinthians 11. 7: 'the woman is the glory of the man') leads him towards the view that woman, considered in her own right, is *different* – subordinate qua bodily, and not fully in the image of God unless joined to a man, her husband. Thus, in one and the same section of the *De trinitate* (book XII, ch. 7), Augustine can quote Galatians 3. 28 ('There is neither male nor female'), and comment that when the rational mind is renewed through incorporative baptism in Christ, 'who would exclude women ... since they are co-heirs with us of grace?' But just before, in deference to Paul in 1 Corinthians 11. 7 (a passage with which he clearly struggles), he can also reason thus:

In what sense are we to understand the Apostle, that the man is the image of God, and consequently is forbidden to cover his head, but the woman is not,

---

[28] I am grateful to Gillian Clark for this insight.

[29] See, again, Ruether, 'Misogynism and Virginal Feminism', 150–83, and Genevieve Lloyd, *The Man of Reason: 'Male' and 'Female' in Western Philosophy* (London: Methuen, 1984), 28, 33. One should compare these accounts with the more nuanced presentations in T. J. van Bavel, 'Augustine's View of Women', *Augustiniana* 39 (1989), 5–53; Kari E. Børresen, 'In Defence of Augustine: How *Femina* is *Homo*?', in B. Brunning, ed., *Collectanea Augustiniana: Mélanges T. J. van Bavel* (Leuven: Peeters, 1990), 411–27; and John Rist, *Augustine: Ancient Thought Baptized* (Cambridge University Press, 1994), 92–147.

and on this account is commanded to do so? The solution lies . . . [in that] the woman together with the husband is the image of God . . . when she is assigned as a help-mate, a function that pertains to her alone, then she is not the image of God; but as far as the man is concerned, he is by himself alone the image of God, just as fully and completely as when he and the woman are joined together into one.

The fatal lines of subordination are seemingly drawn, then: Augustine confronts the paradox of equality and difference, but the dice are this time, in contrast to Gregory, loaded towards the latter, to subordinate difference. He bows, significantly, to scriptural authority, 'order', and subordination. Yet another instinct, equally mandated by Scripture (in Galatians 3. 28), continues to draw him in a different direction. And so the paradox remains.

As for the theme of prayer and spiritual advance in Augustine, secondly, there are differences in the earlier and later periods of his life, but the important point to notice in comparison with Gregory is that Augustine's is a spiritual theology leading to *light* and clarification and insight (supremely beyond this life), not to darkness and incomprehensibility and loss of control. Augustine's later views on prayer, as witnessed by his letter 130 to the widow Proba,[30] are quite different in tone from the contemplative experience of ascent with his mother at Ostia, described in *The Confessions*, book IX. He has now given up his earlier interest in highpoint 'Plotinian' experiences. Prayer is, he says now, 'desire for happiness', and rightly so; but this happiness can only lie *beyond* the darkness (*tenebrae*) of this life. For we long to arrive and to be freed from the corrupted will. Again, we are not travelling into darkness and loss of control here, but *from* darkness into light, into the light of grace which one might appropriately describe as right *divine* control.

[30] *Letters*, ed. Sr Wilfrid Parsons (FC 18; Washington, DC: Catholic University of America Press, 1953), vol. II, 376–401.

We can see, now, how all this fits with one important strand in Augustine's trinitarian theology in books X–XII of the *De trinitate*. Just as paradise or human perfection consists in harmonious mental cooperation of the faculties and no loss of physical or sexual control, so too (on the analogy of the mental activities), memory, understanding, and the will in their mutual cooperation mirror forth *God*. For the mind is the image of the trinitarian God in us, says Augustine: 'Since these three, the memory, the understanding and the will, are therefore not three lives but one life, not three minds but one mind, it follows that there are certainly not three substances, but one substance' (*De trinitate*, X, ch. 11). Thus, as with the level of the human, so at the level of the divine, what matters is harmony and order, unity and cooperation.

There is, however, as with Gregory, one aspect of these correlations that is misleading and does not seem to 'fit' the Augustinian picture overall. For Augustine himself, as has been noted, has a profoundly apophatic sensibility and, over the years, and in the face of the Pelagian controversy, a manifestly intensified theology of prevenient grace. Whereas the measured 'linear' ordering of the triune God in some of Gregory's apologetic writings does not quite seem to *go* with his vision of God in his late exegetical texts and his sense there of the mind's radical slippage into the 'spiritual senses' at the height of the ascent (his apophatic *loss* of control), so too, I suggest, there is a strain in the later anti-Pelagian Augustine that breaks down *his* carefully constructed edifice of controlled cognitive order *in God*. It peeps out, as I have mentioned before, in the last book of the *De trinitate* – the book in which, not coincidentally, Augustine also announces the inadequacy of all of his previous analogies for the Trinity. It is a discourse of an overflowing, enkindling, inflaming, and 'incorporative' flow of the holy Spirit, a 'pouring forth' into our hearts, through which, says Augustine, 'the whole Trinity dwells in us' (book xv, ch. 18). There is not only a strong echo here of Romans 5. 5 and Romans 8. 14–17 (in the outpouring and incorporative flow of the Spirit), but also a sense of even divine 'control' finally being released, the system cracking, undoing itself – although not enough to cause Augustine to question or qualify his biblically directed views about the symbolic subordination of women to men.

Let me now sum up this long section, which has formed the weightier part of this chapter. Throughout it I have been engaged in exploring two substantive themes – themselves complicatedly related. First, I have shown – at least if my *théologie totale* exploration of connected texts and themes on relationship has any validity – that there is a correlated package of gender-laden meanings attached to both Gregory's and Augustine's trinitarianism, such that recurring interests analogically conjoin different levels of their theological thinking. Whereas Gregory stresses the potential *equality*, even superiority, of ascetic women over men (and repeatedly lauds loss of noetic control as the goal of the contemplative), Augustine wavers a bit before subordinating women to a place of controlled dependent orderliness (which does however protect their divinely ordained physical *difference* and their irreducibly significant status in the institution of marriage). The paradox of equality and difference is thus ridden; but it is not in either case being expressed in a way that is easily recognizable to either modern or contemporary gender theory: gender is here being recast, rethought, by both authors in response to different scriptural dictates and in relation to a distinctive trinitarian vision of the Godhead. Yet two very different renditions of gender result.

But secondly, there are also elements in both men's theology (and this will be the basis of my constructive suggestion to come) that press in a certain 'maverick', yet strangely convergent, direction. There is Gregory's 'apophatic turn' into darkness which upends the world's (and even some of the Bible's) sexual stereotypes, and Augustine's returning and uncontrolled effusions of desire and delight at the divine level in the last chapters of his *De trinitate*. Both, it seems, hint at a certain symbolic or analogical alignment of sexual desire and desire for God, rather than demanding a disjunctive choice between them. And both, by chance, point forward to themes in another 'maverick' of the Christian Platonist tradition, Pseudo-Dionysius the Areopagite, whose distinctly daring perception (in the *Divine Names*, ch. 4) of a *divine* ecstatic yearning meeting and incorporating a responsive human, ecstatic yearning, will form the basis of my proposed contemplative trinitarian reconstruction to come.

But I will only hint at that now and return to it in the last chapter; because I want to finish this chapter with a return to modern feminist critiques of the Trinity, and in particular to that much maligned early modern sonnet, Donne's 'Batter My Heart'. For I believe our foregoing analysis may now throw significant light on it, given its standing as an unforgettable poetic rendition of 'Augustinian' trinitarianism. What is still at stake, then, is the earlier feminist concern that – covertly, or even here overtly – the themes of patriarchal power and abuse remain validated in the 'Western imaginary' about the trinitarian God. For what we are again up against, in Donne's distinctly Augustinian theology of desire, is a tragic sense of *disjunction* between human and divine loves, yet one which Donne himself clearly yearns to resolve. And at this point the questions posed at the start of this chapter, about false and authentic theologies of desire, begin to press with new force. What can we learn here from Donne's celebrated example? How does he extend, or modify, his Augustinian inheritance?

'BATTER MY HEART': JOHN DONNE ON THE TRINITY
AND FEMINIST CRITIQUE

I said at the beginning of this chapter that feminist critiques of trinitarianism need to be more nuanced, less simplistic. If our analysis of the history of trinitarianism up till now has done nothing else, I hope it has shown that these problems for trinitarianism cannot be discussed or dismissed in *general*. Neither the claim by Jürgen Moltmann that properly trinitarian thinking per se makes it all right (in contradistinction to what he calls the 'monotheist' ordering: 'Holy Father, Father of the Country, Father of the family'),[31] nor the claim that trinitarianism makes it all wrong (for, as Daphne Hampson has put it: 'the Trinity does not as a symbol embody equality between male and female')[32] quite works, surely, granted the *complexity* that we now recognize in trinitarian traditions, in prayer and art and text and field observation. The multitudinous messages that press on us in any one of such contexts belie this. Nor will a quick shift of pronouns, or the smuggling in of a divine 'feminine' principle, or some bracing talk about 'mutuality' (with a pot-shot or two at 'hierarchy') do the trick either, if what we really need to do is stare the entanglement of sexual desire and desire for God firmly in the face. And this, significantly, is at least what Donne does. Let us then reflect afresh on his sonnet, and see what lessons we may learn from it.

The matter became newly contentious in feminist theology in the 1990s in an article by Mary Grey, in which she argued – following Nancy Chodorow's psychological thesis that boys develop through

---

[31] Jürgen Moltmann, 'The Motherly Father. Is Trinitarian Patripassianism Replacing Theological Patriarchalism?', in J.-B. Metz and E. Schillebeeckx, eds., *God as Father?* (Edinburgh: T&T Clark, 1981), 51–6.

[32] Daphne Hampson, *Theology and Feminism* (Oxford: Blackwell, 1990), 154.

separation from the mother, and girls through relationality and connection – that 'women's relational experience has a triadic basis', while patriarchal notions of transcendence are separative and disjunctive.[33] The particular butt of her critique of 'male' transcendence, so-called, was Donne's 'Batter My Heart':

> Batter my heart, three-personed God; for you
> As yet but knock, breathe, shine and seek to mend;
> That I may rise and stand, oerthrow me, and bend
> Your force, to break, blow, burn and make me new.
> I, like an usurped town to another due,
> Labour to admit you, but O, to no end.
> Reason, your viceroy in me, me should defend,
> But is captive and proves weak or untrue.
> Yet dearly I love you and would be loved fain,
> But am betrothed unto your enemy.
> Divorce me, untie, or break that knot again,
> Take me to you, imprison me, for I
> Except you enthrall me, never shall be free,
> Nor ever chaste, except you ravish me.

'Here', comments Grey, is 'the [male] transcendent God battering from the outside, invited to take the poet by force: this is the model of Christian love – which uses the language of rape and seduction'.[34] This, it seems to her, is negative comment enough to delegitimize Donne's 'trinitarian' God altogether in the eyes of feminism.

One can of course only concur with Grey that such a language of 'battering' is more than capable of nefarious *use*; and that, as she puts it, 'Even the language of love can never be innocent of its social connotations'. That much all can surely agree upon. Indeed, a

---

[33] Mary Grey, 'The Core of our Desire: Re-Imaging the Trinity', *Theology* 93 (1990), 363–72; see Nancy Chodorow, *The Reproduction of Mothering: Psychoanalysis and the Sociology of Religion* (Berkeley: University of California Press, 1978).

[34] Grey, 'Core of our Desire', 365.

significant dimension of my *théologie totale* has been devoted to showing such a set of semiconscious negative connections, and indicating how to resist them. But in fairness to Donne, I think his extraordinary 'Holy Sonnet' is worthy of more profound and sympathetic attention before we dismiss it simply as a 'masculinist' incitement to rape and battery. It is true that one recent American critic, Arthur Marotti, takes the apparent plea for homosexual rape in the sonnet quite literally, and as suitable to a currying of favour in that Jacobean court, where King James's homoeroticism was well known, and his male favourites often able to assume powerful positions. This seems unduly artful an account, however, especially granting, as John Carey notes, Donne's willingness elsewhere to ridicule sodomy with disgust.[35] A much more significant factor, it seems to me, is Donne's truly Augustinian sense of his own bondage of the will: the 'battering' needed is precisely to 'divorce' *him* from his 'enemy'. 'Chastity' is thus impossible without drastic divine intervention. We are much reminded of the *Confessions*. In other words, Donne seems to thematize precisely the sense of the impossibility of aligning sexual desire and desire for God which constitutes the persistent male-constructed *aporia* to which feminist theology aims to attend. Only divine force will overthrow *that* force, Donne believes, given that the forces – divine and human – remain viewed as disjunctive and wrapt in mutual enmity. Without such an intervention, Donne remains a 'usurped town', which language reminds us of his own translation of 'The Lamentations of Jeremy', and of the fallen Jerusalem who has 'sinned, therefore is she Removed, as women in uncleanness be'. Significantly also (rather as in Augustine's treatment of male sex in *The City of God*), Donne finds 'reason' unable to confront the problem:

[35] John Carey, *John Donne: Life, Mind and Art* (London: Faber, 1981), 30, 35.

'Reason your viceroy in me, me should defend, / But is captive and proves weak or untrue'. The only answer, then, again reminding us evocatively of Romans 8, is an *incorporative* divine act – a 'jointure in the knotty Trinity', as Donne puts it in another 'Holy Sonnet' – a truly participative living in the life of God Godself.[36]

These brief reflections do nothing whatever, I am aware, to exonerate Donne *tout court*, if indeed one wants to find in him a butt for precisely the sort of masculinist and violent takeover bid that post-Christian feminism abominates in its reading of the Christian Trinity. And John Carey comments further on a worrying streak in Donne that such a form of feminism would also deride: a 'need for a God who would make him suffer', as Carey puts it, a need perhaps arising from Donne's guilty sense of 'missed martyrdom' as a turncoat Catholic.[37] But I am not concerned myself to unwrite the notes of violence in this memorable sonnet, nor of course to *recommend* them. Rather, I wish to call fresh attention, as Mary Grey does not, to their assumed but underlying theological pathology – the *disjunctive* sense of loves that ostensibly cannot be united, but yet even in Donne are in one moment of grief, at least, so united, when he writes on the death of his beloved wife Anne: 'Here the admiring her my mind did whet, *To seek thee God*'.[38] But here is the exception that proves the rule: the tragic sense of sinful disjunction between human and divine desires is the more normative in the Augustinian outlook which Donne inherits.

It is, then, to this problematic theme of untied – or disunited loves – that we shall return again in our next and last chapter. In this

---

[36] 'Batter My Heart', in John Donne, *The Divine Poems*, ed. Helen Gardner (Oxford: Clarendon Press, 1978), 11; see also 'Father, part of his double interest', 12; and 'Lamentations of Jeremy', 35–48, here 36.

[37] Carey, *John Donne*, 49.

[38] 'Since she whom I love', in Gardner, ed., *Divine Poems*, 14–15, here 15, my emphasis.

current chapter we have examined a paradox which has led us to this final point of reflection: we have first looked again at how 'gender' and 'sex' (as we now call them) are much more intrinsically connected to trinitarian thinking in the classic patristic period than one might assume; but also at how fractured, problematic, and demanding this analogical relation of desires may prove to be in practice: to bring different desires into true 'alignment' in God cannot be done without painful spiritual purgation and transformation, without the power of grace, without a dizzying adventure into the ecstasy of divine unknowing. At the same time we have noted that Gregory and Augustine, ostensibly so different in their account of 'gender' and 'sexuality', nonetheless converge in their celebration of the apophatic mystery of divine grace, one that seems to sweep all before it, even (at least for Gregory) the supposed fixities of human 'gender'. Have we then answered the challenge presented at the start of the chapter? Do we now know when it is proper to abandon the crutches of spiritual infirmity and confidently embrace engagement with a God whose darkness is 'dazzling'?

The contemplative on her knees well knows the messy entanglement of sexual desire and the desire for God. The question is: can the *feminist* contemplative align them in her trinitarian thinking, or must she too, 'divorce, untie, or break that knot again'? To that question, which has haunted us throughout this volume, I turn finally in the last chapter.

* * *

BIBLIOGRAPHIC NOTE

I have already commented on the falsely disjunctive renditions of 'East' and West' trinitarianism in much recent trinitarian scholarship (see the bibliographic note to the Prelude). But this train of thought is hard to shift, once established, and is enshrined in such influential textbooks as Catherine Mowry LaCugna, *God for Us: The Trinity and Christian Life* (San Francisco: Harper, 1991); Colin Gunton, *The Promise of Trinitarian Theology* (2nd edn; Edinburgh: T&T Clark, 1997); Colin Gunton, *The One, the Three and the Many: God, Creation and the Culture of Modernity* (Cambridge University Press, 1993); and Stanley Grenz, *Rediscovering the Triune God: The Trinity in Contemporary Theology* (Minneapolis: Fortress Press, 2004). The late Colin Gunton, especially, strongly advocated the 'social trinitarian' reading of the Cappadocian fathers found in the work of John Zizioulas, and correlatively read Augustine unsympathetically, as the progenitor of later Cartesian individualism: see 'Augustine, the Trinity and the Theological Crisis of the West', *Scottish Journal of Theology* 43 (1990), 33–58. The influential work of Lewis Ayres (*Nicaea and its Legacy: An Approach to Fourth-Century Trinitarian Theology* (Oxford University Press, 2004)), Michel Barnes (especially his article, 'De Regnon Reconsidered', *Augustinian Studies* 26 (1995), 51–79), and Richard Cross (especially his 'Two Models of the Trinity?', *Heythrop Journal* 43 (2002), 275–94) has been important in shifting this old pedagogy of 'East'–'West' divergence; and signs of its demise are now evident in more recent textbooks, such as Anne Hunt, *Trinity: Nexus of the Mysteries of the Christian Faith* (Maryknoll, NY: Orbis Books, 2005); Declan Marmion and Rik van Nieuwenhove, *An Introduction to the Trinity* (Cambridge University Press, 2011); and Paul M. Collins, *The Trinity: A Guide for the Perplexed* (London: Continuum, 2008). Robert J. Woźniak and Giulio Maspero, eds., *Re-Thinking Trinitarian Theology: Disputed Questions and Contemporary Issues in Trinitarian Theology* (London: T&T Clark, 2012) contains essays which straddle the two paradigms and catch the critical moment of debate. There is now a certain danger that, in overreaction to the 'East'–'West' disjunction paradigm, the 'pro-Nicene' communalities of the Cappadocians and

Augustine that Ayres has highlighted will divert attention from what remain as undeniable differences of *emphasis* between Gregory of Nyssa's and Augustine's trinitarian visions: see the astute comments of Khaled Anatolios and John Behr in *Harvard Theological Review* 100 (2007), 145–58. Khaled Anatolios's more extended discussion of the Trinity in Athanasius, Gregory of Nyssa, and Augustine is to be found in his recent *Retrieving Nicaea: The Development and Meaning of Trinitarian Doctrine* (Grand Rapids, MI: Baker Academic, 2011). Anatolios's 'Introduction' (ibid., 1–13) is explicit about the dogmatic tilt of his own project: in a way rather different from that of Ayres, he wishes to trace an essential unity in the story of patristic trinitarianism (as an outcome of the 'exigencies' of Christian life), but in a certain abstraction from surrounding political events.

I mention in this chapter the way that feminist theology in the last part of the twentieth century tended to support the 'Eastern' 'social trinitarianism' project, and to see the 'equality' and 'relationality' of the divine 'persons' as pointers towards a renewed feminist anthropology: see again Jürgen Moltmann and Elisabeth Moltmann-Wendel, *Humanity in God* (London: SCM Press, 1984), and also Elizabeth A. Johnson's justly influential *She Who Is: The Mystery of God in Feminist Theological Discourse* (New York: Crossroad, 1992).

GREGORY OF NYSSA ON THE TRINITY

Recent studies of Nyssen's trinitarianism follow the new trajectory outlined above, resisting the 'social trinitarian' construction; they also move beyond an earlier generation of scholarship's main concern with Gregory's *philosophical* coherence in his polemical or apologetic writings, and embrace a new interest in finding trinitarian clues in his exegetical works. In addition to Ayres, *Nicaea*, and Anatolios, *Retrieving Nicaea* (see above), and the essays in my own *Re-Thinking Gregory of Nyssa* (Oxford: Blackwell, 2003), and *Powers and Submissions: Philosophy, Spirituality and Gender* (Oxford: Blackwell, 2002), ch. 7 (already mentioned), one may specially commend Lucian Turcescu, *Gregory of Nyssa and the Concept of Divine Persons* (Oxford University Press, 2005); Michel R. Barnes, *The Power of God: Dunamis in Gregory of Nyssa's Theology* (Washington, DC: Catholic University of America Press, 2001); John Behr, *The Nicene Faith* (Crestwood, NY: St Vladimir's Seminary Press, 2004), vol.

II, 409–73; Richard Cross, 'Gregory of Nyssa on Universals', *Vigiliae Christianae* 56 (2002), 372–410; Richard Cross, 'On Generic and Derivation Views of God's Trinitarian Substance', *Scottish Journal of Theology* 56 (2003), 464–80; Kevin Corrigan, 'Ousia and Hypostasis in the Trinitarian Theology of the Cappadocian Fathers: Basil and Gregory of Nyssa', *Zeitschrift für Antikes Christentum* 12 (2008), 114–34. Studies which illuminate the intrinsic connection of Gregory's anthropology to his vision of God, or which stress the precise significance of his 'apophaticism' for his trinitarianism, have also enriched the field: see Johannes Zachhuber, *Human Nature in Gregory of Nyssa: Philosophical Background and Theological Significance* (Leiden: Brill, 2000); Giulio Maspero, *Trinity and Man: Gregory of Nyssa's Ad Ablabium* (Leiden: Brill, 2007); and – in rather different, 'postmodern' philosophical style – Scot Douglass, *Theology of the Gap: Cappadocian Language Theory and the Trinitarian Controversy* (Bern: Peter Lang, 2005). Morwenna Ludlow's *Gregory of Nyssa: Ancient and (Post)Modern* (Oxford University Press, 2007), parts I (13–94) and IV (231–91) provide a painstaking analysis of these recent trends in interpretation of Nyssen's trinitarianism and an extensive further bibliography. Lucas Francisco Mateo-Seco and Giulio Maspero, eds., *The Brill Dictionary of Gregory of Nyssa* (Leiden: Brill, 2010) provides a wealth of relevant articles and further useful bibliographies.

GREGORY OF NYSSA ON GENDER, SEX, AND DESIRE

Ludlow's *Gregory of Nyssa*, part III (163–233) also supplies an exhaustive discussion of recent trends in the 'reception' of Nyssen on 'gender', 'sex', and desire, and an acute analysis of the extent to which those trends have been animated by fashion or 'hermeneutical circularity'. Undeniably the root of this modern interest in Nyssen's concept of 'desire' was the inspiration provided by Jean Daniélou's *Platonisme et théologie mystique* (2nd edn; Paris: Aubier, 1944); but it has been taken in many directions since, from Verna Harrison's articles on gender 'complementarity' in Gregory (to my mind, remainingly infused by Jungian insight) – 'Male and Female in Cappadocian Theology', *Journal of Theological Studies* 41 (1990), 441–7; 'A Gender Reversal in Gregory of Nyssa's First Homily on the Song of Songs', *Studia Patristica* 27 (1993), 34–8; 'Gender, Generation and Virginity in Cappadocian Theology', *Journal of Theological Studies* 47 (1996), 38–68 – to Virginia Burrus's stringent postmodern critique of

Gregory's purportedly 'male' symbolic – *'Begotten, Not Made': Conceiving Manhood in Late Antiquity* (Stanford University Press, 2000); and 'Queer Father: Gregory of Nyssa and the Subversion of Identity', in Gerard Loughlin, ed., *Queer Theology: Rethinking the Western Body* (Oxford: Blackwell, 2007), 147–62. My own earlier work in this area attempts to escape both these alternatives (see especially my *Powers and Submissions*, ch. 9), as well as avoiding the misreading of Ruether, 'Misogynism and Virginal Feminism in the Fathers of the Church' (as discussed in this chapter); although I would now want to correct an undue fascination with the fashion for 'gender fluidity', which was a strong feature of the American gender theoretical discussion of the 1990s. As this chapter shows, Gregory's views on body and gender change over time, and with greater spiritual maturity; but they are also modulated by context and pastoral need: his is a *sui generis* view of gender and not one subsumable into modern or postmodern secular categories.

AUGUSTINE ON THE TRINITY

Scholarship on Augustine's theology of the Trinity has undergone fundamental realignments in recent years, not unlike those charted above in relation to Nyssen. Thus what we might call 'philosophical source criticism' – working out which kind of Platonism influenced which part of Augustine's theological writing, and to what extent – has given way to significant efforts in the last two decades to read Augustine's mature work of trinitarian theology, the *De trinitate*, as a theological whole significantly influenced by his scriptural reading. The older approach comes in various guises, from the highly influential but now much criticized book by Olivier du Roy, *L'Intelligence de la foi en la Trinité selon saint Augustin: genèse de sa théologie trinitaire jusqu'en 391* (Paris: Études Augustiniennes, 1966), through to the cruder later British version in Colin Gunton's critiques of Augustine's alleged 'Platonising' relegation of the Trinity (see above): *The Promise of Trinitarian Theology*, esp. 30–55. These kinds of readings of the *De trinitate* tended to focus almost exclusively on the role of the 'psychological analogies' for the Trinity in books IX–XII. The recent reaction against these selective readings in the anglophone context can perhaps be traced to the influential work of Rowan Williams in Oxford, and of his students: his '*Sapientia* and the Trinity: Reflections on the *De trinitate*', in B. Brunning, ed., *Collectanea Augustiniana: Mélanges J. T. van Bavel* (Leuven: Peeters, 1990), 317–32, has been particularly significant. Lewis Ayres's stream of studies, which have been highly significant in creating the 'new canon' of Augustine trinitarian scholarship, can be most easily sought out in his *Augustine and the Trinity* (Cambridge University Press, 2010), a revised version of his Oxford doctoral thesis written under the supervision of Williams. Another revised Oxford thesis, Luigi Gioia, OSB, *The Theological Epistemology of Augustine's De Trinitate* (Oxford University Press, 2008), also confronts du Roy's reading head-on, and argues painstakingly for a holistic and thoroughly theological reading of the *De trinitate* as a text integrally related to the living of the Christian life and yielding a dynamic, because trinitarian, theological epistemology of love anchored in the human as *imago Dei*. The work of Michel Barnes has also been significant in establishing the new reading of Augustine: see for instance his 'Re-Reading Augustine's Theology of the Trinity', in Stephen T. Davis, Daniel Kendall, and Gerald O'Collins, eds., *The Trinity: An Interdisciplinary Symposium on the Trinity* (Oxford University Press, 1999), 145–76; and Michel Barnes, 'Augustine in Contemporary Trinitarian Theology', *Theological Studies* 56 (1995), 237–50. Another astute comparative study is Andrew Louth, 'Love and the Trinity: Saint Augustine and the Greek Fathers', *Augustinian Studies* 33 (2002), 1–16.

Continental approaches to Augustine's trinitarian thought have been strongly affected by the work of Basil Stüder, OSB, and have been particularly marked by the theology of history found in the *De trinitate* as well as the importance of soteriology in reading it – see, for instance, his 'History and Faith in Augustine's *De trinitate*', *Augustinian Studies* 28 (1997), 7–50, and *Augustins De Trinitate: Eine Einführung* (Paderborn: Schöningh, 2005) – although, as Ayres has noted, the latter work still seems inflected by discredited forms of *Dogmengeschichte* (e.g., Augustine's alleged 'unitarian' tendency linked with the psychological analogies). The vast literature on Augustine's *De trinitate* is magisterially surveyed, organized, and analyzed in Roland Kany, *Augustins Trinitätsdenken: Bilanz, Kritik und Weiterführung der modernen Forschung zu 'De trinitate'* (Tübingen: Mohr Siebeck, 2007), which has been published in an abridged translation as *Augustine's Trinitarian Thought: A Critical Reappraisal of Modern Scholarship on 'De trinitate'* (London: Bloomsbury, 2013).

Another strand of Rowan Williams's redirection of Augustinian studies focuses on christology, linking trinitarian thinking with theological anthropology. See, for example, his 'Augustine's Christology: Its Spirituality and Rhetoric', in Peter Martens, ed., *In the Shadow of the Incarnation: Essays in Honor of Brian Daley* (University of Notre Dame Press, 2008), 176–89. The best recent entry point into work on Augustine's christology is Dominic Keech, *The Anti-Pelagian Christology of Augustine of Hippo, 396–430* (Oxford University Press, 2012). For the burgeoning study of Augustine's hermeneutics and exegesis, influenced by this 'new canon', see Michael Cameron, *Christ Meets me Everywhere: Augustine's Early Figurative Exegesis* (Oxford University Press, 2012). The new reading of Augustine's trinitarian thought, especially in its destabilizing of former philosophical source criticism, has influenced a wide range of works by contemporary systematic theologians: see, for example, David Tracy, 'Augustine's Christomorphic Theocentrism', in Aristotle Papanikolaou, ed., *Orthodox Readings of Augustine* (Crestwood, NY: St Vladimir's Seminary Press, 2008), 263–89; Emmanuel Falque, 'Metaphysics and Theology in Tension: A Reading of Augustine's *De trinitate*', in Lieven Boeve, Mathijs Lamberigts, and Maarten Wisse, eds., *Augustine and Postmodern Thought: A New Alliance against Modernity?* (Leuven: Peeters, 2009), 21–55; and most recently Jean-Luc Marion, *In the Self's Place: The Approach of Saint Augustine* (Stanford University Press, 2012).

AUGUSTINE ON GENDER, SEX, AND DESIRE

The work of feminist theologians and scholars, amongst others, has led to a concentrated interest in recent years in issues of gender, sexuality, and desire in all periods of theology, including the theologies of late antiquity. The varieties of feminist, and feminist-inspired, work have led to a wide range of interactions with Augustine's theology – from 'modernist' critiques of his apparent failure to grant women 'equality', through to playful postmodern assertions of the 'queerness' of his theology. As in the case of Gregory, there is a strong danger of gender-theoretical overdetermination. A representative chronological selection of the most stimulating, varied, and significant studies (other than those already discussed in the body of this chapter) would include the now classic study of Kari Børresen, *Subordination and Equivalence: The Nature and Role of Woman in Augustine and Thomas Aquinas* (Washington, DC: University of America Press, 1981), several works by Margaret Miles, starting with her doctoral thesis *Augustine on the Body* (Missoula, MT: Scholars Press, 1979) and the later *Desire and Delight: A New Reading of Augustine's Confessions* (London: Continuum, 1992), followed by 'Not Nameless but Unnamed: The Woman Torn from Augustine's Side', in Judith Chelius Stark, ed., *Feminist Interpretations of Augustine* (University Park: Pennsylvania State University Press, 2007), 167–88; Kim Power, *Veiled Desire: Augustine on Women* (London: DLT, 1995); Gillian Clark, 'Adam's Engendering: Augustine on Gender and Creation', in R. N. Swanson, ed., *Gender and Christian Religion* (Woodbridge: Boydell Press, 1998), 13–22; Willemien Otten, 'Augustine on Marriage, Monasticism, and the Community of the Church', *Theological Studies* 59 (1998), 385–405; David Hunter, 'Augustine and the Making of Marriage in Roman North Africa', *Journal of Early Christian Studies* 11 (2003), 63–85; Karmen MacKendrick, 'Carthage didn't Burn Hot Enough: Saint Augustine's Divine Seduction', in Virginia Burrus and Catherine Keller, eds., *Toward a Theology of Eros: Transfiguring Passion at the Limits of Discipline* (New York: Fordham University Press, 2006), 205–17; Virginia Burrus, Mark D. Jordan, and Karmen MacKendrick, *Seducing Augustine: Bodies, Desires, Confessions* (New York: Fordham University Press, 2010); Virginia Burrus, '"Fleeing the uxorious kingdom": Augustine's Queer Theology of Marriage', *Journal of Early Christian Studies* 19 (2011), 1–20; John E. Thiel, 'Augustine on Eros, Desire, and Sexuality', in Margaret D. Kamitsuka, ed., *The Embrace of Eros: Bodies, Desires, and Sexuality in Christianity* (Minneapolis: Fortress Press, 2010), 67–82. Foundational source texts for all these issues have been Elizabeth A. Clark, *Women in the Early Church* (Collegeville, PA: Liturgical Press, 1983); Elizabeth A. Clark, ed., *Augustine on Marriage and Sexuality* (Washington, DC: Catholic University of America Press, 1996); and Gillian Clark, *Women in Late Antiquity: Pagan and Christian Life-Styles* (Oxford: Clarendon Press, 1993).

CHAPTER 7

The primacy of divine desire: God as Trinity and the 'apophatic turn'

In this, the last full chapter of this first volume of systematics, it remains only for me to gather together the fragments of theological reflection I have scattered upon the mountains, and trust that they constitute at least an interesting foretaste of the larger potential of a *théologie totale*, if not of a full eucharistic banquet. Let me explain at the outset what is still to be attempted here.

First, my explorations of the multilayered evocations of trinitarian discourse in this book have, I hope, convinced the reader of at least this much: that no trinitarian language is innocent of sexual, political, and ecclesiastical overtones and implications, and that it is a primary task of a *théologie totale* to ferret out these implications, and to bring them to greater critical consciousness. The redoubtable Baroness von Blixen (the Danish author of *Out of Africa*, who wrote under the pen name Isak Dinesen) once remarked in a letter that, as far as she was concerned, the Trinity was merely, 'The most deadly dull of all male companies'.[1] Our own investigations have hardly found *dullness* to be the major drawback of trinitarianism; more truly could we characterize it as a heady mixture of 'love and pain and the whole damn thing' (to summon a memorable film title from the 1970s), since no major passion has been absent from the

---

[1] Clara Svendsen, *Notater om Karen Blixen* (Copenhagen: Gyldendal, 1974), 16.

complexity of meanings that we have found trinitarian language and art to disgorge, given the tools of a *théologie totale*.

Yet such a symbolic bombardment should not be seen merely as a theological problem. As we have already found Gregory of Nyssa to exemplify in his later exegetical works, and as the sixth-century 'pseudo-Dionysius' is wont to remind us more systematically (we shall come to him anon), metaphorical profusion can aid, just as much as distract from, the epistemic stripping necessary to right contemplation of the divine. We can start with these outrageous multiple cultural meanings and move, through contemplative purgation, to an ascetic alignment with God's purposes.

But this issue of 'alignmnent', too, to which we constantly adverted in the last chapter, clearly needs further analysis and resolution as this book reaches its end. For it is vitally important not to confuse this quest for the right 'alignment' of sexual desire and divine desire with the false attempt directly to *imitate* the life of the Trinity – an idolatrous project that we have consistently resisted. Because we are embodied, created beings, we may indeed (through the graced aid of the Spirit) 'imitate' Christ, the God/*man*; but we cannot without Christ's mediation directly imitate the Trinity itself.[2] And whereas sexual desire is, as I have all along suggested in this volume, the 'precious clue' woven into our created being reminding us of our rootedness in God, to bring this desire into *right* 'alignment' with God's purposes, purified from sin and

---

[2] There is only one New Testament passage which speaks of 'participation' in God (2 Peter 1.4, using the phrase 'partakers of the divine nature'), and it was to have great influence in later Christian tradition. In comparison, there is only one passage in the New Testament which seemingly demands a direct 'imitation' of God (Eph. 5. 1); but in context (see verse 2) the imitation is really that of Christ. Elsewhere 'imitation' is demanded by Paul and others of themselves, as indirect secondary mediators of the life of Christ: see 1 Cor. 4. 16; 1 Cor. 11. 1; Phil. 3. 17; 2 Thess. 3. 7, 9; see also Heb. 13. 7; 3 John 1. 11. The comparison with contemporary 'social trinitarianism' is significant: there, the project of the direct imitation of 'persons' of the Trinity and their relations is considered central.

possessiveness, something profoundly transformative has to happen. If I am correct, then the contemplative encounter with divine mystery will include the possibility of upsetting the 'normal' vision of the sexes and gender altogether; but it will also include an often painful submission to other demanding tests of ascetic transformation – through fidelity to divine desire, and thence through fidelity to those whom we love in this world.

Let us then remind ourselves about where our last chapter left us, because this will show us what tasks we still have to undertake.

The chapter brought us back once more to the brink of that elusive goal of inner trinitarian *radical* equality towards which we are still fumbling. It exposed two major traditional alternatives for women in the thought of (the 'Eastern') Gregory and (the 'Western') Augustine, highlighting the supposed double bind of either desexed equality, on the one hand, or of sexual subordination, on the other. It then showed, speculatively, how Gregory's and Augustine's views on sexual relationships were in important senses *part and parcel* of their trinitarian constructions, analogically speaking. Both these alternatives witnessed to a certain lack of symbolic adjustment between sexual desire and the desire for God; and yet both writers' systems, we found, culminated in ecstatic moments too, which appeared to transcend even their own categories, and converge towards a vision of God predicated precisely on the notion of incorporative, transformative, *divine* desire. Let us now plot the course of that convergence further, in three moves.

First, we shall explore this ontology of divine, trinitarian, desire somewhat further, by reference to the pseudo-Dionysian writings themselves.[3] This will inevitably involve musing on what the

---

[3] This mysterious author of the late fifth or early sixth century, writing under the 'pseudonym' of the convert made by Paul on the Areopagite hill (Acts 17. 34), wrote

contested Dionysian notion of cosmological 'hierarchy'[4] could mean for the contemporary contemplative – by way of an engagement with the sifting and ordering of all desires – and whether an acceptance of a hierarchical vision such as Dionysius' is compatible with feminist commitments. Second, we shall return, as promised, to the connected and fractious contemporary issue of how to *name* God aright trinitarianly – in liturgy, prayer, and common conversation. And finally we shall trace the implications of all these reflections for the equally divisive issue of the '*filioque*' clause in the Nicene Creed, and for the concomitant understanding of inner-divine 'relations' and 'processions'.

THE PRIMACY OF DIVINE DESIRE

We recall for a moment those places of special theological promise for our trinitarian project that we found in the later thought of Gregory and Augustine respectively. On the one hand there was the extraordinary collapse in Gregory's *Life of Moses* of the human hegemony of reason (when construed as an upward, 'penetrating' ascent), a darkening into apophatic obscurity, and a new and necessary reliance on the spiritual/sensual, combined with a fascinating flip into metaphors of receptivity and fecundity. In short, Platonist 'masculinist' reason was here undone; 'normal' sexual stereotypes defied; and a rich use of all kinds of sexual *metaphor* was aligned with a profound loss of

---

only a few works, but ones of inestimable influence on later Christianity, both East and West (see *Pseudo-Dionysius: The Complete Works*, trans. Colm Luibheid (CWS; New York: Paulist Press, 1987) for Dionysius' *oeuvre* in English). Dionysius' obvious familiarity with the work of the neo-Platonist Proclus has made him a contentious figure in modern Christian assessment: is he therefore *more* Platonist than Christian, and thus a dangerous ally? The view taken here (which is also Dionysius' own, as we shall see) is that that question is a falsely disjunctive one: see Sarah Coakley and Charles M. Stang, ed., *Re-Thinking Dionysius the Areopagite* (Oxford: Blackwell, 2009), esp. 1–26.

[4] A term that Dionysius himself coined for the first time.

every previous certainty at the noetic level about the nature of the Godhead as Trinity. In other words, a releasing of conventional sexual stereotypes, a rich and bombarding application of differing sexual metaphors, and a profounder and more mature sense of God's triune mystery: all appeared to go together in Gregory's last great works of biblical commentary.

Now recall our discussion of Augustine. There, it was the daring return to the obsessive themes of human desire from the *Confessions*, but now raised to the divine trinitarian level, that caused a new and late note to sound at the end of the *De trinitate*, a note of effusive, Spirit-leading divine incorporation: 'When God the Holy Spirit . . . who proceeds from God, has been given to [humanity], He inflames . . . the love for God and . . . neighbour, and *He Himself is love*' (*De trinitate*, xv.17.31, my emphasis).

It is not for nothing that Andrew Louth says of this passage in Augustine that it uncannily anticipates themes in the work of the mysterious late fifth-century writer Dionysius the Areopagite. Louth writes: 'The soul's ecstasy – so important for Plotinus [Augustine's neo-Platonist forebear] – is [here] replaced, we might almost say (to use the language of Denys the Areopagite, which Augustine does not himself use), by *God's* ecstasy in the condescension of the Incarnation and the pouring forth of the Holy Spirit.'[5] Let us now consider, then, this notion in Dionysius of *divine ekstasis*, and his accompanying understanding of how rich metaphorical language for God can combine with what might be called an 'apophatic turn', a principled commitment to divine mystery and unknowability. If I am right, then these themes in Dionysius not only take into themselves the elements in Gregory and Augustine

---

[5] Andrew Louth, *The Origins of the Christian Mystical Tradition* (Oxford: Clarendon Press, 1981), 158, my emphasis. Louth prefers to use the medieval English rendition of Dionysius as 'Denys'.

that seemed to us most spiritually profound, but may also (admittedly with suitable modifications) suggest the outlines of a developed trinitarian metaphysic true to the cardinal insights of Romans 8 from which our analysis began.

The passage in the Dionysian corpus that most concerns us is a famous and disputed one in *Divine Names*, ch. 4. In section 12, Dionysius is discussing the nature of 'yearning' (*erōs*) for God. He is well aware of the criticism of those who would keep *erōs* and *agapē* safely apart. But to this Dionysius responds: 'let us not fear this title of "yearning", nor be upset ... for, in my opinion, the sacred writers regard "yearning" (*erōs*) and love (*agapē*) as having one and the same meaning'.[6] (Dionysius omits, however, to mention explicitly the strong influence on him here of Platonism in general, and especially of the neo-Platonist author, Proclus, on his own use of the notion of *erōs*, for what he wants to do is to argue that his hero Paul also crucially relies on such a notion). Now Dionysius certainly does not straightforwardly align physical sexual (or more broadly, 'erotic') yearning and yearning for God; in fact, in Platonist mode reminiscent of the *Symposium*, he sees the former (physical love) as 'partial' and 'divided', a 'lapse' from the *real* 'yearning' in *God*. There is no quick or easy route from the lower to the higher, no spurious identification: a profound purgation and transformation is required for us truly to participate in divine longing. But the important point is that the protoerotic dimension for him *is* divine. Dionysius explains: 'The fact is that men are [*sc.* initially] unable to grasp the simplicity of the *one* divine yearning, and, hence, the term is quite offensive to most of them. So it is left to the divine Wisdom [*sc.* the Spirit] to lift them and to raise them up to

---

[6] *Divine Names*, IV.12, in *Pseudo-Dionysius*, 81; Dionysius the Areopagite, *Corpus Dionysiacum*, eds. Günter Heil, Adolf Martin Ritter, and Beata Regina Suchla (PTS 33, 36; 2 vols.; Berlin: De Gruyter, 1990–1), vol. I, 157.

a knowledge of what yearning really is, after which they no longer
take offence.' He goes on: 'it is clear to us that many lowly men
think there is something absurd in the lovely verse: "Love for you
came on me like love for women" . . . To those listening properly to
the divine things the name "love" is used by the sacred writers in
divine revelation with the exact same meaning as the term "yearning". What is signified is a capacity to effect a unity, an alliance, and
a particular commingling in the Beautiful and the Good.'[7]

So far, one might say, Dionysius has not made anything greatly
more significant than Plato's move in the *Symposium* to find physical love as a lower 'type' of love of the Form of Beauty, although
Dionysius has also made the added conjunction of Platonic *erōs* and
Christian *agapē* (already anticipated in Origen and Gregory of
Nyssa), which for him is completely unproblematic. A much more
daring metaphysical move comes in the next section, however (ch.
4, section 13). For here Dionysius goes on to attribute ecstatic
yearning not only to human lovers of God, but also, prototypically,
to *divine* love of creation:

This divine yearning brings ecstasy so that the lover belongs not to self but
to the beloved . . . This is why the great Paul, swept along by his yearning
for God and seized of its ecstatic power, had these inspired words to say: 'It
is no longer I who live, but Christ who lives in me'. Paul was clearly a lover,
and, as he says, he was *beside himself* for God.[8]

From here Dionysius makes the further move to attribute *ekstasis*
pre-eminently to God:

It must be said too that the very cause of the universe in the beautiful, good
superabundance of his benign yearning for all, *is also carried outside of*

---

[7] *Divine Names*, IV.12, in *Pseudo-Dionysius*, 81; *Corpus Dionysiacum*, vol. I, 158.

[8] *Divine Names*, IV.13, in *Pseudo-Dionysius*, 82; *Corpus Dionysiacum*, vol. I, 158–9, my
emphasis. The biblical allusion here is to 2 Cor. 5. 13, where Paul says he is 'out of his
mind' (*exestēkōs*) for God.

himself in the loving care he has for everything. He is, as it were, beguiled by goodness, by love, and by yearning, and is enticed away from his transcendent dwelling place and comes to abide within all things, and he does so by virtue of his supernatural and ecstatic capacity to *remain, nevertheless, within himself.*[9]

Going on, we find Dionysius forced to draw on circular metaphors to describe this continuing flow of *ekstasis* and return:

[God] is yearning on the move, simple, self-moved, self-acting, pre-existent in the Good, flowing out from the Good onto all that is and returning once again to the Good. [The divine yearning] . . . shows especially its unbeginning and unending nature travelling in an endless circle through the Good, from the Good, in the Good, and to the Good; unerringly turning, ever on the same centre . . . always proceeding, always remaining, always being restored to itself.[10]

Now the extent to which Dionysius is breaking genuinely new ground here, and the extent to which he is either more Christian or more neo-Platonist in his construal of divine love, are both subjects of perennial dispute; yet arguably they should not be. The celebrated Swedish Lutheran scholar Anders Nygren was notoriously vehement, as we noted earlier, in his rejection of this identification of supposedly self-seeking *erōs* and selfless *agapē*;[11] and while more recent scholarly assessments also rightly attribute most of the component ingredients of the passage to Dionysius' neo-Platonic predecessors, Plotinus and Proclus,[12] theologians such as Louth who are sympathetic to the Dionysian vision find in this ecstatic

---

[9] *Divine Names*, IV.13, in *Pseudo-Dionysius*, 82; *Corpus Dionysiacum*, vol. I, 159, my emphasis.

[10] *Divine Names*, IV.14, in *Pseudo-Dionysius*, 82–3; *Corpus Dionysiacum*, vol. I, 160, my emphasis.

[11] Anders Nygren, *Agape and Eros* (London: SPCK, 1953); see the discussion earlier, in the bibliographic note to the Prelude.

[12] See, e.g., John M. Rist, 'Eros and Agape in Pseudo-Dionysius', *Vigiliae Christianae* 20 (1966), 235–43, esp. 239–41.

dimension of Dionysius' construal of love just as much a distinctively Christian construction.[13] Since we are here more interested in truth than in attribution, there seems no intrinsic reason why both these suppositions could not be true. Why should Christianity and Platonism here *not* genuinely converge and intersect? It has indeed all along been the burden of this volume to suggest such.

What is perhaps even more important for our immediate purposes, however, are the following considerations.

First, we are presented with a vision of a divine incorporative flow which fits our original 'prayer-based' model of the Trinity with exactitude, and yet strangely it is not here given by Dionysius specifically *trinitarian* grammar.[14] The paradoxical divine capacity for perpetual *ekstasis* and return is however precisely the understanding of the relation of Spirit to 'Father' that we gestured towards earlier on the basis of Romans 8. Secondly, although Dionysius is unable, in virtue of his Platonic commitments, fully to align sexual *erōs* and divine *erōs*, he is *also*, in virtue of his Platonic commitments, quite clear that physical desire finds its origins in right divine desire. Thus, as I put it in the Prelude: Dionysius' more ancient vision means that, in contemporary terms, Freud is turned on his head. Instead of 'God' language 'really' being about sex, sex is really about God – the potent reminder woven into our earthly existence of the divine 'unity', 'alliance', and 'commingling' that we seek. This in turn has profound ascetical implications, of course; for no one can move simply from earthly, physical love (tainted as it so often is by sin and misdirection of desire) to divine love – unless it is via a Christological transformation. Thirdly, the crucial notion of *ekstasis* allows an implicit acknowledgement of love across

---

[13] Louth, *Origins*, 170.

[14] It is however clear in Dionysius' other writings that he holds to an ostensibly orthodox Christian trinitarianism.

difference; for it reflects on the moment of divine love across an ontological divide. Dionysius, in fact, says that the ecstatic dimension of love can operate whether or not the parties are equal. Of course, in God's case the ecstasy towards the creation is one of 'superior towards subordinate', as he puts it. But the same logic is shown, he says, 'in the regard for one another demonstrated by those of equal status'.[15] It is unlikely that Dionysius himself had men and women in mind when he talked of 'equals' here. But what if we now extended the potential of his thought on *ekstasis* in this direction?

If the divine ecstasy returning to itself allows redeemed creation to participate in it, and so signals an 'incorporative' trinitarianism, what, correlatively, might be the trinitarian implications of ecstatic love *between* the sexes?

Quite inadvertently, and in another context altogether, the contemporary French feminist Luce Irigaray provides us with a compelling image of human sexual love as precisely 'trinitarian' qua 'ecstatic'; the inadvertent alignment with Dionysius, I suggest, is deeply creative and revealing, and perhaps helps us to move towards a further exploration of the relation of divine and human ecstasy in Christian terms. Commenting critically (and admittedly unjustly) on the thought of the Jewish philosopher Emmanuel Lévinas, Irigaray writes:

He knows nothing of communion in pleasure. Lévinas does not ever seem to have experienced the transcendence of the other which becomes an immanent ecstasy ... The other is [merely] 'close' to him in 'duality'. This autistic, egological, solitary love does not correspond to the shared outpouring, to the loss of boundary of the skin into the mucous membranes of the body, leaving the circle which encloses my solitude to meet in a shared space, a shared breath ... In this relation *we are at least three*, each of

---

[15] *Divine Names*, IV.13, in *Pseudo-Dionysius*, 82; *Corpus Dionysiacum*, vol. I, 159.

which is irreducible to any of the others: you, me and our creation [*oeuvre*], that ecstasy of ourself in us [*de nous en nous*] . . . prior to any 'child'.[16]

If we take inspiration here from Irigaray's insight about the implicitly 'trinitarian' nature even of human erotic ecstasy, then we may perhaps glimpse how human ecstatic loves (*at their best*) might ultimately relate to divine ecstatic love: not by any direct emulation of the trinitarian nature, but by the 'interruption' by the Spirit of any merely 'egological' duality inherent in their relationship, such that the human lovers are themselves aware of a necessary 'third' between them – both uniting them and protecting their integrity in their new ecstasy of exchange. What then is happening may even be a degree of participation in the divine life; but it comes with both the cost and the joy of truly 'ecstatic' attention to the other.

To divert the fifth-century Pseudo-Dionysius in this sort of direction is of course to take some considerable exegetical liberties, albeit – as I suggest – creative ones for contemporary discussion. But it is also to shift one's eyes from dimensions of his philosophy which have most profoundly offended modern feminist sensibilities. For what of the notoriously 'hierarchical' commitments in his thought? Do they not thoroughly undermine afresh any such possibilities of a radical ecstatic *equality* between lovers? Granted the negative status that the term 'hierarchy' has achieved amongst modern feminists and others committed to the political goal of 'equality' for all, it is hardly surprising that Dionysius can be larded with blame even for inventing the word *hierarchia* in the first place. In a 'hierarchy', Anne Primavesi writes in her study of feminism and ecology, 'God is separated from Nature by graded orders of being,

---

[16] Luce Irigaray, 'Questions to Emmanuel Lévinas: On the Divinity of Love', in Robert Bernasconi and Simon Critchley, eds., *Re-Reading Lévinas* (London: Athlone, 1991), 109–18, at 88, my emphasis.

with man "supergraded" over other life on earth'.[17] The result is fatal, she thinks, for ecological consciousness in general, and it even gives to our current blindness a sort of divine justification. Hardly surprisingly, Dionysius is the original culprit in Primavesi's feminist analysis of our ecological woes.

But how are we to assess this problem theologically? Dionysius does indeed have a vision of a *layered* universe in which everyone has an appropriate place – a notion repellent, as Andrew Louth points out in his own excellent study of Dionysius, to anyone with an individualistic or 'social contract' model of society (and repellent to feminism in particular, of course, if women are to be placed at a lower level of subordination to men).[18] Still, several points of rejoinder on Dionusius' behalf need considering.

The first point is that 'hierarchy', like 'power', is a word much in need of nuanced and analytical reflection. Thus it is not obvious that 'hierarchy' in *all* its meanings (Dionysian or otherwise) is, or should be, abhorrent to a modern feminist agenda. Dionysius says, for instance, that 'the aim of hierarchy is the greatest possible assimilation to and union with God ... Hierarchy is a holy order and knowledge and activity which ... participates in the Divine Likeness'.[19] Where hierarchy simply means *order*, then, it is not at all clear that feminism should oppose it. Anyone who has worked in circumstances of institutional chaos knows that some such order, organizationally speaking, is preferable for everyone; it is worldly *sexed* subordination that feminism opposes. And 'ordering' oneself to God, in contrast, as we have examined at some length in the case

[17] Anne Primavesi, *From Apocaplyspse to Genesis: Ecology, Feminism and Christianity* (Tunbridge Wells: Burns & Oates, 1991), 88.
[18] Andrew Louth, *Denys the Areopagite* (London: Continuum, 1989), 132.
[19] *Celestial Hierarchy*, III.1–2, in *Pseudo-Dionysius*, 153–4; *Corpus Dionysiacum*, vol. II, 17–18.

of Gregory of Nyssa, may precisely be the means of undermining and dissolving such sexed subordination.

Second, as the anthropologist Louis Dumont argued in his famous study of the Indian caste system, *Homo Hierarchicus*, our repressive distaste for 'hierarchy' in the modern West may be based on an irrational restriction of the meaning of the word to what Dumont calls 'power hierarchy', an 'artificial organization of multiple activities' involving '*inequalities* of aptitude and functions'. To this idea he contrasts what he takes to be a more basic meaning of the word, as a 'system of [ordered] values', which he takes to be 'indispensable to [any] social life'.[20] Similarly again, Mary Douglas's later work on cultural analysis (which we have already drawn upon in this volume, and which at points itself appeals to Dumont) uses the notion of 'hierarchy' to do something of the same work as the notion of the 'church' type did in Weber's and Troeltsch's typology. According to Douglas, the 'hierarchical society' is not necessarily, let alone intrinsically, a repressive top-down system, but one which has an eye to all its members: 'The distinguishing feature of hierarchy', writes Douglas, 'is that every decision is referred to the well-being of the whole. A whole transcending its parts is what hierarchy means'.[21] Again, such commitments seem, in contrast to patriarchal 'top-down' hierarchy and abuse of male power, a potentially positive means of blessing.

But the third, and most important point in relation to 'hierarchy', is that classic feminist theology has often implicitly and mistakenly *identified* divine 'hierarchical power' with worldly male power – thus ironically replicating the very ontological fallacy that it rightly

---

[20] Louis Dumont, *Homo Hierarchicus: The Caste System and its Implications* (London: Paladin, 1972), 54, my emphasis.

[21] Mary Douglas, 'Thought Style Exemplified: The Idea of the Self', in *Risk and Blame: Essays in Cultural Theory* (London: Routledge, 1992), 211–34, here 226.

critiques in its masculinist opponents. The God of 'hierarchy' then becomes by definition a male dictator God who needs cutting down to size and remaking according to an existing feminist agenda, rather than a God of infinite ontological difference, of ecstasy, and of endless divine creativity. Yet for Dionysius' hierarchy, God/the Good is precisely not one of the arranged and ordered created beings (a very Big one), subject thereby to its own rules of either reiterated repression or its opposite; on the contrary, God is by definition the Source of all that is, the One who places each 'order' of being precisely where it is destined to flourish in ecstatic response to the Spirit's own ecstatic lure.

So there is a paradoxical thesis at stake here in relation to the Dionysian notion of 'hierarchy'. On the one hand I want to defend this idea of hierarchy in a particular sense in the *human* realm, and argue that we cannot do without it, if we are to *order* our values aright – order them appropriately, 'orient' them, towards God. That itself involves a lifetime's undertaking of discernment and (graced) practice. On the other hand, and in a properly Nicene spirit, I continue sternly to resist the notion of hierarchy in the *Godhead*. Yet much of this book has been taken up in showing that even those who profess the Nicene spirit are – whether consciously or unconsciously – often fatally abrogating it, and then reading that same distorted power message into the human realm.[22] And therein lies the real rub. When humans come, in contrast, into *authentic* relation with God as Trinity through the Spirit, their values and orders of 'hierarchy' change; they are not *imitating* God thereby, but rather

---

[22] And one might say that this problem has even been intensified by the 'social trinitarianism' fashion: the trinitarian 'persons' then become 'personalities' with specific power agendas, rather than personal entities so subtly distinguishable qua inherent 'relations' that one can at best talk of each attracting the possibility of verb-forms, and then only in mutual 'co-inherence' with each other.

being radically transformed by ecstatic participation in the Spirit. So what is being broken here is the idea that a false patriarchal hierarchy in the Trinity should be emulated by a false patriarchal hierarchy in the church or world (*that* is the anti-'hierarchical' battle that must ever be fought). But what is also being broken, more challengingly to the 'liberal' mind, is any idea that by magicking the idea of 'hierarchy' away altogether there can be an enforced feminist rearrangement of God and the world. God, qua God, cannot be cut down to ontological size to fit a false feminist fear of divine transcendence. In short, we cannot get this vision of powers and submissions right by political or theological manipulation or fiat; we can only get it right by *right* primary submission to the Spirit, with all the purgative costliness that involves.

Is this then simply 'business as usual' as far as naming God is concerned? By no means. But again, this may take a bit of explaining.

NAMING GOD AS TRINITY: DAZZLING DARKNESS, NOETIC SLIPPAGE, AND THE STRANGE CONTEMPLATIVE TRANSFORMATION OF PATRIARCHAL MEANING

For along with this paradoxical approach to hierarchy must go a concomitant, and equally paradoxical, approach to naming God. On the one hand, Chapter 5 showed afresh, and with renewed impact, that 'the medium is the message' in the way we subliminally image God: the words we mouth in the liturgy, the pictures we gaze upon, the 'orthodoxies' we profess, can mandate and remandate repressive patriarchy even as some other (supposedly enlightened) message is being announced rhetorically from the pulpit or podium. In this sense, it might seem that our words and pictures need to change *first* to express the deeper reality of a Trinity beyond patriarchy. On the other hand, if words and pictures are merely changed by political and feminist fiat, however well intentioned, the purgative process of renewal in the Spirit is short-changed, the 'renewal' spiritually *faux* and inevitably hijacked by passing worldly fashion. Ultimately there are no short cuts in the battle against repressive patriarchy: the demons have to be slain one by one, and indeed over and over; and it is the task of us all to slay our own demons.

But that does not mean that we are left without resources and strategies for profound spiritual change too. If one asks, 'Does this approach "leave everything as it is" in terms of the traditional naming of God?', the answer is 'Yes and no (*but above all no*).' No, first and foremost, because in the mysterious ongoing contemplative surrender to Dionysius' 'ray of divine darkness'[23] the psychic bag and baggage which we bring to our prayer, its hauntings by parents, lovers, and friends, good and bad, saintly and sinful, is by slow degrees retrieved, sorted, and held up for healing. Of course, this is an arduous and sometime tortuous lifetime's endeavour, and can never be hurried;[24] but the wounds (whether of neglect or abuse) that may for some of us at first have attached themselves inexorably and painfully to the 'Father' language of the Trinity are, precisely in the interruption of the Spirit's distinctive undertaking, progressively laid open to healing in concert with the invitation by Christ into his 'glorious liberty', his 'birth-pangs' for the sake of the whole world's salvation. Such is the gracious logic of the prayer of

---

[23] *Mystical Theology*, I, in *Pseudo-Dionysius*, 135; *Corpus Dionysiacum*, vol. II, 142.

[24] Any priest or counsellor who has listened to the intractable sufferings of those who have endured sexual abuse will know that no glib optimism is in order here. It is never appropriate to *impose* the use of either 'Father' or 'Mother' language for God on those who are still shattered by abusive memories. But Christian hope is also demanded of us; and in my experience, creative and sensitive pastoral solutions can be devised to encourage those who are so suffering to continue to partake of sacramental and ecclesial support.

incorporation à la Romans 8, as has been stressed from the very opening of this volume.

This approach cannot of course occlude the element of authority in the simple givenness by the church of the language of 'Father', 'Son', and Spirit – which some on feminist grounds would reject altogether. But nor does it prevent us rejoicing – as Dionysius himself insists upon most vehemently – in a glorious accompanying profusion of metaphors of all kinds – zany, illogical, even irreverent – to help us tie the knot in our handkerchief of memory that *God* is beyond all positive and negative attributes we may hope to lard upon God. The naming of God as Trinity, however, has an importantly different status from the metaphoric profusion or delicious illogicality that our better liturgical reformers may occasionally use with delicacy and power to bounce us out of our unconscious ongoing idolatries. For, as Thomas Aquinas so acutely puts it, 'Father' is used 'appropriately' (*proprie*) of God when the word is used of inner-trinitarian relations; whereas when 'Father' alone is used of God it is technically 'inappropriate' and therefore metaphorical (even in the Lord's Prayer).[25] Its appropriateness inner-trinitarianly means that the *true* meaning of 'Father' is to be found in the Trinity, not dredged up from the scummy realm of human patriarchal fatherhood: as Jesus himself insisted so evocatively, 'Call no man Father *except* God alone' (Matthew 23. 9).

[25] It is in *ST* I, q. 13 that Thomas expounds his famous distinction between analogical and metaphorical naming of God, and stresses that the latter, when used for God, is technically inappropriate (though still highly evocative and meaningful: the Bible is full of such metaphors) because drawing on *creaturely* prototypes. Later, at *ST* I, q. 43, 5 ad. 2, Thomas underscores in contrast the particular (analogical) appropriateness of naming God as Father *in the Trinity*. See J. Augustine DiNoia, 'Knowing and Naming the Triune God: The Grammar of Trinitarian Confession', in Alvin Kimel, ed., *Speaking the Christian God: The Holy Trinity and the Challenge of Feminism* (Grand Rapids, MI: Eerdmans, 1992), 162–87, for a sensitive discussion of this issue in Thomas Aquinas. (I do not however share Fr DiNoia's final systematic conclusions.)

But this is still a hard saying; for societal associations cannot be 'fixed' by a mere repression of father language for God (what I have sometimes called the 'Tipp-ex' approach to liturgy, one which merely 'whites out' what offends); nor can it simply be compensated for by well-meaning 'maternal' projections and additions (and in any case, there are so many whose abuse or neglect has been at the hands of their mothers, not their fathers). To be sure, the free poetic use of maternal language, especially if conjoined paradoxically with paternal language, can in some circumstances have an exhilaratingly releasing effect on the imagination, as long as it is not allowed to harden into its own dogmatism. But we have seen enough of the complexity of this issue by now to know that the question of naming God 'appropriately' (*proprie*) is not resolvable by any one isolable strategy, nor indeed at any one distinguishable level of engagement. The strategy of metaphorical profusion (or visual interdeminacy or movement in the artistic realm) at one – culturally accessible – level of imaginative engagement needs to be *conjoined* with rigorous, nuanced theological and philosophical understanding of the precise semantic character of creedal *trinitarian* naming, at another.[26] Both strategies are needed; but even they do not exhaust what is under-lyingly an invitation to engage a Reality that is itself triune. And what is at stake here, at base, is a slow but steady assault on idolatry which only the patient practices of prayer can allow God to do *in* us: in the purgative kneeling before the blankness of the darkness which nonetheless dazzles, the Spirit is at work in this very noetic slippage, drawing all things into Christ and recasting our whole sense of how language for God *works*.

---

[26] See my *Powers and Submissions: Philosophy, Spirituality and Gender* (Oxford: Blackwell, 2002), ch. 7, and also the analytic philosophy of religion approach to the Trinity, *tout court*.

So what seemed at first like a trinitarian formula with little life in it but much traditional patriarchal authority insidiously associated and imposed, loosens its grip as an external imposition and begins to beome a Life into which to enter. As we enter, our presumptions about 'Fatherhood' strangely start to change ... and at last we follow Jesus into an exploration of the meaning of 'Fatherhood' beyond all human formulations.

But is there not still feminist false consciousness, even in such an acceptance of 'Father' language in the Trinity at all? Not I believe on the terms I have described; for as has been repeatedly stressed in this book, the silence of contemplation is not a shutting down of resistance to human abuse and horror, but rather the incubator for the strength and courage to resist it. Likewise, in the same silence we learn to use 'Father' *proprie*, and *only* as 'Father' in Trinity; we learn to approach this mystery as that which is more intimate to us even than we are to ourselves, as source – *the* source – of infinite tenderness and joy; and we learn to endure the ongoing noetic slippage that ever reminds us of that fact, and that dazzles us with its unspeakable presence.

At the heart of this book has been a paradoxical assertion that 'orthodoxy' is very rarely what it seems. The potential for cultural and patriarchal distortion is endless, and the mere 'complementary' addition of some new, well-intentioned, focus on the Spirit or 'feminine' language for God is not in itself going to shift this problem. A deeper sense of our own capacity for self-deceiving idolatry (yes, even potentially a feminist idolatry) has to come into play, precisely in and through the 'purgations' of prayer: only the primacy of *divine* desire can attend to this deeper problem. Likewise, and as Freud above all knew so well, 'to kill the Father is to remain with and reaffirm the rule of the Father'; so there has to be another way out other than enforced repression. So now we know why 'true orthodoxy' is so elusive. It can *only* occur when the idolatrous twoness of the patriarchal dyad is broken open to transformation by the Spirit.

'Can a feminist call God Father', then?[27] One might more truly insist that she, above all, *must*; for it lies with her alone to do the kneeling work that ultimately slays patriarchy at its root.

CHOOSE YOUR FIGHTS: RETURN TO THE FILIOQUE

The last trinitarian question to which we must turn in this volume is one that has bedevilled ecumenical relations across the centuries. In adding, 'and from the Son' (of the Spirit's procession from the Father) to the Nicene Creed, did the West not only abrogate the agreement that such changes could only occur at an ecumenical council, but also falsely construe the inner-trinitarian relations altogether?

We must first press the utterly practical but also profound spiritual question here: what is really at stake in the *filioque* dispute? Are the 'East' and the 'West' really divided over the nature of the 'processions' of the 'persons' in God, even when they share a 'Nicene' faith in the Trinity?[28] When polemical and political 'hardenings' have not got in the way (as they so often have, especially

---

[27] This is the title of a justly famous essay by my colleague Janet Martin Soskice: 'Can a Feminist call God "Father"?', in Teresa Elwes, ed., *Women's Voices: Essays in Contemporary Feminist Theology* (London: Marshall Pickering, 1992), 15–29. While Soskice and I agree that a feminist *can* call God 'Father', we have somewhat different reasons for arguing *why*.

[28] In what follows in this last section of the book, I shall continue to use the terms 'East' and 'West' in a stereotypic and somewhat ironic mode: as any close historical reading of the history of debates on trinitarian 'processions' will show, the Greek- and Latin-speaking churches evidence a much greater internal diversity and mutual overlapping influence than this disjunctive trope would suggest: see especially the magisterial treatment of this theme in Yves Congar, OP, *I Believe in the Holy Spirit* (3 vols.; London: Chapman, 1983).

since the ninth century and the so-called 'Photian schism'),[29] it has always been the East's main and best concern that the Spirit's power and distinctiveness not in any way be undermined or gainsaid – that the Spirit veritably be the irreducible locus of primary human transformation and the turning of human desire, just as I have sought to urge afresh in this volume. And when the West has been at its best, it has been most concerned that the unity of the Godhead and the complete equality of the 'hypostases' be preserved, such that the Spirit be as *intrinsically* related to the Son as to the Father, and that the Spirit in no way bypass the full implications of Christ's divine life. Thus the West has vigorously defended what we might call the utter mutual *infusion* of all three 'persons': Father, Son, and Spirit.

Yet has not the East had an equally 'Nicene' investment in such a principle of 'mutual infusion'? Certainly it has, though with occasional different forms of emphasis and expression. Cannot both these vital emphases, then, the so-called 'Eastern' and 'Western', be maintained simultaneously? Certainly they can, and moreover they must be, if the original Nicene project is not to lapse into theological incoherence. The fact that an early Eastern theologian as profound and insightful as Cyril of Alexandria defended something like Augustine's 'double procession' of the Spirit from Father *and Son*[30] shows us that faithful expositors of the biblical witness and of the Nicene tradition, both 'East' and 'West', always wanted to insist that the Spirit's 'procession' could not bypass the Son: after all, Gregory of Nyssa himself had urged that the Holy Spirit proceeds

[29] It was only at this point that it was insisted by an Eastern Patriarch that the Holy Spirit proceeded from the Father *'alone'*, a polemical view which effectively undid the rich potential for agreement between earlier patristic formulae on the Spirit's procession, East and West.

[30] See Congar, *I Believe*, vol. III, 35–6.

from the Father *through the Son*.[31] How different, then, was this from the notion of the Spirit as proceeding from both Father and Son, yet from the Father principally (*principaliter*), as Augustine had taught?[32]

Unfortunately, however, it is not quite good enough to say, as so many good-hearted ecumenists of the modern period before me have done, that the different emphases of 'East' and 'West' can now be seen to be complementary and thus ultimately mutually coherent. In one sense this supposition has all the truth of an established truism; and yet there remain two things wrong with this path, admirable and good and right as it is in spirit.

On the one hand it fails to do justice to the profundity of polemical divergence that Orthodox and Catholic exponents of trinitiarian theology have indeed exemplified, already in the later patristic period and sporadically since, as they have from time to time dug into their characteristic institutional trenches – trenches which are on both sides hardened into a false sense of patriarchal control and superiority. And on the other, it fails to grasp a nettle (or rather a potential new inspiration) that could even now be turned to ecstatic theological advantage for the coming Great Church.

---

[31] As Nyssen puts it in one celebrated passage: 'Again, we recognize another distinction with regard to that which depends on the cause. There is that which depends on the first cause and *that which is derived from what immediately depends on the first cause*. Thus the attribute of being only-begotten without doubt remains with the Son, and we do not question that the Spirit is derived from the Father. For the mediation of the Son, while it guards his prerogative of being only-begotten, does not exclude the relation which the Spirit has by nature to the Father' (Gregory of Nyssa, *An Answer to Ablabius*, in E. R. Hardy, ed., *Christology of the Later Fathers* (Philadelphia: Westminster, 1953), 266, my emphasis; GNO III/1, 56).

[32] See *De trinitate*, xv.17.29; xv.26.47. See the discussion in Lewis Ayres, '*Sempiterne Spiritum Donum*: Augustine's Pneumatology and the Metaphysics of Spirit', in Aristotle Papanikolaou and George E. Demacopoulos, eds., *Orthodox Readings of Augustine* (Crestwood, NY: St Vladimir's Seminary Press, 2008), 127–52, here 146–52.

What I mean is this. If the argument that I have mounted in the earlier part of this volume is right, then the mainstream churches, *both* 'East' and 'West', have always and perennially been tempted to draw back from the full implications of human submission to the Spirit's *primary* divine power. So it is not the '*filioque*' problem but something more radical with which we have to do here. To put it provocatively: even to *say* '*filioque*' is to imply a remaining subordination of the Spirit. Even to say '*filioque*' is to presume that a privileged dyad of Father and Son is already established, and that the Spirit then somehow has to be fitted in thereafter. This, we might say in latter-day paradoxical retrospect of Chapter 3 and its arguments, is the ironic 'Nicene' tragedy of the Holy Spirit.

Moreover, when this problem is then run through a gendered and culturally produced lens, the correlated human problem, as has been demonstrated afresh at some arduous length in this volume, is obvious: a 'Father–Son' pre-eminence is established as the Rule of Patriarchy, into which a subordinated 'femininity' struggles to find a place, even as it is also at times paradoxically adulated and pedestalized as a form of 'man-made' human perfection (whether as a 'feminized' visualization of the 'person' of the Spirit, or as the Virgin Mary as the Spirit's substitute). Anyone who wants to deny this will, at the very least, have to give some tortuous explanations of the iconographical evidences gathered in Chapter 5. The answer is not, then, to add this man-made 'femininity', and stir. Something more profound, more rich and strange, is required of us.

So what is the alternative?

I wrote at the end of Chapter 1 that it is an implication of trinitarian thinking at its most robust and daring that its ontological threeness always challenges and 'ambushes' the stuckness of established 'twoness': of male and female, of 'us' and 'other', of 'East' and 'West', and even of God and world (for in the cosmological disturbance of the incarnation the Spirit destabilizes even that 'certainty' of ontological difference afresh, not by demolishing the utter ontological distinction, but by reinvesting it with participative mystery). In and through the Spirit, such 'fixities' of our human thinking are ever challenged and queried; in and through the Spirit we are drawn to place our binary 'certainties' into the melting pot of the crucible of divine – not human – desire. The same logic, we now see, applies no less to how we try to 'manage' the processions of the divine life in trinitarian speculation, to polemicize one rendition of these over against another – precisely in order to re-establish yet another binary (of 'East' and 'West'). So what if we allow the radical lure of the Spirit to draw us into a new realm of transformation more deeply than these hallowed disjunctions allow – more deeply even than good-hearted ecumenical attempts to mediate them can envisage?

What we do know, of course, is that our trinitarian God is *One*, and that the ultimate route to blessed human oneness with that One in the Christic 'mystical body' must refuse any *idolatrous* stuckness in two, whether that takes the form of neglecting the Spirit in the Godhead, or of bogging down in human binaries which themselves resist the power of the Spirit. Yet, as has been repeatedly stressed, to add a 'third' in God is not to spice any possibly idolatrous or patriarchal twoness with a hint of 'feminine' (let alone 'Eastern') promise; rather, it is utterly to resist the idea that the Spirit is *subordinately* 'third' in the first place. It is to submit to an adventure into God in which the Spirit *leads* by surprise, adventure, purgation, and conviction.

When I am asked, then, whether I stand by the 'Western' *filioque* in the Nicene Creed or whether I express my solidarity with the 'East' by refusing to mouth it, I find that I cannot even answer that question – precisely because it is the wrong one to ask. This is not

because I have made a crass mistake in confusing the so-called
'economic' and 'ontological' understandings of the Trinity.[33]
Instead, I find I am first drawn to reinvite all parties concerned to
submit themselves afresh to the duty and delight of the life of the
Spirit itself; for herein we shall surely find, as we did in Chapter 4,
that any attempt to evade the implications of the divine Son's
Passion will inexorably go awry. What we discover in the adven-
ture of prayer, in contrast to these other routes, is a gentle but all-
consuming Spirit-led 'procession' into the glory of the Passion and
Resurrection, a royal road to a 'Fatherhood' beyond patriarchalism.
And thus, if then asked to pronounce on 'procession' *in* the
Godhead, I can only start with the Spirit's invitation into that
Godhead. Thus I start with the presumption of the Spirit's mutual
infusion *in* Son and Father.

The propulsion of my argument then leads almost inexorably to
one radical ontological conclusion: that there can be in God's
trinitarian ontology no Sonship which is not eternally 'sourced'
by 'Father' *in the Spirit* (in such a way, in fact, as to query even the
usual and exclusive meanings of Fatherly 'source', as already indicated).[34] To argue thus is to complete the purification from 'linear'

---

[33] To say that we are led into the Trinity 'first' by the Spirit of course implies an 'economic'
approach – that is, at the level of divine revelation and human response within time and
history; whereas for God in Godself we must think more probingly about whether and
how it is appropriate to parse the 'Father' as 'first' and as *sole* 'source' of the other two
'persons', as the biblical 'economic' language in its linear mode clearly suggests. Even
though we stand by the insistence that 'the economic Trinity *is* the 'immanent (or
'ontological') Trinity', the latter (the 'ontological') clearly cannot simply be *reduced* to
the former (the 'economic'): there must be that which God *is* which eternally 'precedes'
God's manifestion to us. And hence the speculation that follows here.

[34] I am glad to acknowledge my broad concurrence here with the important proposals of
Thomas G. Weinandy, *The Father's Spirit of Sonship: Reconceiving the Trinity* (Edinburgh:
T&T Clark, 1995), and remain grateful for the discussions I enjoyed with Fr Weinandy
in Oxford during 1991–3. I do not however share Weinandy's latter-day 'Harnackian'
suspicion of 'Platonism' (or Thomist 'Aristotelianism') as supposedly major culprits in
the history of classic trinitarianism and its relative neglect of the Spirit; as I have argued

subordinationism to which post-Nicene theologians constantly strove, though never with complete or unambiguous success (see Chapter 3). Indeed, were we to speculate further about the 'processions', we would not only need to speak thus of the Son eternally coming forth from the Father 'in' or 'by' the Spirit (rather than the Spirit proceeding from the Father merely 'and', or 'through', the Son, as in classical 'Western' and 'Eastern' language); but, more daringly, we would also need to speak of the Father's own reception back of his status as 'source' from the other two 'persons', precisely via the Spirit's reflexive propulsion and the Son's creative effulgence. Here, in divinity, then, is a 'source' of love unlike any other, giving and receiving and ecstatically deflecting, ever and always.

Thus, divine 'processions' cannot, according to the vision outlined in this book, ever be about *patriarchal* hierarchy; they are about the perfect mutual ontological desire that only the Godhead instantiates – without either loss or excess. Here is a desire not of need or imposition but of active plenitude and longing love. But it is finally only the clarification of the place of the Spirit in the Trinity which can resist the (ever-seductive) lure back into patriarchal hierarchy.

Is this mere talking in riddles? I say not. But it is certainly talking in a way that necessarily escapes *clear* human grasp or control, since although there are hallowed analogies for it, they are precisely that – hallowed analogies only, as both Gregory of Nyssa and Augustine insisted with equal vehemence at the end of their life's work. And if what I have argued in this book has any cogency, then we must start afresh with our celestial number system, and allow the Spirit's primary propulsion to allow us to rethink, even now,

above, the marriage of biblical inheritance and pagan philosophical clarification need not be regarded as a regrettable convenience, but more truly as an evolutionary strengthening, given the right philosophic insights. The deeper problem lies in rightly locating the *intrinsic* role of the Spirit in the Father–Son relationship.

trinitarian number in God, and just as much, and correlatively, number in the human realm of gender.

It has been the daring invitation of this book to make that problematic 'third' in God the 'first' in human encounter, not because the Spirit is thereby jostling *competitively* with the Father to be the primary ontological source, but because we humans have to cleanse our hearts and minds of any suggestion that the paternal divine 'source' could ever involve that sort of rivalry: 'source' here has become ecstatic goal as much as ecstatic origin, propelled inherently towards the transformative appearance of the God/Man. If, finally, we make this mind-shift, then everything changes.

* * *

BIBLIOGRAPHIC NOTE

THE RENEWAL OF DIONYSIAN STUDIES

The publication of a modern critical edition of the works of Dionysius in 1990–1 has sparked off a resurgence of studies into the texts of Dionysius and their various receptions. This interest has coincided and intermingled, not always knowingly or informedly, with an efflorescence of interest in 'negative theology' allied with postmodern scepticism at the universalizing certainties of modernity (see again, Chapter 1 above).

The critical edition noted above is Günter Heil, Adolf Martin Ritter, and Beata Regina Suchla, eds., *Corpus Dionysiacum* (2 vols.; Berlin: De Gruyter, 1990–1). The much awaited *Sources Chrétiennes* edition, edited by Ysabel de Andia, has yet to appear. A major shift in recent studies of Dionysius' texts has concerned the question of the extent and nature of their use of various 'Platonisms'. The paradigm-shifting work of Orthodox scholars Andrew Louth and Alexander Golitzin is especially important here: see Andrew Louth, *Denys the Areopagite* (London: Geoffrey Chapman, 1989); Alexander Golitzin, *Et Introibo ad Altare Dei: The Mystagogy of Dionysius*

Areopagita with Special Reference to its Predecessors in the Eastern Christian Tradition (Thessaloniki: Patriarchikon Idruma Paterikōn Meletōn, 1994); Alexander Golitzin, 'Dionysius Areopagita: A Christian Mysticism?', *Pro Ecclesia* 12 (2003), 161–212; and Alexander Golitzin, '"Suddenly, Christ": The Place of Negative Theology in the Mystagogy of Dionysius Areopagites', in Michael Kessler and Christian Sheppard, eds., *Mystics: Presence and Aporia* (University of Chicago Press, 2003), 8–37. Golitzin's work has also led to a significant collaborative scholarly enterprise arguing that the origins of Dionysius' work, and much Eastern Christian spirituality, are to be found in the 'matrix' of Second Temple Judaism; for the first fruits, see Basil Lourié and Andrei Orlov, eds., *The Theophaneia School: Jewish Roots of Eastern Christian Mysticism* (St Petersburg: Byzantinorossica, 2007).

The most recent investigation of the various receptions of Dionysius, both East and West, can be found in the essays in Sarah Coakley and Charles M. Stang, eds., *Re-Thinking Dionysius the Areopagite* (Oxford: Wiley–Blackwell, 2009). Other important surveys of Dionysius' reception can be found in broad-sweep works such as Ysabel de Andia, ed., *Denys l'Aréopagite et sa postérité en orient et en occident* (Paris: Institut d'Études Augustiniennes, 1997); Ysabel de Andia, ed., *Denys l'Aréopagite: Tradition et métamorphoses* (Paris: J. Vrin, 2006); and T. Boiadjiev, G. Kapriev, and A. Speer, eds., *Die Dionysius-Rezeption im Mittelalter* (Turnhout: Brepols, 2000). Other, more narrowly focused, works on aspects of Dionysius reception include: Paul Rorem and John C. Lamoreaux, eds., *John of Scythopolis and the Dionysian Corpus: Annotating the Areopagite* (Oxford: Clarendon Press, 1998); James McEvoy, *Mystical Theology: The Glosses by Thomas Gallus and the Commentary of Robert Grosseteste on 'De Mystica Theologia'* (Leuven: Peeters, 2003); L. Michael Harrington, *A Thirteenth-Century Textbook of Mystical Theology at the University of Paris* (Leuven: Peeters, 2004); and Paul Rorem, *Eriugena's Commentary on the Dionysian Celestial Hierarchy* (Toronto: Pontifical Institute of Mediaeval Studies, 2005).

Tamsin Jones Farmer, 'Dionysius in Hans Urs von Balthasar and Jean-Luc Marion', in Coakley and Stang, eds., *Re-Thinking Dionysius the Areopagite* (213–24), begins the work of teasing out the intertwined stories of the receptions of Dionysius and the contemporary interest in apophaticism, a story she deepens in her *A Genealogy of Marion's Philosophy of Religion: Apparent Darkness* (Bloomington: Indiana University Press, 2011), and which is also examined in Johannes Zachhuber, 'Jean-Luc Marion's Reading of Dionysius the Areopagite: Hermeneutics and Reception History', in Morwenna Ludlow and Scot Douglass, eds., *Reading the Church Fathers* (London: T&T Clark, 2011), 3–22. One of the best current entry points into recent Dionysian scholarship is Charles M. Stang, *Apophasis and Pseudonymity in Dionysius the Areopagite: 'No Longer I'* (Oxford University Press, 2012), a study which questions the usual modern way of thinking about pseudonymity.

Highly influential in the recent upsurge of interest in negative theology has been the work of my predecessor in Cambridge, Denys Turner, *The Darkness of God: Negativity in Christian Mysticism* (Cambridge University Press, 1994); Denys Turner and Oliver Davies, eds., *Silence and the Word: Negative Theology* (Cambridge University Press, 2002) is a rich collection of essays on the turn to 'apophaticism' in contemporary theology. For the terminology of 'apophatic rage', see Martin Laird, '"Whereof we speak": Gregory of Nyssa, Jean-Luc Marion and the Current Apophatic Rage', *Heythrop Journal* 42 (2001), 1–12.

There have been various recent attempts to analyze and systematize the different kinds of apophatic theology, amongst them Bruce Milem, 'Four Theories of Negative Theology', *Heythrop Journal* 48 (2007), 187–204; and Bernard McGinn, 'Three Forms of Negativity in Christian Mysticism', in John Bowker, ed., *Knowing the Unknowable: Science and Religions on God and the Universe* (London: I. B. Tauris, 2009), 99–121. I take up and expand McGinn's analysis in my 'Dark Contemplation and Epistemic Transformation: The Analytic Theologian Re-Meets Teresa of Avila', in Oliver D. Crisp and Michael C. Rae, eds., *Analytic Theology: New Essays in the Philosophy of Theology* (Oxford University Press, 2009), 280–312.

NAMING GOD AS 'FATHER'

Feminist theologies have produced many and varied responses to the issue of the use of male names and pronouns used of God. Seminal for my work has been Janet Martin Soskice, 'Can a Feminist call God "Father"?', in Teresa Elwes, ed., *Women's Voices: Essays in Contemporary Feminist Theology* (London: Marshall Pickering, 1992), 15–29, although – as I explain above – my approach ultimately differs subtly but importantly from Soskice's. The essays contained in Alvin Kimel, ed., *Speaking the Christian God: The Holy Trinity and the Challenge of Feminism* (Grand Rapids, MI: Eerdmans, 1992) are a mixed bag (see my review, *Journal of Theological Studies* 47 (1996), 389–94); but the chapter by J. Augustine DiNoia, OP, cited above, is philosophically nuanced and theologically important in relation to the metaphor–analogy distinction. I have also found Catherine Osborne, 'Literal or Metaphorical? Some Issues of Language in the Arian Controversy', in Lionel R. Wickham and Caroline P. Bammel, eds., *Christian Faith and Greek Philosophy in Late Antiquity: Essay in Tribute to George Christopher Stead* (Leiden: Brill, 1993), 148–70, of great interest in this connection, as is Peter Widdicombe, *The Fatherhood of God from Origen to Athanasius* (2nd edn; Oxford: Clarendon Press, 2000), new preface and 256–9. On the issue of the use of gendered language in worship, I have found Ruth C. Duck, *Gender and the Name of God: The Trinitarian Baptismal Formula* (New York: Pilgrim Press, 1991) stimulating. Particularly influential treatments of these issues from the perspective of feminist systematic theology are Elizabeth A. Johnson, *She Who Is: The Mystery of God in Feminist Theological Discourse* (New York: Crossroad, 1992), and Sallie McFague, *Models of God: Theology for an Ecological, Nuclear Age* (Philadelphia: Fortress Press, 1987) – again, writers whom I respect but from whom I part company on this topic, as is evident throughout this volume. For a collection of articles on this issue from a broadly Roman Catholic perspective which remain classics, see Johannes-Baptist Metz and Edward Schillebeeckx, eds., *God as Father?* (Concilium 143; Edinburgh: T&T Clark, 1981). Other monographs by male authors which attempt to resolve the issue of gendered naming of God, especially in the liturgical context, are: David S. Cunningham, *These Three are One: The Practice of Trinitarian Theology* (Oxford: Blackwell, 1998) (a proposal for dispensing with parental language in the Trinity); Anselm Min, *Paths to the Triune God: An Encounter between Aquinas and Recent Theologies* (University of Notre Dame Press, 2005) (a sensitive reflection on Aquinas's importance for feminist decisions about liturgical language); and David Lyle Jeffrey, *Houses of the Interpreter: Reading Scripture, Reading Culture* (Waco, TX: Baylor University Press, 2003) (a more conservative Protestant defence of 'Father' language as mandated by Jesus).

The renewal of trinitarian theology in the twentieth century, as well as the thawing of ecumenical interactions in the same period, has led to many re-examinations of the controversies surrounding the *filioque* since the schism of 1054. I have acknowledged my indebtedness to Yves Congar OP's *I Believe in the Holy Spirit* (3 vols.; London, Chapman, 1983) throughout this study, especially as this issue concentrates specifically on pneumatology. Very useful overviews of the problem of the *filioque*, both historical and systematic, can be found in Brian Daley, SJ, 'Revisiting the "Filioque": Roots and Branches of an Old Debate, Part One', *Pro Ecclesia* 10 (2001), 31–62; Brian Daley, SJ, 'Revisiting the "Filioque": Part Two: Contemporary Catholic Approaches', *Pro Ecclesia* 10 (2001), 195–212; and most recently and thoroughly, A. Edward Siecienski, *The Filioque: History of a Doctrinal Controversy* (Oxford University Press, 2010). The most fulsome study of the Council of Ferrara-Florence (1438–45), which came so close to resolving the issue between East and West, remains Joseph Gill, SJ, *The Council of Florence* (Cambridge University Press, 1969). Recent systematic theological proposals to do with the Spirit's procession and the *filioque* which cohere most closely with the radical line I pursue in this chapter are (as noted above) Thomas Weinandy, *The Father's Spirit of Sonship: Reconceiving the Trinity* (Edinburgh: T&T Clark, 1995), and Robert D. Hughes III, *Beloved Dust: Tides of the Spirit in Christian Life* (New York: Continuum, 2008). See also Robert D. Hughes III, 'Catching the Divine Breath in the Paschal Mystery: An Essay on the (Im)Passibility of God, in honor of Elizabeth Johnson', *Anglican Theological Review* 93 (2011), 527–39.

For early ecumenical interactions on the topic of the *filioque*, see Lukas Vischer, ed., *Spirit of God, Spirit of Christ: Ecumenical Reflections on the Filioque Controversy* (London: SPCK, 1981); for a more recent survey, see Michael Böhnke, Assaad Elias Kattan, and Bernd Oberdorfer, eds., *Die Filioque-Kontroverse: historische, ökumenische und dogmatische Perspektiven 1200 Jahre nach der Aachener Synode* (Freiburg: Herder, 2011). Ralph Del Colle, 'Reflections on the *filioque*', *Journal of Ecumenical Studies* 34 (1997), 202–17 attempted an important eirenic solution from the point of view of his Spirit Christology, and this still repays reflection. At the instigation of John Paul II, the Vatican statement, 'The Greek and Latin Traditions Regarding the Procession of the Holy Spirit' was produced by the Pontifical Council for Christian Unity and published in *L'Osservatore Romano* on 20 September 1995 (3, 6), and it has further stimulated work on this topic. For an Orthodox response, see John Zizioulas, 'One Single Source: An Orthodox Response to the Clarification on the Filioque', published online at http://agrino.org/cyberdesert/zizioulas.htm (last accessed 22.12.12); and for a further Roman Catholic response, see David Coffey, 'The Roman "Clarification" of the Doctrine of the Filioque', *International Journal of Systematic Theology* 5 (2003), 3–21.

Coda: conclusions and beyond

I want to end with a recapitulation of my contentious insistence, made at the outset, that contemplation as an ascetical discipline, a regular and repeated act, must attend the insights of any feminist *théologie totale*. For the *true* 'apophatic' is not just a verbal play, let alone a merely political ploy, but that towards which we are lured – it is 'mystical theology' itself, in Dionysius' terms. And if I am myself right, such a sustained *askēsis* of prayer has at least six theological implications, which draw together the central theses of this volume and immediately open on to the next.[1] Let me end, then, with six succinct theses, six recapitulated implications of such a regular silent waiting on the divine. It would be appropriate to see these six features as a systematic unfolding of the *first* mark of a *théologie totale* on 'contemplation', as outlined in Chapter 2 of this volume. These features also point forward to the second volume, since they represent the human, cognitive correlate of what we have here taught about the Trinity, and so demand further critical attention philosophically.

PRIVILEGING CONTEMPLATION: SIX THESES

Thesis 1: *The contemplative is one who is forced to acknowledge the 'messy entanglement' of sexual desire and the desire for God.* A very

---

[1] The second volume will be centrally concerned with the epistemic status of claims such as these.

340

little time on one's knees in silence will be sufficient to convince one of that. But this has more commonly led to a fearful disjunction of the two realms than to their alignment. It was Bernard of Clairvaux, after all, who was (in his sermons on the *Song of Songs*) the great medieval reinvigorator of the quest for God expressed in daring erotic metaphor, but who also wrote (in Sermon 65): 'To be always with a woman and not to have sexual relations with her is more difficult than to raise the dead. You cannot do the less difficult; do you think I will believe that you can do what is more difficult?' Herein lies a fundamental pathology, a disjunction that feminist contemplative theology ever seeks to resolve. But it is also the mystics, in their more outré moments, who have pointed the way through this tragic divide: Dionysius with his language of divine desire, Eckhart with his daring sexual metaphors of the birth of Christ in the 'virgin' soul, Julian with her 'mothering' Christ within the Trinity. All seem to chafe at the edges of acceptable trinitarian 'orthodoxy'; all seek to face or resolve the dilemma of sexual desire and desire for God. But it cannot be resolved without the ascetical transformation of human desire.

Thesis 2: *The contemplative acknowledges the leading activity of the Holy Spirit, and so jealously guards the distinctness of the third 'person'.* Trinitarianism, we have seen, is always in danger of reduction, the loss of the wafting 'pigeon', the apparent redundancy of a hypostatized relationship. But where the distinctness of the third is well guarded, so too there is a certain institutionally subversive element that is also well guarded. So, ironically, the 'church' type needs its contemplative subversives if it is to reinvigorate its trinitarianism and expand its notion of the 'Son' beyond the idolatrous male. Or, as Troeltsch put: the 'church' type needs the 'sect'. Both are legitimate outworkings of the gospel; yet the 'mystic' type who recalls both to contemplative practice will always stand at the edges of institutional acceptability, always be pressing to an 'orthodoxy' beyond mere propositional assent.

Thesis 3: *The 'apophatic turn' has the capacity not only to undermine gender stereotypes, but to lead to a form of ever-changing modellings of desire for God.* 'A love affair with a blank', such as contemplation is,[2] is a strange subversion of all certainties, a stripping, often painful, of what one previously took for granted. As Gregory of Nyssa's rich example shows, this 'blank' is capable too of undermining and transcending presumptions about gender roles, of shifting the boundaries of expectation and acceptability. Divine desire, and human desire for the divine, is more fundamental than gender.

Thesis 4: *Contemplation entails an expansion of the 'self', a subversion of disengaged reason.* The act of contemplation involves a willed suspension of one's rational agendas, a silent waiting. What fills the waiting over time is a kind of seepage in the self, a recognition of rich unconscious elements, a transcendence of narrow rationality. In Gregory of Nyssa the Platonic 'Man of Reason' is already toppled; new dimensions of the affective self – the 'spiritual senses' – are explored. This has, I believe, a new and profound significance in a period when, simultaneously, postmodern philosophy is obliterating the Enlightenment vision of the autonomous reasoned self, and feminist women are wondering whether they are being asked to lose an 'autonomy' they never enjoyed. Contemplation points to an expanded view of the self rooted in the trinitarian God.

Thesis 5: *Contemplation reorders the passions.* Contemplation involves a great risk: it implies a loss of *repressive* control, but at the same time it engenders a reordering of the passions such that

---

[2] This is Dom Sebastian Moore's wonderful rendition of the experience of dark contemplative practice, to which I remain indebted: see his 'Some Principles for an Adequate Theism', *Downside Review* 95 (1977), 201–13.

'control' finds new and significant coinage as *right* direction and purification of the passionate nature. To this extent, Augustine's perennial concern with 'control' is indeed justifiable. For ethically, some such notion of 'self-control' is vital. Without an accompanying ascetical dimension, a *praxis* of ordering of the passions into some kind of 'hierarchy', the suggested trinitarian language of *erōs* would be more than capable of abuse and distortion; and indeed we have already acknowledged that it is impossible to guard completely against this danger. Hence *the hermeneutics of suspicion never comes to an end*. Doubtless this is why the 'church' type in Christianity has always been nervous of conceptualizing the divine in terms of the erotic. Contemplation makes great ethical demands – to lose one's life in order to gain it, to turn the other cheek, to love one's enemies. It is not a form of disengagement, but of passionate *reordered* engagement.

And finally, thesis 6: *Contemplation presents us with a trinitarian model of power-in-vulnerability*. Contemplation is an act of willed 'vulnerability' to divine action. In it, one cooperates with the promptings of divine desire. There is no force; indeed, any force or anger both kill the subtle act of contemplation stone dead. The contemplative steps wilfully into an act of reflexive divine love that is always going on, always begging Christomorphic shape. This engenders divine power not as 'force' but as Christo-form 'authority'. This, if I am right, is fully compatible with the rightful goals of a distinctively Christian feminism; it sustains but also transcends the ongoing, elusive quest for 'equality' and the simultaneous acknowledgement of 'difference'.

Despite their format, these theses are not uttered dogmatically but tentatively, for the contemplative can hardly afford to speak otherwise. As such, the practice of silence is actually a place of regained *courage* to speak as a feminist, and not just a place of welcome rest and restoration from the theological slings and arrows. Thus the commitment to silence is also, paradoxically, the commitment as a theologian to give voice – but tentatively, and in a changed key. My own words are not an 'interruption' themselves; they are – at best – an invitation, uttered out of the abyss of the divine 'interruption' of the Spirit.

* * *

Glossary of technical terms and names

The definitions given here are my own, and I have deliberately kept them as clear and simple as possible. A useful point of further reference for the meaning of theological terms is Ian A. MacFarland, David A. S. Fergusson, Karen Kilby, and Iain R. Torrance, eds., *The Cambridge Dictionary of Christian Theology* (Cambridge University Press, 2011).

agapē (Greek):   love that is unselfish, fulsome and in principle universal (as enjoined in the teaching of Jesus).

apophatic: saying what something is *not* (Greek *apophasis*, 'denial, negation').

Arianism: the teaching that Christ was a creature and not fully God in the same sense as the Father (named from Arius, an Egyptian presbyter of the early fourth century).

asceticism: a programme of discipline and self-denial (Greek *askēsis*, 'exercise, training'); ascetic(al).

atonement: the remedy or defeat of sin effected by Christ through his life, death and resurrection.

binary: involving just two, as in *binary choice, binary opposites*. May also be used as a noun, meaning a pair of alternatives demanding a disjunctive choice.

Cappadocian fathers: the three fourth-century theologians Basil of Caesarea, Gregory of Nazianzus, and Basil's brother Gregory of Nyssa (all born in Cappadocia, now Eastern Turkey), most usually associated with the development of the orthodox doctrine of the Trinity in response to later Arianism.

cataphatic: saying what something *is* (Greek *kataphasis*, 'affirmation'); the opposite of *apophatic*.

contemplation: prayer or communing with God that does not use ordinary propositional language, but rests in silence or near silence; distinguished by Christian theologians from *meditation*: prayerful reflection on Scripture.

deconstruction: *broadly*, analysis of a text that is philosophically sceptical about its inherent truth or meaning; or criticism that subverts the received understanding of a text. In the particular and technical use of the French postmodern philosopher Jacques Derrida: a critical exposure of binary and hierarchical elements in philosophical thinking for the sake of averting political violence and injustice.

deferral: again, in the technical use of Jacques Derrida, the idea that words and signs can never fully summon that to which they refer; *or* a refusal to allow semantic meanings to settle or become static.

desire: the physical, emotional, or intellectual longing that is directed towards something or someone that is wanted.

economic Trinity: *see* Trinity.

epistemic: relating to knowledge or to *epistemology*, the branch of philosophy concerned with the nature and possibility of knowledge (Greek *epistēmē*, 'knowledge, understanding').

erōs (Greek): love that is marked by desire and longing, especially sexual desire; often contrasted with *agapē*.

eschatological: relating to the 'end' (Greek, *eschaton*), sometimes of an individual in death, but more usually of the world and humankind, associated in Christian theology (*eschatology*) with the final judgment.

essentialism: the belief that objects or persons have essential properties, different from accidental ones, that can be discovered and defined.

exegesis: the interpretation or analysis of a text; exegetical.

feminism: any movement or theoretical approach committed to overcoming economic, cultural, societal, or psychological disadvantages for women; feminist.

filioque: the doctrine that the Holy Spirit proceeds from the Father *and the Son* (Latin *filioque* in the Nicene Creed), maintained by the Western church but not the Eastern.

foundationalism: in epistemology, the view that certain basic beliefs are not dependent on other beliefs but are justified in ways that inherently cannot be mistaken. (*Non-foundationalism* denies that such basic beliefs can be identifiable or valid.)

gender: in common parlance, one's identity as 'male' or 'female' considered in relation to cultural norms, or 'constructed' through them. See Chapter 1 for further analysis and specifically theological discussion.

gnostic: relating to any religious system that makes salvation dependent on arcane knowledge (Greek *gnōsis*), and specifically to various ancient schools of 'Gnosticism' rejected as Christian 'heresies' in the second and third centuries.

hegemony (Greek *hēgemonia*, 'command, power'): predominance; especially the position asserted by a powerful group over against a weaker one; hegemonic.

hermeneutics: the theory of interpretation of texts.

hermeneutics of suspicion: an attitude towards texts that is sceptical about their surface appearance and seeks to reveal authors' unstated and in particular improper motives.

heterosexism: the belief that opposite-sex relationships are the only normal and acceptable ones; also called heteronormativity.

homoousios (Greek):   the adjective in the Nicene Creed that describes the relationship of the Son to the Father, literally 'of the same substance'; in English 'consubstantial' or in modern Western church use 'of one being'.

hypostasis (Greek: among other meanings, a 'being', 'individual', 'entity'):   in trinitarian theology, a 'person', denoting in each case the Father, Son, and Holy Spirit ('three *hypostases* in one Godhead'); and in orthodox Christology, denoting Christ as a single individual ('one hypostasis in two natures' or 'a hypostatic union of two natures').

immanent Trinity: *see* Trinity.

incarnation: Christ's becoming a human being, or taking flesh (Latin *caro*, 'flesh'; but the orthodox doctrine holds that Christ was 'fully man', not only the possessor of a human body).

lex orandi (Latin):   the 'law of praying', the logic of the practice of prayer and worship, especially as the accompaniment and basis for the *lex credendi* the 'law of believing'.

liberalism (in theology):   an attitude of tolerance and openness to new ways of thinking; opposed to traditionalism merely for the sake of adherence to authority.

locus (Latin 'place'):   in systematic theology, a central theme in theology (e.g., the doctrine of the Trinity, Christology, etc.) which demands a distinct treatment and reflection.

masculinism: in critical theory, the ('hegemonic') view that men's insights positions in society are superior to women's.

metaphysics: a broad category in philosophy relating to any topic which goes beyond what is visible or analyzable in physical terms (literally, 'after or beyond physics').

modalism: the doctrine (condemned as heretical since the third century) that the distinct 'persons' of the Trinity are not permanent but only 'modes' or aspects in which God as a single person has operated from time to time.

Montanism: a Christian movement originating in the late second century (named after its first leader Montanus) that practised on the one hand ecstatic and apocalyptic prophecy and on the other hand a strict ascetical discipline.

noumenal/phenomenal: a technical distinction in Kant's philosophy between things as they appear to us ('phenomena') and as they are in themselves ('noumena'), the latter being according to Kant unavailable as objects of knowledge.

nouvelle théologie (French 'new theology'): a movement of renewal in Roman Catholic thought in the twentieth century characterized by a return to biblical and patristic sources (*ressourcement*) and a resistance to rigid modernistic readings of Thomas Aquinas.

ontological: relating to being or the nature of being or existence (ontology); in metaphysics, relating to the ultimate nature of God, the world and self.

ontological Trinity: *see* Trinity.

participation: the gift of partaking in God's nature to which Christians are invited through grace and discipline; see also *theōsis*.

patriarchy: any system in which men are dominant and rule over subordinate women.

Pelagianism: the doctrine (rejected explicitly by the Western church generally since the fifth century) that people can choose good and reject evil by their own efforts and apart from God's grace.

perichorēsis (Greek): the mutual indwelling of the 'persons' of the Trinity in each other.

person (trinitarian sense): a divine personalized entity ('Father', 'Son', or 'Spirit') distinct enough to have a verb associated with it, but without the possibility of any separation in activity, or difference in divine characteristics, from the other two 'persons'.

pneumatology (Greek *pneuma*, spirit): teaching about the Holy Spirit.

post-colonialism: critical theory that analyzes writings of the colonial period and after it to expose motives of imperialism, exploitation, and racism.

postmodernity: the condition of thought or society *after* whatever is conceived as 'modern', most usually marked by fragmentation, pluralism, and the loss of coherent ideologies.

procession (trinitarian sense): within the Trinity, the generic technical term for the way in which each 'person' relates to the other two by distinguishing forms of relationship; more specifically, the term used particularly of the Holy Spirit who according to the Nicene Creed 'proceeds' from the Father (or, in the West, 'from the Father and the Son').

recapitulation: a conception of atonement according to which Christ has undone the disobedience of Adam and restored the human condition to its unfallen state.

relation (trinitarian sense): the technical term for speaking about the only distinguishing features other than number of the three 'persons' in the *ontological* Trinity, e.g., as the 'Father who generates the Son', the 'Son who is the only-begotten of the Father', the 'Spirit who proceeds from the Father'.

relativism: a theory of knowledge according to which propositions have no absolute or universal truth or validity and have to be evaluated in the context of their expression; or a similar theory about moral choices being right or wrong only circumstantially.

Sabellianism: another name for *modalism*, associated with a shadowy third-century figure Sabellius.

semiotic: in the technical sense of Jacques Lacan, the realm of diffuse thought and creative imagination repressed by the male symbolic, and especially associated with 'femininity'.

sex: one's biological identity as male or female (or 'intersexed'); often compared with *gender* (but the distinction is rendered problematic in postmodern gender theory, given the social 'constructions' of gender which occur even in identifying a person's 'sex').

sexuality: a modern word with wide evocations, ranging from those of sexual 'orientation' of erotic desire through to actual physical intercourse.

social trinitarianism: the understanding of the Trinity in terms of the relations of the persons with each other according to the model of human relations in church or society.

Socinianism: a rationalistic and anti-trinitarian movement at the time of the Reformation, named for its two founders Lelio and Fausto Sozzini.

soteriology: teaching about the nature of salvation.

spirituality: in contemporary parlance, religious practice and experience, especially as distinguished from assent to doctrine or ecclesiastical authority.

subordinationism: any system of trinitarian doctrine that assumes or teaches that the Father is greater than the Son, or the Father and Son greater than the Spirit.

substance: in the doctrine of the Trinity, the English word (through Latin *substantia*) commonly used to translate Greek *ousia*, and denoting the single being common to the Father, Son, and Holy Spirit.

symbolic: as understood by Jacques Lacan, the form of thinking unconsciously imposed as culturally normative, and particularly associated with the male: propositional, clear, analytic, demonstrable: compare semiotic.

systematic theology or systematics: the study or exposition of theology as a coherent whole usually including the traditional doctrines of God, Christ, atonement, the Holy Spirit, etc.

théologie totale: a new form of systematic theology that attempts to incorporate insights from every level of society and to integrate intellectual, affective, and imaginative approaches to doctrine and practice; see the discussion in Chapters 1 and 2.

theōsis (Greek, lit.,'becoming God'): in Orthodox theology the union with God that is made possible by Christ and that is the goal of a life of spiritual discipline; see also participation).

Thomism: Christian teaching that adopts the theological system of Thomas Aquinas (thirteenth century), some of its modern forms being known as neo-Thomism.

Trinity: God understood in Christian thinking as 'three in one', the three 'persons' being Father, Son, and Holy Spirit, fully united in one divine 'substance', and distinguished from each other only in number and 'relation'. Different perspectives on this doctrine (trinitarianism) include the economic (concerned with how the three 'persons' operate in the realm of history – the 'economy of salvation' – towards humankind), and ontological or immanent (concerned with the eternal nature and inner relationship of the three 'persons').

Scripture index

General index

Abraham, 199
agapē, 8, 345
Ahern, Geoffrey, 164
Aletti, Jean-Noël, 149
Allison, Henry, 96
Almond, Gabriel, 94
Amayem, Mohamed Abou el-, 204
Anatolios, Khaled, 149, 302
Andia, Ysabel de, 334, 335
Anglican ecclesiology, 31, 163, 165, 166. *See*
    Church of England
  field studies in parishes, 163–86
  as hybrid of 'sect' and 'church', 168
aniconism, 199, 263–4
anima
  and 'feminine' stereotype, 240
Annales School of History, 35, 62
Anthony of Egypt, 135, 145
anti-foundationalism, 16
Aphrahat, 201
apophaticism, 23, 44, 45, 46, 62, 273, 293,
    303, 312, 335, 336, 345. *See* Trinity
  and desire for God, 342
  as undermining gender stereotypes, 342
  true, 340
Appleby, R. Scott, 94
Aquinas, Thomas, 38, 61, 63, 89, 324
Arian Baptistery at Ravenna, 201
Arian controversy, 133, 196, 345
Arius, 108
Arnold, Matthew, 69, 93
asceticism, 3, 11, 15–20, 54, 345
Ashton, Cyril, 188
Athanasius of Alexandria, 4, 124, 135, 145
  on the Holy Spirit, 135, 138
atonement, 345
Augustine of Hippo, 3, 4, 145, 175, 268, 269,
    273, 278, 279, 280, 288, 289, 300,
    310, 311, 329, 333, 343

apophaticism of, 293
on body, 276
on desire, 278, 306–7
on desire for God and sexual desire as
    aligned, 295
on gender, 274, 289–92, 306–7
incorporative model, 294
life, 275
on prayer, 292
on sex, 276, 278, 290, 306–7
on the Trinity, 143, 279, 293, 304–6
on women, 274, 278, 291
Ayres, Lewis, 28, 149, 273, 301, 302, 305,
    329

Babka, Susie Paulik, 263
Balthasar, Hans Urs von, 40, 61, 149
baptism in the Spirit, 169
baptism of Christ, 118, 199, 201
Barker, Eileen, 93
Barnes, Michel R., 301, 302, 305
Barth, Karl, 18, 27, 39, 40, 41, 61
Basil of Caesarea, 138, 139, 145
Bates, Stephen, 31
Bauer, Walter, 28
Bavel, Tarcisius J. van, 291
Behr, John, 302
Belting, Hans, 264
Benedict XVI, 72
Benhabib, Seyla, 97
Berg, Hans van den, 204
Berger, Peter, 94
Bernard of Clairvaux, 341
Bernstein, Richard J., 97
biblical exegesis, 8, 25, 53, 127, 347
binary, 53, 57, 91, 282, 345
Blake, William, 255, 262
Blixen, Baroness von, 308
Bock, Gisela, 97